NOLO Products & Services

Books & Software

Nolo publishes hundreds of great books and software programs on the topics consumers and business owners want to know about. And every one of them is available in print or as a download at Nolo.com.

Plain-English Legal Dictionary

Free at Nolo.com. Stumped by jargon? Look it up in America's most up-to-date source for definitions of cutting edge legal terminology. Emphatically not your grandmother's law dictionary!

Legal Encyclopedia

Free at Nolo.com. Here are more than 1,200 free articles and answers to frequently asked questions about everyday consumer legal issues including wills, bankruptcy, small business formation, divorce, patents, employment and much more. As *The Washington Post* says, "Nobody does a better job than Nolo."

Online Legal Forms

Make a will or living trust, form an LLC or corporation or obtain a trademark or provisional patent at Nolo.com, all for a remarkably affordable price. In addition, our site provides hundreds of high-quality, low-cost downloadable legal forms including bills of sale, promissory notes, nondisclosure agreements and many more.

Lawyer Directory

Find an attorney at Nolo.com. Nolo's unique lawyer directory provides in-depth profiles of lawyers all over America. From fees and experience to legal philosophy, education and special expertise, you'll find all the information you need to pick a lawyer who's a good fit.

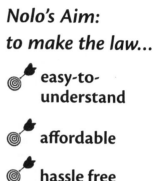

Nolo's Aim:
to make the law...

easy-to-understand

affordable

hassle free

Keep Up to Date!

*Old law is often bad law. That's why Nolo.com has free updates for this and every Nolo book. And if you want to be notified when a revised edition of any Nolo title comes out, sign up for this free service at **nolo.com/legalupdater**.*

"Nolo is always there in a jam."
—NEWSWEEK

Save Your Small Business

10 Crucial Strategies to Survive Hard Times
or Close Down & Move On

Ralph Warner, J.D. & Bethany K. Laurence, J.D.

FIRST EDITION   JULY 2009

Editor   MARY RANDOLPH

Cover and Book Design   SUSAN PUTNEY

Proofreading   ROBERT WELLS

Index   MEDEA MINNICH

Printing   DELTA PRINTING SOLUTIONS, INC.

Warner, Ralph E.
   Save your small business : 10 crucial strategies to survive hard times or close down &
move on / by Ralph Warner & Bethany Laurence. -- 1st ed.
       p. cm.
   Includes bibliographical references and index.
   ISBN-13: 978-1-4133-1041-2 (pbk. : alk. paper)
   ISBN-10: 1-4133-1041-9 (pbk. : alk. paper)
   1. Small business--Management. 2. Business planning. 3. Business failures--Prevention.
I. Laurence, Bethany K., 1968- II. Title.
   HD62.7.W376 2009
   658.4'012--dc22
                        2009011899

Acknowledgments

This book wouldn't have been possible without Toni Ihara's assistance, encouragement, and good ideas.

We are also indebted to a number of businesspeople who generously shared their ideas and experiences, including Chuck Drulis, Laura and Kiran Singh, Rich Stim, Lori Clawson, and Kay Klaczynski.

Stephen Elias, author of Nolo's *How to File for Chapter 7 Bankruptcy,* provided big assistance in reviewing our debt and bankruptcy materials, as did Terri Hearsh in checking our financial calculations. And finally, and most importantly, our Nolo editor Mary Randolph did the inspired nipping, tucking, and reorganizing necessary to make our manuscript truly shine.

Table of Contents

Your Small Business Companion

"I am not my business, and my business is not me." Now close your eyes and repeat that three times.

Got it? We hope so, because treating your business and its chances of survival in an objective, arm's-length manner is your best chance to make good strategic decisions in these difficult economic times.

Start by facing the fact that in the next year or two, hundreds of thousands of small businesses will fail. Some will go bankrupt, while many more will simply close the doors for the last time. Enterprises that were struggling long before the economic downturn began are all but doomed. But many other businesses can be saved if their owners act quickly and decisively to cut expenses, increase low-cost marketing, and revamp their entrepreneurial models to allow them to succeed in this recessionary environment.

In a nutshell, this book will give you objective tools to help you decide whether it makes most sense to continue, hibernate, close, or sell your business. If you decide to continue, we will help you start shoring up your business, with ten strategies you can start to implement right now to get your business back on track.

Some of our suggestions are tried and true. You may know that you need to cut expenses fast and hard so that overhead won't gobble up your reduced profits, but we'll tell you where to look first to make cuts (and what to leave alone). Other strategies will require you to fundamentally rethink your business, so you can develop innovative new goods and services and reach new markets. No question, accomplishing this will be challenging—but if your existing entrepreneurial model is failing, you know that your very survival depends on changing it.

In addition to providing what we hope is advice that will help you save your business, this book will give you the essential legal information you need to prioritize your debt payments, protect your family's personal assets, renegotiate your debts, and, if necessary, file for business or personal bankruptcy. With a little effort, you'll learn information that may prove crucial to keeping a roof over your head and a car in your driveway.

Getting Started

If objectivity is the key to developing a viable survival plan, how will you achieve it, especially at a time when so many around you are panicking? We recommend a three-step approach.

Step 1. Create a business survival plan. For example, if in the past six months, sales have been down 30%, your plan should convincingly explain how your business will be able to cut expenses, increase sales, maintain or reestablish an adequate profit margin, and manage (or attract more) cash so that in X months you'll be both profitable and have enough money in the kitty to bring past-due bills current.

Step 2. Prepare a current profit-and-loss statement and cash flow analysis. This is explained in detail in the appendix. You can't do the planning or take the action that will be needed to turn around a recession-battered business unless you fully understand your business's key numbers. It's like trying to land a plane in dense fog without instruments—you'll encounter the ground eventually, but it won't be pleasant.

Step 3. Establish an advisory board. This is a small group of knowledgeable small business advisers, people with enough entrepreneurial experience to understand your profit-and-loss statement and to review and challenge your survival plan. (More about who to enlist as your advisers in Chapter 1.)

It's tough to run your own business during an economic meltdown. But just as in the Great Depression, in the next months and years, millions of entrepreneurs will figure out how to successfully accomplish it, and by doing so will put themselves in a position to thrive when good times return. We'll help you develop and implement the best possible plan to cut costs, increase marketing, and develop the basic entrepreneurial strategies necessary to succeed. And if success in your business niche just isn't possible right now, we'll show you how you can take the legal and practical steps necessary to close down in a way that preserves your dignity, your business relationships, and your personal assets—and lets you move on to the next venture.

Can You Save Your Business?

"In this business, by the time you realize you're in trouble, it's too late to save yourself. Unless you're running scared all the time, you're gone."
BILL GATES

The economic tsunami that has engulfed America and much of the world means that the revenues of many small businesses have dropped precipitously, in some cases 40% or more. Because most small enterprises are marginally profitable in the best of times, and only a miniscule number have the chunky financial reserves necessary to survive a significant period of losses, it's obvious that many will close.

But the good news is that many businesses will survive—and some will emerge from the economic downturn stronger and better positioned to thrive. Here let's look at your main options: selling, hibernating, or hanging in there until better times return. If one of them will work for you, you won't have to close your doors.

Stepping Back to Plan for the Short and Long Term

As a crucial first step toward creating a survival plan, your business's key stakeholders should take an objective look at its prospects. No question, in the middle of an economic meltdown, it can be tough to take the time to plan. But just as you'll never grow a garden by pouring more and more water onto sand, you won't turn around a failing business simply by working 15 hours a day and worrying the other nine.

To decide whether or not your business has a future, it's absolutely essential that you separate your personal hopes and dreams from your business's honest prospects. If you don't, you will likely end up throwing good money after bad while needlessly dragging yourself (and your family) through an extended period of unhappiness. In short, this is a good time to repeat this book's mantra: "I am not my business, and my business is not me."

After you have your objective hat firmly on, create an advisory committee of experienced businesspeople. This is important because, even if you do a reasonable job of separating your ego from your business's problems, your advisers are likely to be more rational and, if you choose well, collectively more experienced and business savvy than you are. In other words, this really is an instance where a group can arrive at a better decision than an individual.

Creating Your Advisory Board

There is no one-size-fits-all rule for establishing an optimum advisory group, but we favor keeping it small, with three to five members. If your business is incorporated, some or all of the people on your board of directors may be well positioned to play a role as an adviser. If board members don't have the necessary skills, or you don't have a board because your business is a sole proprietorship, LLC, or partnership, you'll need to look elsewhere. Try to find:

- Experienced small business people in your community who you know and trust and who, in turn, respect your business.

- A loyal customer with deep business experience who values your business and is willing to help. Every business worth saving has supporters. Don't be afraid to enlist yours.

- An objective, business-savvy family member with the time and desire to help.

- SCORE, a nonprofit organization that provides free in-person and online mentoring to small businesses. Check out what they offer at www.score.org.

It's best to approach each potential mentor personally and explain that your goal is to have a group of objective advisers who will meet with you periodically to review your business and financial plans. If you'll need a considerable time commitment in the beginning (for example, a full-day meeting followed by monthly two-hour sessions), make this clear up front. Offering to pay a small stipend per meeting or per hour will be appreciated even by people who don't need the money, because it tells them you value (and won't abuse) their time. If your finances are too tight to afford that, consider offering some other form of compensation, such as free products or services, or, if you are incorporated, a small stock grant.

Now let's focus on how to decide whether your business is savable. You wouldn't be reading this if your sales hadn't dropped, probably steeply, so we'll begin with the assumption that your business is performing poorly. Recognizing that you are undoubtedly trying to make sense of a confusing, overlapping, and perhaps contradictory array of business and personal issues, it will help clarify matters if you think about how to proceed over the short, medium, and long term.

Short term: one to six months. In the short term, your job is to either develop an objective and realistic plan to get the business back to breakeven or, if that's not possible, to close or sell it. In general, you shouldn't allow losses to accumulate beyond six consecutive months. The only major exception to this rule is when a clear-eyed investor is willing to put new money into the business under a long-term turnaround plan.

Medium term: six to 18 months. If you can make the cuts necessary to get back to breakeven in six months, you'll need to return your business to profit, usually through a combination of more cost cutting, adopting effective new marketing initiatives, and, if possible, pivoting your business so that its goods and services are more desirable to penny-pinching customers. But if your locale or industry faces a deep recession, the best you may be able to do during this next year is to continue to break even. As long as you can pay your household expenses, and you and your advisers conclude that the business has a bright future, sticking with it may make sense.

Long term: beyond 18 months. Your long-term plan must return your business to profit. No matter how much your ego is tied to your business and how much you believe it will eventually succeed, there's no long-term future for a business that doesn't make money. Cutting costs and increasing marketing may keep your business alive for the short term, but chances are good that to return it to solid profitability, you'll also need to adopt a series of business-enhancing innovations.

To plan for the short-, medium-, and long-term future of your business, you need to do some basic financial work. First, complete a profit-and-loss statement and a cash flow analysis. (The appendix tells you how.) Second, read the rest of this book with special attention to the chapters on innovation and marketing. And third, run your conclusions past your advisory board.

Selling Your Business

In good economic times, it can be tough to sell even a profitable small business. When times are tough and a business begins losing money, arranging even a bargain-basement sale is usually impossible. But as with anything, there are exceptions. A business with a great reputation, market position, or excellent location might be salable even when profits have disappeared.

The key to selling anything, including a business, is that it must provide value to the buyer that the buyer can't get in another, cheaper way. A copy shop or Thai restaurant that's losing money probably can't be sold, because it would probably be cheaper to start from scratch, assuming anyone wanted to enter a highly competitive business where an existing enterprise was doing so poorly.

But businesses that have well-established local brands and have been historically profitable retain at least some value even when they don't make money. Take, for example, a well-established plumbing supply company that suffered significant losses when the recession dried up new construction. It might be salable based on the value of its brand and the loyalty of its customers. This would be even more likely if a competitor saw buying it as a chance to corner the local plumbing supply market, gaining significant pricing power.

EXAMPLE: Randolph Colocation Services provides the infrastructure necessary to support e-commerce websites. This includes ensuring that a site has stable and redundant electrical power, enough bandwidth to work fast, good security, and other services.

When the recession hit and business suddenly dropped 20%, Randolph, which had just committed to build two new facilities nearby, lost both a key investor and a major line of credit. Suddenly, instead of dreaming of becoming a large and lucrative market player, Randolph worried about scraping up enough money to make the next payroll. Seeing that Randolph was in trouble, two well-funded local competitors called with offers to purchase. Both realized that grabbing Randolph meant picking up hundreds of existing business customers and becoming well-positioned to dominate the local market—even though Randolph would continue to lose money until the new facilities could be successfully integrated or dumped.

RESOURCE

Information on selling. *The Complete Guide to Selling Your Business,* by Fred Steingold (Nolo), is an excellent step-by-step guide. It will help you decide whether it makes more sense to approach likely purchasers yourself or hire a business broker to do it for you. It also takes you through a typical sales contract clause by clause, identifying the key issues you'll need to negotiate.

CAUTION

Cut expenses while planning to sell. A deal to sell your business isn't final until the ink on the signatures is dry and the money is in the bank, things that can often take several months. In the meantime, it's crucial to limit your losses by cutting expenses hard and fast to avoid losing as much money as you reap from the sale. (More on this in Chapter 3.)

Putting Your Business in Hibernation

Some money-losing businesses that are likely to have bright prospects once economic times improve can sensibly be put to sleep for a period of time rather than killed. The idea is to cut costs to the bone and keep the business functioning at a minimal level, while concentrating your entrepreneurial energy elsewhere.

EXAMPLE: Chuck and Samantha, young architects with just a few years' experience at a large firm, open their own shop, C&S Design, to specialize in designing cultural centers, museums, and public safety spaces for small cities. After quickly getting two decent commissions, business dries up as cities facing depleted tax revenue delay new projects and bigger architectural firms, losing commercial work, increasingly target this niche.

Less than a year into the recession, Chuck and Samantha are out of money and out of hope. Their last chance for survival hinges on their belief that new commissions will quickly materialize after the two innovative buildings they have designed are finally built. But when municipal funding cutbacks delay both projects, it's clear that C&S is not going break even, to say nothing of make money, anytime soon.

They decide to close down. But after talking to their advisory board, one of whom is an older architect who has been through several boom-and-bust economic cycles, they instead decide to hibernate their business. To this end, they give up their way-cool loft and, at very low cost, rent a corner of a friend's studio to keep a business address and a place to meet any prospective clients. And they decide to limit themselves to submitting three public sector proposals per year and entering one large judged competition—just enough to keep their firm's name out there. In the meantime, both take temporary contract jobs with larger architectural firms to earn enough money to keep their kids fed. With the help of employed spouses and supportive parents, they plan to put C&S Design to sleep for a year or two and then recommit to it full time when the economy picks up.

Saving Your Business

Chances are that, like most small business people, you are an optimist—pessimists usually work for someone else. It follows that when a recession wallops your business, you are likely to be overly sanguine about the future. Even if your business is melting down in front of your eyes, you might too easily conclude that sales will pick up next week, next month, or next spring. Sorry, but when economic times are bad and threatening to get worse, the opposite is more likely to be true. Just as in boom times your happiest projections may consistently be surpassed, chances are that when many things are going wrong, more will. To make changes and cutbacks fast enough to bring income in line with expenses, we not only recommend that you take off your rose-tinted glasses, but that you step on them.

Every small business rests on a set of fundamental and often simple commercial assumptions such as these:

- When dogs get sick, owners take them to a vet.
- When cars are filthy, people wash them.
- When people are hungry at the beach, they buy food.

This much is obvious. But what can be less obvious is that when a recession hits, the assumptions behind many successful small businesses become invalid or lose much of their power.

EXAMPLE: Pam operates an upscale children's clothing boutique in a trendy resort town. Her fundamental business assumption is that grandparents on vacation will pay top dollar for cute outfits to take home as presents for their grandkids. But six months into the recession, Pam realizes that this is no longer true. Because only about half as many older tourists are visiting the town as previously, and many are traumatized by their shrinking retirement plans, the days of free-spending grandparents are plainly over.

So, with her sales down 50% and her lease expiring, and no reasonable prospect of returning to profitability in the next six months, Pam has a big sale and closes down. She knows she'll eventually open another business, but for now she'll spend more time with her own grandkids.

Once you honestly face up to the fact that boom times may not return for many years, you need to either close down, sell, or quickly develop and implement a realistic plan to turn your business into a survivor. Almost always this means identifying your business's profitable core and shucking off all or most activities that are not part of it. For instance, a publisher of regional guidebooks with a dozen well-established, profitable titles, and many others that barely break even, might be hit hard when a recession cuts into the area's tourist business. It will need to quickly redesign its business plan around income produced by the core titles that still make money. This is true even though it will mean laying off valued employees, canceling speculative new titles, and pruning the backlist.

EXAMPLE: Jack owns Racafrax Roofing, a company with 32 employees, when the recession hits and orders dry up. Immediately laying off 20 employees, moving to a tiny, cheap office, selling two of his four trucks, and hiring a local lawyer to send threatening but very effective letters to his past-due accounts stops the worst of the bleeding, but Jack is still losing money. Realizing most residential and commercial customers are putting off major roof replacement work, Jack focuses on repairs, a fussy lower-profit business he used to avoid. But now, every time it rains, Jack leaflets entire neighborhoods. With water pouring in, Racafrax gets lots of emergency calls, most of which he can deal with before the next rain when the process starts all over.

Although Jack misses the days when big jobs produced big profits, he can return a much smaller Racafrax to modest profitability just seven months after it began losing money. Then, six months later, when two other local roofers who haven't hustled as hard go out of business, Jack realizes that Racafrax is back in the black for good. True, the local economy will have to recover before significant profits return, but he knows he'll be there when they do.

Once you and your advisers decide that your hard-hit business has a decent chance of survival if you act fast, you'll want to follow these often overlapping steps.

Cut costs. You must urgently slash costs to fit your new lowered income projection. Depending on your situation, this can involve cutting every possible expense, moving to a less costly location, laying off employees, aggressively collecting past due debts, and a host of other penny-pinching techniques discussed throughout this book.

Change your strategy. You need to promptly face up to the fact that your business's current strategy is failing and then fundamentally change it. There are as many ways to do this as there are small businesses, but when times are tough a common theme is to pivot a business so that it's more in tune with the recessionary environment. To attract the newly frugal "recessionista" customers, you'll typically want to convince them that your business is all about providing value, reliability, and frugality. For example:

- Millie's Way Cool Boutique might devote half of the store to "Way Cool Vintage" clothing.

- Ihara Marine, which offers full-day charter trips, might add lower cost half-day fishing trips priced to fit shrinking family vacation budgets.

- Elegant Lighting of Lakeport might reconfigure itself as the Lakeport Green Lighting Center, offering environmentally conscious choices.

- James & Cirelli, a small business law firm, might start handling business bankruptcies, lease workouts, and bad debt collections, and tell clients that fees will be $50 per hour less until the economy recovers.

Come up with new marketing ideas. You'll need a low-cost and highly effective marketing campaign to reach out to recession-shocked customers. Your strategies must hinge on understanding who your best customers are, how to reach them most effectively, and how to provide incentives for them to purchase goods and services on which you make a decent profit. (Chapters 7 and 8 discuss this.) Here are a few examples:

- A yoga studio that offers existing customers a 10% discount for bringing in a new student.
- A boutique that offers periodic "Present-Buying for Guys" classes (husbands and boyfriends), along with a 15% after-class discount coupon.
- A roofer who advertises low-cost gutter cleaning in affluent neighborhoods, letting him at the same time give each homeowner a free roof assessment highlighting areas that need immediate attention.
- A hardware store that features low-cost holiday lights to attract people to the store's high-margin Christmas ornament section.
- A jewelry store that features three watch battery replacements for the price of two and, in the process, attracts thousands of dollars worth of higher-margin repairs on jewelry that customers bring along.

Special Considerations for Different Kinds of Businesses

Okay, now that you have begun to come to terms with what you'll need to do to rescue your business, let's look more closely at the typical problems and opportunities faced by the most common kinds of small businesses: retail, service, wholesale, construction, and franchises. Although you may be tempted to read only the material most relevant to your business, many ideas overlap, so take a moment to at least skim it all.

Retailers

Even when the economy is strong, it's hard to make a decent living running an independent retail business. The long-term trend that makes it tough for the little shop owner to survive began way back in the mid-19th century, when department stores began selling a wide variety of mass-produced consumer goods. It hugely accelerated in the decade after World War II with the advent of large discount chains, and went into hyper-drive in the last two decades with the marriage of computerized "just-in-time" inventory systems to low-cost but highly reliable foreign production.

Today there can be little doubt that if for no other reason than price, most Americans prefer to shop at the huge, low-cost megastores that have all but taken over the retail environment. The proof can be seen both in the empty storefronts that line the main streets of America's small cities and the crowded parking lots of the Walmart, Home Depot, Staples, and other big-box retailers. The main exceptions to the inexorable march of the megastore have been niche businesses that sell products not available from the big players: luxury goods or specialty items such as Balinese imports, fly fishing gear, or high-end bicycles.

Unfortunately, when times are tough, specialty goods retailers are extremely vulnerable to a devastating drop in sales even as their fixed costs, including rent and insurance, remain high. For example, stores that sell fancy kitchenware, lingerie, or wine all offer goods that newly frugal customers can do without or replace with less expensive alternatives. (When times are hard, lingerie is called underwear, and women wear last year's or shop at Target.)

In all but the most upscale neighborhoods, these businesses face the double whammy of many customers who can no longer afford boutique shopping and others who, even though they still have money to spend, find that it's suddenly cool to consume less and patronize consignment stores. And then there is the increasing competition from online niche retailers, who because of their nationwide reach can often offer a huge array of specialty goods at extremely attractive prices. The upshot is that many retailers, especially those that sell upscale items in areas hard hit by layoffs or a drop-off in the tourist business, have little chance of survival and are best abandoned early.

EXAMPLE: Frederika owned Fancy Food, a store that featured organic and other upscale food for dogs and cats. But with half a dozen local competitors, Fancy Food never made more than a modest profit. Then several large local employers cut workers and closed facilities, hurting her customer base. Almost immediately, Fancy Food's monthly sales dropped, first 25%, then 35%, and finally more than 40%.

To try to turn the situation around, Frederika, who by this time was almost out of cash, came up with a plan to increase her marketing for lower-priced brands. But after talking to her advisory board, she realized that even if sales fully recovered (unlikely given that Costco and Walmart were nearby), the far lower profit margins on budget food would still result in a substantial loss. Facing this truth, Frederika closed down.

On the other hand, retailers who have kept overhead low while providing convenient access to essential products may do just fine when times are hard. For example, people who do fix-it projects themselves rather than hiring a contractor might actually buy more from a local hardware, electrical supply, or paint store, especially one with deep community roots and the marketing savvy to compete with the discounters. True, some shoppers will be tempted to switch to the big-box retailer at the edge of town, but local providers who have lasted this long have learned how to emphasize service, convenience, and marketing to keep most customers loyal.

Enough generalizations. To get a good idea as to whether your store has a chance to survive until the economy improves, do these two things:

- Identify the month your sales suffered a significant drop. Then find the average sales for each month since, extrapolating for a full 12 months if the decline is more recent. For instance, if sales started to decline eight months ago and have averaged $15,000 per month since, figure that yearly sales will be $180,000, unless you have a good reason (for example, that sales are still declining) to adjust this number up or down.

- Run a profit-and-loss statement and a cash flow analysis based on your new sales numbers (see the appendix for instructions).

The results should give you a pretty accurate confirmation of what you may already know—whether or not your business is savable. If, even given declining sales, you are still within shouting distance of breakeven, chances are you can cut costs and increase marketing to get back in the black. But if a huge sales drop has decimated your balance sheet, trying to keep going until business eventually improves may be as unwise as it is impossible.

EXAMPLE 1: John and Becky run a wine shop specializing in high-priced imported wines not available at mainstream retailers. Last year they made $50,000 on sales of $450,000 and hoped to improve significantly on this in the current year. Then, as America's financial system began to melt down, sales started dropping 5% to 10% per month, finally leveling off at an annual rate of $350,000. John and Becky do a detailed profit-and-loss statement and cash flow analysis based on this lower sales number and find that they are now losing $20,000 per year.

After checking with their advisers, John and Becky decide to take a number of steps to get the business back at least to breakeven. If they can, they have an assurance that Becky's dad will lend them money for their personal expenses for the next year, an amount that will be subtracted from Becky's eventual inheritance.

Here are the steps Becky and John take:

- They contact their landlord and show him their balance sheet. In part because he fears having an empty shop if they go under and in part because he likes their spunk, he agrees to lower the rent 10%.

- They lay off their one part-time employee and go to a five- instead of six-day schedule.

- They increase the number of moderately priced but still unusual wines. This is not so much calculated to make money (lower priced wines are less profitable), but to bring customers into the store, where at least some of them would also buy a more upscale and profitable tipple.

- They adopt a number of low-cost marketing techniques (see Chapter 8), the first and most successful of which is to write a forthright letter to everyone on their mailing list explaining that they are on the edge of insolvency and asking for help. They also include a 30%-off coupon good for any bottle over $20. Hundreds of people, concerned that their favorite little wine shop might close and wanting to help the nice couple who ran it, respond, with a surprising number purchasing a case or more. The result is that John and Becky have their best month of the year.

EXAMPLE 2: Phyllis runs an upmarket women's clothing boutique called Festoon, out of a hole-in-the-wall shop near a large university. After making money 20 years in a row, Festoon suffers six consecutive losing months. When a larger boutique goes out of business around the corner, Phyllis considers moving and turning half of the new shop into an upmarket vintage clothing store.

But after talking extensively with her advisers, she decides that with her house paid for, some money in the bank, and Festoon's lease running out in three months, her best bet is to have a three-month going-out-of-business sale, put her store fixtures in storage, and consider reopening at a lower-rent location when the recession finally exhausts itself. Fortunately, when her long-term customers hear Festoon is closing down, they flood the store and all but demand Phyllis stay open through the holidays. The resulting profit from the going-out-of-business sale is much larger than Phyllis's previous losses, meaning that she has a nice nest egg to cushion her temporary retirement.

Services

A house painter, roofer, electrician, lawyer, or other service provider whose overhead costs are only a small percentage of gross sales—and who cuts back quickly after experiencing a significant sales drop—usually has an excellent chance to survive. That's because in a service business where overhead is low (and can usually be reduced), even a small sales uptick resulting from a properly targeted, low-cost marketing campaign will mean a substantial fattening of the bottom line.

Another way of saying this is that if you can charge a substantial hourly rate, with little or no overhead, you'll normally be able to hang in there even if sales initially plunge as much as 40% to 50%. Of course you still need enough income to put bread on the table, and may even need to take a part-time job to do it, but especially if your business is both established and historically profitable, it will probably survive. That's because for most quality service businesses, continued success depends on the accumulation of positive word of mouth. That's something that in hard times you might be able to leverage as part of a marketing plan to reach out to long-term customers, asking them for both their personal support and their help in recruiting others. (This may not be true if your business is the new kid on the block.)

If your company provides services that can easily be put off, however, you can face a customer meltdown in tough times. So if you paint houses, detail cars, install garage doors, landscape gardens, or cater business events, no matter how hard you are willing to work, you need a convincing survival plan.

It might involve repositioning your business to deliver services that penny-pinching customers still are willing to pay for—for example, a veterinarian might contract with a city to provide services at the animal shelter.

You might also have a difficult time if, by industry tradition, your company does the work first and bills later. That's because when times are hard, inevitably some customers will pay late and others not at all. That's why it's often crucial to quickly revisit and tighten credit policies before bad debts mount. One way to do this is to require a substantial up-front deposit as well as appropriate progress payments. To help long-term customers adjust to your new rules, it's helpful to also extend a discount.

EXAMPLE: The Myers & Pedroilla law firm informs its clients that in recognition of hard economic times, it is lowering its hourly fee by $50 per hour. But because it's impossible to both charge lower prices and wait to be paid, M&P is simultaneously moving to a new billing routine in which clients are asked to pay half of the estimated cost of their legal task up front and the other half within seven days of completion. As a result, M&P loses a couple of significant clients, but when one of them goes bankrupt a few months later owing its new law firm $35,000, M&P knows it made the right choice.

A sales meltdown is more difficult to overcome if you run a service business with a relatively high overhead such as a hair salon, car repair shop, dry cleaners, car wash, or bed and breakfast. Like retailers, the cost of keeping the doors open and the business staffed can gobble up all of your declining income and more, resulting in a substantial loss. In Chapter 2, we discuss how to make cuts quickly, something that all businesses with substantial overhead must do.

Because in our 21st-century commercial world it's a lot easier to make money selling services than goods, most service providers have many local competitors. Always remember that you're not operating in a vacuum. Recall the old joke about the three hikers who, while walking in the forest, encounter a huge, hungry tiger. The first slumps to the ground and says, "We're as good as dead—no one can run faster than a tiger!" The second, who can't argue with this, collapses next to him. But that's when the third, who is already running away as fast as she can, shouts over her shoulder, "I don't need to run faster than the tiger, only faster than you two!"

If you equate hard times with the tiger and your direct competitors with the hikers, the point is simple—chances are your business will survive if you outlast at least a good number of the other businesses that provide similar services. Even in a declining market, lots of people will still get their hair cut and colored, have spots removed from their clothing, or get their nails done. Lucky ones will even be able to afford a few days' vacation. It follows that if your business can stay open until others close, you may even do better than you did when times were good.

How can you outperform your rivals? Start by making a list of your direct competitors. You have doubtless known most of them for years. But don't forget that when times are hard, many cash-strapped consumers look for cheaper alternatives. So if you operate an upscale hair salon and never previously thought of the local Supercuts outlet as a competitor, you may need to think again, depending on just how depressed your local economy is.

Then make a short list of the strengths and weaknesses of each competitor. This might include their customer base, reputation, employee relations, cost structure, and marketing savvy.

Finally, come up with a realistic plan to outperform and outlast a percentage of them. (We discuss the possibility of lowering your overhead by combining operations with a favorite competitor in Chapter 11.) Once your plan is made, run it by your advisory board. Here are some examples:

- Cedar Cleaners, whose business is hard hit by the recession, decides that it has the financial resources to survive two years of low, or even no, profits. Accordingly, to keep its long-time customer base loyal, it runs a sale per week (sleeping bags, drapes, formal wear, quilts, and so on) to keep volume up, even though profits take a hit. When, after a year of deepening recession, two other dry cleaning establishments close, Cedar is able to regain pricing power and return to solid profitability. Once the local economy finally improves, Cedar has its most profitable year ever.

- Two bed and breakfasts in the same seashore town combine marketing efforts, sending "three nights for the price of two" offers to their combined mailing lists, merging their websites, and even taking turns doing breakfast. On the website they provide loads of information to make it easy for people organizing weddings, family reunions, and small business getaways to book both inns at once.

Construction

In a deep recession, tiny construction outfits with good marketing savvy and energy often survive, and some even do well. That's because a fair number of home remodels and other smaller jobs tend to go forward even when new housing and commercial construction is put on hold. True, small construction outfits may have to shrink even more, but because most already operate out of a home office and have little overhead, they can cut costs by simply hiring less labor.

Slightly larger construction outfits in the 20 to 70 employee range, however, often face severe problems. Not only is their overhead higher, as a percentage of sales, but they also typically rely on suddenly iffy bank lines of credit to smooth out payment cycles. Some fail for a combination of reasons, the most important of which is that much of the new residential and commercial construction they typically rely on grinds to a halt at the same time that they don't cut expenses nearly fast enough.

EXAMPLE 1: Six months into the recession, new business at J&B Concrete begins to drop precipitously as residential and commercial construction severely contract. At the same time, payments to J&B for cement jobs begin to slow down as everyone from prime contractors to several municipal governments begins to hoard cash. Out of loyalty to longtime office workers and estimators, J&B is slow to cut overhead, hoping against hope that, as it always had, business will soon pickup. As a result, monthly payments for rent, equipment, and staff exceed income.

J&B turns to its bank with a request that it increase their line of credit. Instead, after seeing that J&B's negative cash flow already violates an existing loan covenant, the bank cancels the credit line. J&B immediately lays off 60% of its staff, tries desperately to collect on past-due receivables, and asks everyone from their landlord to trade creditors to accept late payment. But even though some of these efforts show promise, J&B runs out of money two weeks after the line of credit is canceled. They're unable to pay even their diminished payroll, so the state labor commissioner closes them down, and a bankruptcy filing follows.

When you realize that from start to finish, J&B's crash from solvency to bankruptcy took just five months, you'll understand just how financially fragile many construction outfits are. Nevertheless, had J&B moved faster to shrink overhead, it might have survived. So in, let's give J&B a second chance.

EXAMPLE 2: When J&B has its first bad month, the owners meet with their experienced advisory board and explain that with construction drying up everywhere, business is only likely to get worse. Following their advisers' good advice, J&B immediately cuts office staff from ten employees to three. In addition, it sells $100,000 worth of equipment, using the receipts to pay off several equipment loans. Telling the landlord they plan to move in six months when their lease was up elicits a counter proposal that they sign up for another two years at a 25% rent reduction, which J&B accepts. Applying an aggressive full-court-press strategy to their lagging accounts receivable, they collect many of them and sell several more to a factoring company that specializes in collecting from municipalities and other public entities.

Then, with their balance sheet more or less in order, Jim and Bart meet with the bank and present their plan to further shrink the business as necessary with the goal of quickly returning to profitability, no matter how deep the cuts need to be. Their loan officer, saying that he appreciates J&B's determination to take the steps necessary to operate in the black, renews their line of credit. When several other local concrete outfits go under, J&B's business stabilizes. After several months of savvy, low-cost marketing efforts focused on smaller home remodeling projects and solar panel installations, business actually improves.

Restaurants

In most parts of America, there are at least one-third more restaurants than the local market can support. In hard times, when cutting back on eating out is near the top of most people's "spend less" list, in some areas up to 50% won't make a profit sufficient to sustain themselves.

Established eateries, especially those whose equipment is paid for, have the best chance of survival. Fancy new restaurants that borrowed heavily to pay for upmarket kitchens and pricey décor are the most vulnerable, because they have little room to cut prices. Even a small dip in patronage can make it impossible to meet debt payments, to say nothing of making a profit. For those restaurants lucky enough not to have high fixed costs, closing down a couple of the slowest days of each week may be the best option, since it will avoid paying out more in staff and supply costs than it takes in. But this strategy won't work if you've got $1,000 a day in fixed costs whether you're open or not.

Start by asking yourself "How do I make money?" Is it mostly on the weekends, on nights when the curtain goes up at the local theater, on the á la carte side of the menu, or on fancy coffee drinks, or does 80% of the profit come from the bar? (See Chapter 5 for more on how to answer this question.)

Assume for a moment that, like a lot of restaurants, you make more money selling alcohol than food. If so, the strategy for a midpriced community-based restaurant might be to create specials and events—even some that reduce profits on food to zero—that keep the place full, figuring that once folks come in they'll order their two glasses of wine (or whatever). Although we discuss marketing in detail in Chapter 8, examples and ways to bring in diners include:

- A Beggar's Banquet Tuesday, where you cook up only three entrées, but cut prices in half.
- Kids' Night, where you provide free kids' meals in your banquet room along with free babysitting.
- Thursday Singles' Night, where women eat free—the idea here of course is that where single women go, men will follow. And organized as a buffet where people can grab some food and sit at communal tables, chances are your booze profits will more than make up for the cost of the women's food.

Obviously these strategies won't work for a restaurant suffering from a dearth of tourists or a drop-off in business at the nearby convention center. But the questions you must ask remain the same: "How do I make money?" and "What can I do to preserve and build on this most important part of my business?" Hopefully you'll find some good ideas in the rest of this book in the chapters on making a profit, innovating, and marketing.

Wholesalers and Importers

By definition, wholesalers, importers, and other middlemen face a number of risks when the economy seizes up and their customers suffer. There is little new we can suggest by way of survival strategies if your entire business is rapidly shrinking. For example, a wholesaler that provides a wide range of sealants to the commercial construction industry may simply no longer be viable if local construction all but stops, and an importer of handwoven Indonesian fabric may go under if decorators are no longer willing to pay its premium price.

But, if despite a short-term sales decline, yours remains a viable field, here are the survival strategies you'll want to consider.

Quickly reduce overhead to fit your reduced sales volume. As part of figuring out how to do this, consider combining warehouse operations with another wholesaler.

Sell only to people who pay their bills on time. This means staying relentlessly current on your customers' economic situations and may mean cutting off some previously good customers. But as a middleman who operates on a relatively thin profit margin and who must pay suppliers on time, you simply can't afford to be in the collections business.

Reduce inventory. Turning over inventory too slowly and tying up precious cash is the bane of all wholesale operations, so get rid of some inventory so that precious cash is not sitting in your warehouse. If slow-selling goods have already accumulated, offer whatever deals you need to move them, even at a substantial loss. Wishful thinking won't serve here. No matter how little your excess inventory is worth now, it will likely soon be worth less.

Consider adding hot-selling product lines. Even in a severe recession, some things sell well. So while the market for expensive sweaters may take a big hit, sales of yarn to make sweaters may boom, meaning that the first regional sweater wholesaler who adds knitting supplies may do well. In short, take the time to think hard how you can reposition your business to be in better tune with the times.

Improve your marketing. Cutbacks alone will rarely return a business to profitability. To do that you'll also need to adopt the marketing strategies necessary to move more product. So hit the phone, hit the Internet, hit the bricks, and do whatever else you must to keep sales humming. (See Chapter 8 for ideas.)

Franchises

The biggest problem with many, if not most, franchise operations is depressingly simple: Franchisors charge too much for a business that doesn't have enough value to justify the high up-front and ongoing costs. In a recession, many franchises won't have enough income to cover the cost of capital and ongoing franchise fees. If yours is a typical franchise, you'll have agreed to pay the franchisor 3% to 6% of your monthly gross revenue (big-name fast food operators, such as Wendy's, McDonald's, Burger King, and Subway typically charge between 8% and 11.5%), plus a few more cents on your sales dollar for the franchisor's marketing efforts. You may also have obligated yourself to buy goods and services either directly from the franchisor or from an approved supplier, meaning you'll almost surely be paying more than if you bought them on the open market.

Add it all up, and you're likely sending the franchisor eight to ten cents of every dollar you take in. This is obviously a huge added burden if your business has begun to lose money, because unlike an independent business you need to make not only an operating profit, but also enough extra to pay the franchisor.

What to do? As with any business, cutting payroll and other expenses is a priority. But even here your hands may be partially tied if you have agreed to buy pricey goods and services from the franchisor. If cost cutting isn't enough to get your operation back in the black, there may be little else you can do. That's because, unlike independent businesses where you are free to tinker with the product, prices, and marketing strategy, your franchise agreement may contractually obligate you to follow a paint-by-number business plan. Targeting your best customers and engaging in your own guerilla marketing techniques to reach them, whether technically allowed by your franchise contract or not, is probably your best hope of reversing your sales decline. (See Chapters 7 and 8.)

If, given your best effort, your operation is hemorrhaging money, think about selling. (You'll probably need the franchisor's approval.) Obviously, selling is difficult when a business is losing money, but you may have some hope if there are successful operators of the same franchise in your area, you have a good location, and you sell cheap. That's because a franchise operation with a number of outlets may have the management savvy and deep pockets to succeed where you could not.

If you can't make a quick sale, your only choice is usually to shutter the business, add up your debts, and move on. (See Chapter 12.) ●

Don't Ignore Bad News

*"Take all the time to reflect that circumstances permit but when the time
for action comes, stop thinking."*
ANDREW JACKSON

S mall enterprises are incredibly sensitive to both good and bad fortune.
Catching an important entrepreneurial trend or operating in a
booming locality or business sector can result in quick growth and
outsized profits. Unfortunately, the opposite is also true. When the local
economy sours, or for some reason your business niche falls out of favor,
profits can turn into losses faster than the neighbor's pest of a cat disappears
when you reach for the garden hose.

It's exciting and fun to expand a successful business by hiring additional
employees, buying more equipment, renting new space, and doing all the
other things necessary to grow. But there is precious little joy in quickly
downsizing a business that has become overextended, especially one that has
borrowed heavily to fund expansion, only to find that a declining market
won't sustain it. Unfortunately, entrepreneurs whose businesses are suddenly
caught in stormy financial seas typically start by either denying they are in
trouble or underestimating its severity. The result is that many businesses
that could have been saved by rigorous early action quickly become so debt-
burdened that they die unnecessary deaths.

Why You Can't Wait

Huge, once highly profitable companies such as Ford or Kodak can see their
market position deteriorate for years or even decades without closing. But
small entrepreneurs rarely, if ever, have the luxury of being able to similarly
ride their declining businesses slowly into the sunset. In the small business
world, if revenues drop significantly for more than a few months, you must
promptly both cut expenses and address the causes of the decline. If you
don't, you risk quick and brutal failure.

How do you know when it's time to cut back? As a hands-on entrepreneur,
you should immediately know about—or better, anticipate—negative news
such as a precipitous sales drop, the loss of a big contract, the failure of a

large account to pay on time, or the emergence of a tough new competitor. The problem is rarely spotting the disturbing event or trend, but admitting to yourself that it is serious enough to require quick and decisive action. For example, the owner of the small Reader's Corner bookstore who learns that Barnes & Noble is planning to open a superstore on the next corner is all too likely to hope for the best while carrying on business pretty much as usual. Similarly, the operator of a hotel in a pricey tourist area might do little or nothing even when future bookings drop by 30%.

Whistling a happy tune in the face of entrepreneurial adversity, especially a true recession, won't work. Once you see clearly that your business faces a boulder-strewn road, you must immediately come up with a workable plan to either clear the rocks, choose another path, or sensibly deal with the problem in some other way. Depending on your business and the severity of its financial problem, this might involve quickly cutting overhead, moving to a cheaper location, selling pricey equipment, introducing a new product or service, developing a better way to reach customers, cutting office expenses, selling the business (or a part of it), or closing down, before business losses gobble up all your family's assets.

But because survival depends on quickly reversing losses, what you do is usually less important than how fast you act. Delay even a couple of months too long and fast accumulating debt can turn the boulders in your path into gravestones.

EXAMPLE: All Wooden, a company that builds and replaces wooden windows in older houses, has operated successfully for 38 years when the recession hits. New orders slow dramatically; customers begin to pay late if at all. Owners Janet and Bill try to avoid layoffs by undertaking an expensive cable TV ad campaign. When that fails to bring in many new customers, they again consider layoffs, but decide to wait 60 days in the hope that business will improve.

But in less than a month, the bank, pointing out that All Wooden is in violation of two major covenants (they were operating at a loss, and their debt-to-equity ratio was out of balance), pulls their line of credit. Janet and Bill try to find a factor to buy their receivables, but because many of them were past due, there are no takers. With little cash and a gaggle of suddenly aggressive creditors, All Wooden files for bankruptcy.

Cut Costs, Change Direction, Quit, or Sell

What exactly should you do when hard economic times cause your enterprise to suddenly operate in the red? Commonly you'll have three choices:

- cut expenses and increase low-cost marketing in an effort to return to profit
- take the business in a promising new direction, or
- close down.

In addition, the owners of a minority of troubled small businesses that have obvious long-term value may have a fourth choice, to sell.

Let's look at all four in some detail.

Cut Back

When times are good, it's easy to expand too fast or be too casual about controlling costs. Like a victorious army that advances so quickly it outraces its own supply lines, a rapidly growing business can easily become a victim of its own euphoria, snatching defeat from the jaws of victory. It can become financially, personally, and logistically overextended if, for example, owners open a second café, hire more production workers, or ambitiously expand a website. And when this occurs, you become highly vulnerable to any significant drop-off in business.

Even if a business hasn't been on a growth binge, a long period of financial success often leads owners to tolerate inefficient and sometimes even downright sloppy business practices. For example, the head of a solidly profitable time-share management company in a booming resort area might pay himself and key employees generous salaries and lavish perks, while still expecting to take off Fridays to play golf. He'll quickly be in trouble when the real estate boom goes bust.

As you might expect, both in war and business, the best antidote for advancing too fast or managing too loosely is to pull back quickly and consolidate your initial success. Executing a strategic retreat can work particularly well when your expansion hasn't locked in high capital costs. But if your car dealership, furniture store, or financial management company has maxed out its credit and increased its expenses to move to a fancy new sales complex, simply cutting the number of employees and other expenses won't solve your problem. You'll either have to figure out a way to keep sales growing, sell to someone who can, or find a way to shed your newly acquired overhead costs.

Likewise, opening a second or third location or otherwise substantially expanding just before an economic downturn hits almost always leads to serious economic troubles. If your new location, new product line, or expanded operation isn't quickly profitable, your survival usually depends on shutting it down. If you don't, you are at high risk of transferring precious time and energy from the successful part of your business to the new piece that is sucking your cash while killing your profits, almost always a terrible strategy.

EXAMPLE: Just before the recession hit, Alexia, the owner of Patina, an upscale hair salon that earned good profits for over a decade, decided to open a branch on the other side of town. Facing several entrenched competitors at the new location, Alexia lost money from day one, something that suddenly threatened Patina's survival when business at her original shop dropped 25%. Alexia wanted to close her new shop, but had agreed to a pricey two-year lease and bought a shop full of expensive equipment.

With the help of her lawyer, Alexia convinced the landlord that Patina faced bankruptcy if the lease couldn't be terminated—with the result that, in exchange for a payment equal to four months' rent, he canceled the remainder of the lease. Then Alexia moved the fancy new work stations to her old shop, selling the older equipment to a low-rent shop in the next county. Helped by a short-term loan from her mother, Alexia had just enough money left to hang onto her still-profitable core business.

Assuming for now that your business's situation is still sufficiently sound that a cutback plan can work, you'll want to focus energy and resources on your profitable core competencies while shucking off other money- and energy-draining activities. To develop your back-to-basics business plan, start by looking at the profit margins of each key area of your little empire. You'll probably find that the areas that made you successful in the first place are still your cash cows. For example, a coffee shop that added dinner to its traditional breakfast and lunch business just a few months before the local economy turned sour might find that most of its profits are still made before 2:30 p.m. and that the new dinner business, no matter how excellent its long-term prospects, is causing unsustainable losses. Fine—cut dinner, take a hard look at lunch, and reemphasize coffee and breakfast. When the operation is profitable again, and sunnier economic times return, take another look at expanding into pork chops and pasta. (For help on this, see Chapter 5.)

Although there is no one-plan-fits-all business formula to cutting costs in bad times, most businesses should cut expenses by at least as much as lost income. For example, if sales drop 30%, you'll want to quickly cut costs by that many dollars. In a very small business, this will almost always mean cutting your own pay as well as trying to minimize every possible expense. At the same time, you'll want to work hard to increase sales. (For help with that, read about innovation in Chapter 6 and marketing in Chapter 8.)

> **TIP**
>
> **Cut first, market second.** Don't forget that when you cut spending, you save 100 cents of every dollar. Marketing can bring in profitable new sales, especially for low overhead service businesses, but you never get to keep 100 cents of every dollar. Chapter 3 discusses many strategies for cutting costs.

Take Your Business in a New Direction

In some situations, cutting expenses will simply forestall failure, not prevent it. Pivoting your business so you can face the recessionary era is essential, especially where it's obvious that failure is inevitable if you stick to your old business model. Innovating in tough times is hard to do, especially when your company is already under financial pressure, but your chances of success will improve if you are moving with, not against, the spirit of the times. (More on this in Chapter 6.)

For example, a lawyer might shift from advising business startups to helping entrepreneurs with the legal problems that frequently accompany downsizing. Or the owners of a rural bed and breakfast with a substantial mortgage, who are hit by too much local competition and an area-wide economic downturn, could combine expense cutbacks with a new recession-sensitive marketing strategy, such as using the Internet and other outreach efforts to market to urban families looking for an affordable place to hold family reunions, weddings, or retirement events.

If your business is in danger of failing despite expense cutbacks, we suggest a two-step approach to analyze whether a major change of direction may save you. First, inventory and list your enterprise's core skills and competencies. Second, assess whether or not you can market them in new and affordable ways. For instance, if Wang Flooring spots a potentially lucrative opportunity to sell a suddenly popular new type of kitchen flooring to existing customers, or an existing commercial floor product to new home-remodeling customers, exploring whether either will work quickly and on the cheap is probably its best survival strategy.

EXAMPLE 1: Sandrine, Mavis, and Paul formed SMP & Associates to design websites for e-commerce companies. For two years, business was so good SMP's headcount ballooned to 30, and it was about to sign a lease for office space in a pricey area. Then the credit meltdown scared potential customers, who axed new projects, and new business dried up. Still, for months, the partners believed they could survive until business picked up by completing SMP's many existing contracts. But when two of their best remaining customers suddenly declared bankruptcy and a third simply closed without paying its bills, SMP's owners concluded that SMP was no longer viable.

That's when Mavis mentioned that River People, a nonprofit environmental group whose board she chaired, needed help with its website. With nothing else on the horizon, SMP made River People a quick proposal and landed a fair-sized job, albeit at an hourly rate far lower than they were used to charging profit-making enterprises. Based on this success and a few days of calling other area nonprofits, the partners decided that redeploying their skills to design state-of-the-art websites for nonprofits was their best strategy to stay in business, at least until higher-margin commercial business again became available.

To get started, they made a list of the 20 largest health, environmental, and education groups in the area. Next, they studied each organization's website, easily spotting a number that badly needed improvement. Then they pitched SMP's design services, taking the time to do quick redesign specs for the largest nonprofits. Although many of these potential customers claimed to have absolutely no funds to improve their sites, a half dozen changed their minds when Mavis explained how River People had quickly raised the needed money through a focused membership appeal.

Over the next six months, SMP continued to work with a number of nonprofits, still intending to eventually return to the profitable world of e-commerce. But then, at an owners' meeting one fine spring day, a funny thing happened. In the middle of outlining his planned proposal to a potential client in the children's health field, Paul announced that he was having so much fun working for people who really stood for something that he didn't want to do anything else. When Mavis and Sandrine agreed, the owners realized that they hadn't just temporarily adjusted their business plan in reaction to a financial emergency, they had fundamentally changed it.

EXAMPLE 2: Jorge and Guillermo thought they would be tremendously successful when they opened Los Padres Grill, a midpriced Mexican restaurant across from a university's large complex of married-student housing. With the exception of a McDonald's, there was no real competition nearby. Initially quite successful, the grill's monthly numbers began to display red ink when the recession hit and anxious families cut their eating-out budgets. After four bad months, each one worse than the last, Jorge and Guillermo realized they had to either quit or try a different approach.

With the help of a small loan from their uncle, they converted their sit-down restaurant to a takeout place with just a few tables. Because customers now lined up at a counter to order food, there was no need to provide table service. Prices could be reduced, which somewhat improved their student business.

But still, because only the dinner business was marginally profitable, it was obvious Los Padres Grill needed to quickly develop additional markets or close down. Jorge and Guillermo decided their best bet was to increase sales to people who worked in the light industrial area just north of the campus. Taking a few days to talk to workers at an auto body shop, metal fabricating company, wholesale plumbing supply outfit, and similar businesses, the partners learned that few workers patronized Los Padres at lunch primarily because they were too busy to take a formal lunch hour. Instead, they grabbed a sandwich off a roving lunch truck or brought food from home. To improve access to their food, Jorge and Guillermo converted Guillermo's truck into "the Los Padres Taco Wagon" complete with warming ovens, coolers, and food display units.

Now able to take its food to customers, Los Padres' business immediately improved, something that encouraged Jorge and Guillermo to further diversify into catering. Reasoning that even in tough times virtually all small businesses sometimes order food for meetings and celebrations, and financially challenged students occasionally have parties, the partners created a menu of reasonably priced catered meals. When flyers were distributed at all businesses on the Taco Wagon's route and throughout the student housing complex, orders quickly began to come in.

Sell Your Business or Its Assets

Very few owners of economically troubled small businesses have the opportunity to sell their business as a whole. But if your company has a valuable asset, such as real estate, intellectual property, a respected brand, or valuable equipment free of debt, you may be able to sell it. You'll be able to pay off your debts and, if you are truly fortunate, end up with a few dollars in your pocket.

While you explore whether it's possible to profitably sell your business or its assets, you will almost always need to also cut expenses quickly. That's because finding a buyer and completing a sale will almost always take time, something you don't have if losses are mounting. There's not much point in selling your business or its valuable property only to have all of the proceeds go to pay your creditors.

Close Down

For a variety of reasons, including new competition, a changing marketplace, or most frightening, a recession-driven loss of customers and pricing power, many small businesses won't survive. Sadly, when an economic tsunami hits and customers stop spending, many small businesses fail despite the fact that their owners work hard and do lots of things right. In these circumstances, even formerly highly successful businesses can sail into weather too heavy to survive. In short, if you are the owner of a terminal business, your best course of action is to repeat "I am not my business, and my business is not me," as you close the doors for the last time.

Perhaps it will help you maintain your perspective if you think about the many New York City tourist-based businesses that failed after 9/11. Suddenly, with no out-of-towners to ride their excursion buses, sign up for their theater tours, or buy their souvenirs, many either qualified for government assistance or closed down. Only you can decide whether your business occupies a niche that can outlast a severe downturn, but especially if business has dropped by 40% or more, chances are the decision has been made for you. For example, if a recession decimates your sales of luxury watches, there may be little you can do to survive—unless you come up with a successful new marketing campaign, perhaps one that focuses on value, practicality, and durability and that can convince wealthy penny-pinchers that it still makes sense to purchase a fine watch.

Decide How Much to Cut Expenses

If you believe that your business still has a heartbeat, you have probably already acted to reduce expenses. But if, like most entrepreneurs, you're optimistic about the possibility of a quick turnaround, you probably haven't cut enough. The result is that as hard times get harder, you'll have to cut again, and deeper. But whether you're doing it for the first, second, or even the third time, moving quickly to cut expenses without killing an already troubled business is no easy task.

Your first step is to decide how much you need to cut. Approach this by creating a worst case, a middle case, and an optimistic budget for the next three, six, and 12 months. (To learn how to do a profit-and-loss forecast, see the appendix.) Then gather your advisers and go over these numbers. Chances are, after challenging all of your assumptions, they'll recommend that you go with a version of your budget close to your worst-case scenario, reasoning that your chances of survival are far better if you err on the conservative side.

EXAMPLE: Because of government budget cuts, sales of your public-library-centered consulting business have dropped 25% in the last three months with no rebound in sight. Obviously, your budget for the immediate future should reflect at least this reduced income. But unless you have been quickly able to diversify your business to create a new and profitable income stream, it is wise to assume that income will drop further, since there is no sign your decline has bottomed out. If, as might be sensible, you predict that sales will be down 40% for the year, it follows that to balance your budget you'll need to cut expenses at least by that amount and probably significantly more.

But where will all your savings come from? Here are some of the main areas to look to when you need to cut costs:

- discretionary spending (nonessential maintenance and employees)
- rent (landlords are more willing to renegotiate a lease in an economic downturn)
- capital costs (put off that new equipment purchase), and
- payroll (you might not need to lay anyone off—instead, temporarily cut back salaries and hours).

Cutting expenses, of course, is easier said than done. Chapter 3 includes a long list of creative ways to back on specific kinds of spending without crippling your business.

Act Slowly to Reverse Cutbacks

After you've had to make painful cuts in jobs and salaries, you would be only human if you were tempted to quickly reverse them should business even modestly improve. This is understandable, especially when you hope to rehire employees whose personal budgets you know are miserably stretched. But there are at least two reasons why this is not a good idea.

First, if significant cutbacks were needed in the first place, it will almost certainly take many months and possibly a year or more to bounce back to health, even should the economy pick up or other factors that triggered the need to downsize begin to dissipate. And before you should even think about increasing expenditures, your business not only needs to return to profitability, but also to dig itself out of its financial hole. In many instances, you'll also want to repay at least a good portion of borrowed money, catch up on deferred maintenance, and replace dodgy equipment before you give a thought to restoring benefits, hours, paychecks, and especially, hiring more employees. For example, if you have borrowed $50,000, deferred the purchase of $25,000 worth of new equipment, and failed to repaint your tatty-looking building, you've got lots to spend money on before adding to your payroll expense.

A second reason not to restore jobs and pay too quickly is to avoid the possibility of a double dip. If, after a couple of months, your business again underperforms, it will be emotionally devastating to you and your staff to have to reimpose cuts. To say your credibility as a leader will be shot is an understatement.

In addition, rehiring laid-off workers will almost always be a lower priority than restoring at least some or hopefully all of the pay and hours of the employees who have stuck with you during the hard times and worked extra hard to achieve the recovery. Indeed, if you really did adopt a good process to cut your least important functions and your most inefficient people, it might not make sense to reverse these decisions, no matter how much business prospects improve. Instead you would be smarter to employ fewer, more efficient workers at the same time you lift the pay of those who have experienced cutbacks. (See Chapter 9.)

EXAMPLE: When the snow fails to arrive by December that year, John and Adelle, owners of the HillTop Lodge, are forced to lay off several maids and restaurant workers and make an across-the-board salary reduction. Finally, in the last week of February, the mountains surrounding HillTop Lodge experience a deep snowfall. Even though business immediately improves, John and Adelle decide to keep a lid on costs until they can reduce their maxed-out bank line of credit. So except for rehiring a couple of essential room cleaners and restaurant staffers, they and HillTop's managers continue to fill in behind the front desk and grab the now happily jingling phones. Adelle, who has learned to make a killer martini, decides that she can handle a few more months behind the bar.

Only when a long and busy spring ski season gives way to an equally good summer, allowing HillTop to reduce its line of credit to a comfortable level, do John and Adelle restore half of the salary reductions. A month later, when business stays good, they hire back the assistant reservations manager. But they decide to stick with a number of the economies imposed during the downturn, including contracting out maintenance and snow removal instead of paying a full-time maintenance employee. Finally, when bookings for the fall "color season" come in strong, they decide to restore all salary cuts to their pre-drought levels and hire a weekend bartender. At Christmas, with business still strong, everyone who had survived the tough year receives a small bonus, along with a personal note from John and Adelle thanking them for their loyalty.

Control Your Cash Flow

"Anybody who thinks money will make you happy hasn't got money."
DAVID GEFFEN

When times are tough, cash becomes king, emperor, czar, and grand vizier rolled into one. Suddenly, in a few weeks or months, what was once abundant in your small business can become difficult to get and hard to hold onto. This sudden cash contraction is usually caused by some or all of the following: poor sales, lower profit margins, past-due accounts receivable, bloated inventory, restricted or lost credit lines, and the impossibility of raising more investment capital.

If you've decided to soldier on, you need to trim expenses quickly so that they match your lowered income. (See Chapter 2.) And to make informed decisions, not guesstimates, about how much to cut, you should by now have created a formal profit-and-loss statement and a cash flow analysis (see the appendix).

Now it's time for the next step, which is to focus on your current cash position with an eye to improving it. If cash is flowing out of your business significantly faster than it's coming in, you'll have a very short window in which to fix the problem, assuming it's fixable at all. Viewed most broadly, you need to examine three aspects of your cash flow:

- how and when cash comes into your business
- how and when it goes out again, and
- where it gets tied up in the meantime (in inventory and equipment, for example).

How much cash does your company need? Because businesses are so different, there is no one-size-fits-all answer. But generally speaking, when a deep downturn hits and sales drop, you need at least enough cash to survive six months. That gives you enough time to cut expenses, increase marketing, and quickly develop innovative new products or services. Don't panic—this doesn't mean you need to have six months' revenue in hand now. What you do need is the confidence that you can somehow produce enough cash or credit to cover any shortfall between what you'll take in and what you'll pay out during this period.

Keep Paying Your Bills on Time

When a business begins to run short of cash, it's common for the owners to start paying bills—sometimes even federal and state taxes—late. We hope we don't need to explain why skirting tax obligations is an absolute no-no and a clear sign that you are at (or past) the point where you should close down. (But if you're unconvinced, see Chapter 4 for more on why shortchanging the IRS is a terrible idea.)

Even paying garden-variety bills late is almost always a poor approach, for all the reasons discussed below. But perhaps the biggest benefit of keeping current on your accounts payable is that doing so tells you that you are making the decisions necessary to keep your business viable. Maybe being able to pay your bills on time means you have developed a successful guerilla marketing campaign, moved to a low-rent location, sold unneeded equipment, laid off employees, refinanced an equipment lease, held a killer inventory reduction sale, or cajoled your customers whose accounts are overdue into bringing them current. Whatever you're doing to cope with your cash problems, if the result is that you can pay your creditors on time, it is a clear sign that you are following a winning survival strategy.

Why Paying on Time Makes Sense

But what about the argument some small business commentators make that by keeping accounts current you are paying out money before you absolutely have to—something you can't afford to do in tough times? Sorry, in the real world of small business this is nonsense for at least six important reasons.

Saving Your Good Name

The cost of paying on time is low as compared to almost anything else you can do to maintain a good reputation in your business community. When you pay late, you kick your cash problem down the road a few months at great cost to your credibility, something that is crucial to preserve in tough economic times. To survive, your business will eventually have to pay its debts, so by putting them off a few months you gain nothing but risk losing your good reputation.

Saving Money

Paying early can get you discounts that net you more cash then you could earn in interest by holding onto the money longer. Don't be shy about asking for deeper discounts than your vendors initially offer. Especially if you have the cash to pay early, you should be able to achieve reductions as high as 10% to 15%.

EXAMPLE: A few months after the recession hit and new construction plummeted, Solar Supply LLC's bank threatened to pull its line of credit. This was avoided when the company's founders loaned Solar Supply a substantial sum. Now with both the loan money and line of credit to draw on, Solar Supply had adequate cash, but no profits. So after making lots of money-saving cutbacks, Solar Supply called its ten largest vendors with a simple proposition: For the next six months, Solar Supply will pay on delivery for all orders, in exchange for a 15% discount. Five vendors—themselves short of cash—immediately agreed, and two more said yes when it became clear they would otherwise lose the business. The three holdouts were easily replaced by companies that realized that when times are tough, everyone has to give a little.

Ensuring Excellent Future Service

Every working day, you (and every other small entrepreneur on Earth) form judgments about the businesses you come into contact with, judgments that are particularly crucial at a time when many businesses are in financial trouble. For example, you likely have thoughts like these on a regular basis:

- Business A produces a reliable product.
- Business B's employees can be relied on to show up when they say they will and work overtime if that's what it takes to finish a job.
- Business C constantly comes up with new and innovative services that frequently anticipate our needs.
- Business D always seems to be understaffed by surly employees who never return phone calls.
- The owner of Business E is great, but some of his younger employees are not properly trained.
- Damn Business F. Another day is here, and its check isn't.

When these thoughts run through your head, you'll doubtless question whether you ever want to deal with business D, E, or F again. And if you had to choose one of these less-than-stellar outfits to head your blacklist, we bet it would be Business F. That just makes good sense. Tough as it is to cope with late deliveries, unreturned phone calls, inexperienced workers, or even poor quality products or services, it's far harder to survive without being paid. This is doubly true for a business in a field where payment isn't due until after goods or services are provided. Here, if payments are substantially late, a business can actually fail even though its bottom line shows it to be profitable.

You want to be a company that other companies want to do business with. For example, if your business suddenly needs to ask a print shop to turn around a flyer in a few hours, you'll have a much better chance of getting them to say yes if you paid your last bill the day it was due.

Encouraging People in Your Network to Recommend Your Business

Keep in mind that it's not just your satisfied customers (people who pay you money) who tell others about your business. All the people who work for and with you can also be powerful recommenders. This includes everyone you cut a check to, from your landlord and insurance broker to the owner of the restaurant down the street that occasionally caters your meetings. If they feel positive about your business—something that is greatly aided when you pay their bills promptly—each can become a significant marketing ally.

EXAMPLE: Doug, an insurance broker, goes to great lengths to help Bluebelle Web Design find an insurance company willing to customize a standard business policy to meet Bluebelle's special needs. Joan, Bluebelle's president, is so impressed with Doug that after the policy is finally in place and Bluebelle is billed, she ignores the ten-day payment terms and immediately mails the premium check, along with a note of thanks. Now it's Doug's turn to be pleased. Later that week, when he attends a service club meeting and the subject of small business websites comes up, he favorably mentions Bluebelle to what amounts to a roomful of potential customers. As a result, Joan picks up two excellent new accounts.

Building and Keeping a Positive Credit Profile

If your business is new and tiny, you might assume the rest of the commercial world doesn't even know you exist. Not so. Almost from day one your small business will leave tracks in the commercial sands. For example, if you incorporate, form an LLC, hire employees, or apply for a bank loan, credit card, or trade credit, you'll quickly appear on the radar screen of Dun & Bradstreet and similar data collection organizations. These outfits gather and sell credit information about virtually every American business. Among other things, they note what your business does, how many employees it has, who owns it, and, probably most important, its credit and bill-paying history. In short, your bill-paying profile is available to anyone who pays a modest fee.

Who would buy such a report? Especially when economic times are tough and many businesses are losing money, the answer is: Virtually all of your creditors and potential creditors, including banks that are considering lending you money, companies reviewing your application to lease equipment, and suppliers, wholesalers, and other businesses from which you have requested credit. True, an excellent payment record alone won't guarantee that you'll receive a bundle of commercial credit or a particular loan; other information is also important. But if Dun & Bradstreet reports that you habitually pay late, your credit application is sure to raise a red flag and greatly increase the likelihood that you'll have to pay cash up front.

Getting a Payment Cushion

Paying on time acts as an effective rainy day fund if and when you face a serious reverse like losing a major client, having a horrible sales month, or dealing with the bankruptcy of someone who owes you a lot of money. That's because in case of emergency, you'll have a payment cushion of several months: If you've paid promptly over the years, you'll have built up a substantial reservoir of goodwill and respect with creditors. They are likely to support you when you can't pay on time if you can show them a convincing plan to solve your temporary cash problem.

EXAMPLE: Frank's Marine Services, a long-term customer of your engine repair business, faces a difficult business patch because a charter company went bankrupt owing it $40,000. Frank has always paid you early or on time, so chances are you will be as accommodating as possible—certainly far more generous than you would be if Benji's Boat Repair, your most feckless customer, asked for similar help.

What to Do When You Must Pay Late

Sometimes, despite your best efforts, you might not be able to pay all your bills on time. For example, you might be forced to delay some bills a month or two while you deal with a one-time problem like a lost line of credit, a tax lien, or closing a money-losing part of your business.

In this situation, your best strategy can be stated in three words: communicate, communicate, communicate. Don't wait until you receive a third dun letter to talk to the people whose check is not in the mail; pick up the phone as soon as you know you have a problem. Talk to the person who has real authority to manage accounts receivable to briefly explain what the problem is, how you're solving it, and when you expect to be able to pay. If you can make an immediate partial payment, even a small one, it's absolutely essential that you do so. As the old saying goes, it always pays to put your money where your mouth is.

> **TIP**
>
> **Don't overdramatize your business problems.** Occasionally, people who can't pay a bill on time are tempted to detail every miserable thing that prevents them from doing so. Better to briefly explain a good reason for the holdup and focus on when you will be able to send a check. Otherwise, you risk convincing the creditor that things are so bad they should immediately cut off future credit.

How to Create More Cash

If paying bills (especially tax bills) late is a terrible idea, what are some more effective ways that a cash-strapped business can keep its checking account in positive territory? Generally speaking, all suggestions fall into two broad categories: spend less and take in more. And in businesses that maintain inventory, there is the added wrinkle of not allowing too much cash to be tied up in a warehouse or shop.

Spend Less

Especially in a recession when customers are scarce, the quickest way to raise cash is not to spend it. There are many ways to reduce the amount of money flowing out of your business—and implementing just a few can make a big difference.

Eliminate Discretionary Spending

If you planned to paint your building, buy new equipment, or hire additional employees, don't. Only if a particular expense is essential to carrying out a crucial marketing or diversification plan should you go ahead. In virtually every other instance, just close your checkbook.

Even if you've made a contractual commitment to spend money, you can try to negotiate your way out of it. If you are willing to pay a reasonable buyout fee, it's legal and honorable. After all, once clued in to your financial problems, the other party may be happy to accept a partial payment from you rather than risk your business failing and receiving no payment at all. If the other party simply won't renegotiate, accept a reasonable buyout offer, or otherwise work with you, you or your attorney may need to point out that if you can't stem the flow of red ink, bankruptcy may be your only option.

Buy More Carefully

All businesses buy things. It should go without saying that it will help pre-serve cash if you buy in smaller quantities and negotiate lower prices. But given that prices usually go down when volume goes up, accomplishing these things together may seem impossible.

But when times are tough and suppliers are hungry for business (especially from companies that pay on time), you'll be surprised at how many will lower prices, if you ask and don't take no for an answer. Don't overlook basic expenditures, such as phone service, electricity, copying, janitorial services, and payments to a variety of independent contractors.

Even for smaller purchases, often it's best to ask for bids (prices) from a number of suppliers, including your old standbys. And don't sign a long-term contract with the first vendor who offers you a better deal. If someone eager to get your business offers you a lower price, the vendor you use now will probably try to keep your business by going lower still.

Look for a Cheaper Credit Card Processing Service

If you take credit cards, chances are that you pay your processor too much, thus every day giving up cash you desperately need. Because many banks quote a complicated menu of charges to handle different types of credit cards, it can be confusing and time-consuming to compare prices, something deliberately calculated to give bank sales reps a huge advantage over often extremely busy merchants.

As a general rule, if you solicit a number of bids and buy your own processing equipment, you'll save a significant amount. But because getting several bids may take time you don't have, here are a couple of shortcut ideas. First, if you raise the issue at a local merchants meeting or industry trade group message board, you might find that someone else has done the comparison shopping for you. Second, check out the prices offered by Costco Services and compare them to what you pay now. Costco may not always be cheapest, but it's known for offering a high-quality service at a competitive price.

Stop Paying for Equipment You Don't Need

When times are good, it's easy to commit to buying or leasing expensive equipment—trucks, cars, bulldozers, electronic gear, forklifts, and so on. Take a hard look at everything you own, especially items you're still paying for. Sell everything you don't absolutely need. Even if you sell a vehicle for less than you owe and must make up the difference to pay off the loan, you'll often net large cash savings over time. And if you still need the item from time to time, you can probably rent it by the day for far less.

Don't forget leased equipment. If you are leasing equipment you don't absolutely need, ask the leasing company to renegotiate payments or cancel the lease in exchange for taking back the equipment. If no one takes your requests seriously, don't be afraid to involve a lawyer, who should be experienced in explaining that without quick cooperation, your business may fail. Especially if the leasing company believes you might close down and file for bankruptcy, it will likely make you a better offer or take the equipment back.

> **TIP**
> **Share equipment with other businesses.** Consider the possibility of partnering with another small business if you could sensibly share equipment. Chapter 12 discusses the potential financial advantages of combining some or all of your operations with a competitor. Sharing the cost of expensive equipment is one of them.

Renegotiate Your Lease or Move

Renegotiating an ongoing lease to get a lower rate is rarely easy. But especially if the poor economy has caused tenants in your area to be thin on the ground and your lease will be up for renewal soon, chances are good that if pushed, your landlord will give you a better deal.

Even if you have a long-term lease, try to renegotiate. If properties are emptying out around you and you open your books and show your landlord that, without a reduction in rent, your business won't survive, he or she may be willing to accommodate you. One possibility is to propose a significantly lower rent for the next year, with a built-in increase to kick in when and if your sales return to normal levels.

EXAMPLE: Cleveland and June run Ambrosia Gifts at the Fairview Shopping Mall. Sales have fallen 40% but they must keep paying their lease, common area fees, advertising surcharges, and a small percentage of sales to the mall, the gift shop falls hopelessly into the red.

Believing that mall management will never negotiate a more favorable lease, they decide to close the store immediately and then research whether to file for bankruptcy. But to their surprise, no sooner do they notify Fairview Mall of their intentions than the mall, which by this time has a number of empty shops, offers to cut their rent and fees by 50% for the next 12 months. The deal convinces June and Cleveland that with a more energetic and creative marketing effort, they have a chance to survive.

Be careful not to trade a short-term rent reduction for a significantly longer time commitment, because you can't know for sure that this adjustment will be sufficient to keep you going. In exchange for your requested reduction, your landlord may ask for your personal guarantee (even if you are organized as an LLC). Giving it could imperil your personal credit. (See Chapter 4 to understand why when times are hard, it's particularly important to keep business and personal debts legally separate.)

> **TIP**
> **Consider having a lawyer or other third party negotiate for you.** Unless you have a personal relationship with your landlord, it can often help to let someone else do the negotiating. A lawyer will know how to reassure the landlord that your business can survive if you resolutely reduce expenses, while at the same time suggesting that if you can't quickly reduce expenses, bankruptcy may be your only option. (See Chapter 13 for a discussion of how to get out of a lease.)

Sublet Unneeded Space

If your business is losing money, your real estate may now be your most valuable asset—make sure it's producing every penny of income it can. Especially if your business downsizes, rent out unused space if your lease allows it (you may need to obtain your landlord's prior consent). You might even want to look at moving your business to another location and renting out your entire building.

You might conclude that it would be impossible to find a subtenant because, in a recession, other businesses also have surplus space. But it can put real dollars in your pocket to think again. List your vacancy online and canvass your area for a subtenant who can no longer afford space of its own.

Be creative. Even formerly fiercely competitive retailers may survive by operating out of the same space or combining office, warehouse, or even small manufacturing operations. (See Chapter 11 for more on how a recession profoundly changes the competitive landscape.)

Cut Employee Perks

If you haven't canceled extras, from company-paid cars, parking spaces, and club dues to the daily newspaper and bottled water, you may be beyond help. Once again, examine every check your business writes. Even when cuts are more symbolic than significant, such as no longer buying pizza for meetings or renting parking spaces for employees, working hard to chop every possible expense sends an important message to everyone associated with your business that you are determined to do what it takes to survive.

Cut Employee Benefits

Benefits should be the first place you look to cut employee costs. For example, if your business matches your employees' contributions to a 401(k) plan up to $1,000 per year or it has other generous benefits such as paying health club memberships, alternative wellness programs, or a pricey dental plan, seriously consider eliminating them. Although painful, when times are tough it's better to cut most benefits rather than lay off people.

The one big exception is your medical plan. If you provide one, do your best to keep it, even if you have to cut your premiums by raising employee contributions and co-pays. For most people, health insurance is an essential part of their personal safety net, and if you don't provide it, they will look for an employer that does. (More on this in Chapter 9.)

Cut Your Pay and That of Highly Paid Employees

Payroll is the biggest expense for many small businesses. If this is true for your enterprise, it follows that cutting other expenditures is unlikely to produce the savings your troubled business needs. Sooner or later—and the sooner the better—you'll need to reduce the size of your payroll.

In bad economic times, when jobs are scarce, it's usually possible to cut pay by a small percentage and not lose employees. The first person to take a pay cut should be you (and if your spouse works for the business, both of you). Even if your compensation is already modest, so that cutting it won't save much, trimming your own salary is sure to get employees' attention—and their respect—in ways a dozen dire financial pronouncements never will. Next, sit down with any well-paid employees to help them confront the need to voluntarily accept similar reductions. Depending on pay levels and other circumstances, a cut of 10% to 20% is often reasonable. But be very reluctant to cut the pay of people at the bottom of your scale. Not only is this the decent thing to do, it helps you keep experienced employees who, if forced to take less, would probably look for another job.

This cut-from-the-top approach usually makes sense for several reasons. First, it should help you save money without losing essential employees. Second, and perhaps more important, it sends a message to everyone connected to your company that you and other managers take personal responsibility for coping with tough times.

EXAMPLE: John and Adelle own and operate the HillTop Lodge, a 60-room country motel near a ski resort. Although the motel does decent business year-round, in most years the lion's share of profits are made from the winter ski crowds, who cheerfully pay high-season rates and eat and drink everything in sight. After a decade of hard work, during which they invested most profits back in the business, John and Adelle were finally able to pay themselves and several key employees comfortable salaries. Then came the year when the snow failed to arrive in their corner of the woods, and the skiers went elsewhere. It didn't take many weeks of brown slopes and terrible business before John and Adelle realized that HillTop was in serious trouble.

Calling a meeting of their five highest-paid employees, they suggested freezing all nonessential expenditures, such as replacing older but still serviceable equipment and repainting several hallways and rooms, as well as cutting nonessential items such as subscriptions to periodicals and memberships in trade organizations. They even decided to ask several employees to turn in their cell phones. In addition, they resolved to severely cut the budget for outside services, transferring work to employees who now had time on their hands. Next they announced they were cutting their own pay by 20% and asked all managers to accept a 15% reduction. A couple of people grumbled, but all they had to do was look out the window to understand the problem. Respecting John's and Adelle's determination to take the biggest hit, they accepted their lower paychecks.

This strategy isn't just for small businesses, by the way. To save jobs, shipping giant FedEx froze 401(k) contributions and cut all salaried employees' pay for 2009. The company's CEO took the biggest percentage pay cut, 20%. Other top executives were cut by 7.5% to 10%, and the rest of the salaried employees got a 5% hit. Hourly workers weren't affected. The company made these cuts even though it was profitable—it was looking ahead to an expected downturn in shipping caused by the sluggish economy.

Cut the Work Week

Another way to spread the economic pain while saving jobs is to cut the work week. For example, going to a four-and-a-half day work week saves 10% of payroll; a four-day week saves 20%. Similarly, putting a freeze on overtime hours will save you money.

If your employees are highly motivated to see your business through to better times (and appreciate the fact that the cuts avoid or reduce layoffs), the change won't significantly reduce productivity. People will realize that to keep your enterprise afloat they need to work a little harder and smarter to accomplish the same amount of work in less time. A few employees may quit, but in a deep recession most will be disposed to hang on to what they have.

Lay Off Employees

Cutting jobs and showing loyal employees the door is never a pleasant prospect. But for many businesses where payroll is the biggest cost, it's the only realistic way to achieve needed savings.

In the big business world, a CEO can order 10,000 job cuts without ever meeting anyone who gets laid off. But reducing a small workplace entails the excruciating task of laying off people you know well and are on friendly terms with. It's so hard that some businesspeople watch their business fail rather than wield the axe. But to survive, you must accept the proposition that your duty to your employees is limited by economic reality. Remember, you hired employees in an effort to make a profit, not to pay them in all circumstances forever.

Always cut jobs, not people. Things are likely to go downhill further and faster if you base your cuts on the personal needs of the people who work for you, sparing those who have the most sympathetic personal problems. If you keep them, then it means you'll be cutting those who are more efficient or needed. Far better to look at the tasks that need doing and the people who can do them best.

In a very small enterprise, it will fall to you to decide which jobs must go. But if you depend on others to help with management decisions, it's extremely important to solicit their help in deciding who you should lay off, unless of course you have decided that the manager must also go. They, not you, probably have the best frontline knowledge of which tasks are essential and which expendable. And because they are the ones who will be responsible for accomplishing the essential work with a smaller staff, they are likely to be highly motivated to hold onto the most talented workers who can do the most for the company. (Chapter 9 discusses how to plan and conduct layoffs.)

EXAMPLE: Returning to the HillTop Lodge, it becomes clear to John and Adelle that to survive, it isn't enough to cut discretionary expenses and managerial pay. To plan deeper cuts, Adelle, the financial officer, prepares a revised budget based on their newly drafted worst-case income scenario. This rebudgeting reveals that to achieve balance, an additional $200,000 needs to be cut, pronto.

Some staff reductions are obvious, such as laying off several maids and restaurant workers who, given the lack of guests, aren't needed. To help plan other staff cuts, John and Adelle convene an off-site meeting of their key employees. Fortunately, when these employees share their opinions about how best to reduce staff, a consensus emerges. For example, Constantine, the head cook and restaurant manager, suggests that while things remained slow, the jobs of bartender and restaurant host be combined.

Then Phyllis, the reservations manager, suggests that while business is in the dumps she can handle bookings without an assistant. She points out that occasionally, this change will mean that customers will get a message machine promising a prompt call back, but given the low volume of calls, this shouldn't be a serious problem. Finally, John proposes taking over many routine maintenance tasks himself, allowing HillTop to eliminate the position of in-house maintenance person.

The result of these and several other job consolidations and cuts is to save $200,000 in salaries without significantly reducing essential guest services or eliminating key employees who will be needed as soon as business eventually picks up. All told, ten people—including Adelle's niece, who worked as a part-time desk clerk—lose their jobs.

Increase Marketing, Cut Costs

When sales drop, you need to increase your marketing outreach. But it's not usually cost-effective to do this by paying for expensive advertising or other high-cost techniques. Instead, your cash preservation strategy should usually dictate cutting conventional marketing costs while relying instead on low-cost guerilla marketing efforts that, among other techniques, enlist your loyal customers in helping rescue your business. (Chapter 8 has lots of suggestions.)

Cut Business Travel

Assuming your business still does a significant amount of travel, cut it at least in half. Just committing to this will force you to focus on eliminating the least profitable half.

Reduce Professional Fees

Handing out money at $300 per hour is no way to save your business. Ask your lawyer to give you a recession discount and, if it's not forthcoming, shop around for someone who will. And make sure you understand what your lawyer's minimum billing interval is. If it's 20 minutes (meaning you are billed a minimum of 20 minutes for every call), bunch your questions together so you use all of the time you'll have to pay for. And if, as part of a plan to reduce expenses or deal with anxious creditors, you need your lawyer to negotiate on your behalf, do a little negotiating of your own and ask the lawyer for a flat fee stated in advance.

When it comes to accounting services, don't pay for bookkeeping that you can do much cheaper in house or by hiring a part-time bookkeeper. And again, as with every vendor, be aggressive in asking for a recession discount from your accountant, and if you don't get it, bid out your account.

Cut Printing Costs

Every business we've ever seen prints far too many copies of far too many pieces of paper with the result that lots end up in the trash. And consistently printing too much isn't the only money-eater; lots of businesses pay far too much even when they print exactly what they need. For example, if you're printing 3,000 copies of a four-color catalog at a printer down the street, chances are you can cut your bill in half by using two colors and getting bids from half a dozen area printers. And when the lowest bid comes in, ask how they can cut it further, possibly by using a slightly unusual type of paper left over from another job or waiting a few days until their equipment will be idle.

Ask Creditors to Write Off a Portion of What You Owe

If you are far behind on your bills, and especially if you think you may have to close down because it will be impossible to catch up, consider asking your creditors to write off a portion of your debt.

Your pitch should normally be along these lines: "Our company can't survive the economic downturn with its current debt load. But following our new frugal business plan, we can survive and prove to be a good long-term customer if our debts can be reduced on a one-time basis." The creditor may be willing to accept as little as 40 to 60 cents on the dollar, especially if it believes you may go bankrupt without help—or if you have found a new source of income to tide you over (perhaps a hard-headed investor who will invest only if you reduce your debt load).

Because it can be difficult to beg for debt forgiveness at the same time you promise that your business can operate in the black if you receive it, it usually makes sense to involve a small business consultant or a lawyer with business and bankruptcy experience. A call from a lawyer may be just what a creditor needs to realize that your offer is far better than a notice of your bankruptcy filing. (You can check Nolo's Lawyer Directory for in-depth attorney profiles of local lawyers.)

If you don't have cash to pay off a portion of your debt, you'll have a lot less leverage when it comes to trying to convince a creditor to write off part of it. As an alternative, you may be able to convince a creditor to instead convert your debt to a term loan with low initial payments, or, if your creditor really believes in your future, to trade debt for an equity stake in your corporation or LLC.

> **TIP**
>
> **Open your books to your creditors.** Creditors will be far more likely to support your survival plan by writing off a portion of your debt if they really believe you are taking the hard steps necessary to return your business to profit. It follows that your best course of action is often to open your books and show them.

> **CAUTION**
>
> **Don't convert business debt to personal debt.** If your business is a corporation or LLC and asks creditors to restructure current debt, the creditors may in turn ask for your personal guarantee. Agreeing to this is probably unwise, especially if you have valuable personal assets and your business may fail anyway. Read Chapter 4 for more on this.

Cut Back on Insurance Expense

Faced by tough economic times, the last thing you want to do is eliminate essential insurance coverage for fire, theft, and liability. But by increasing deductibles and canceling less essential coverage for things like business interruption or the death of a key employee, you may be able to reduce your overall payments. It makes more sense to scrimp on insurance if your business is organized as an LLC or corporation than it does if you are a sole proprietor or partner and therefore personally liable for business losses.

Also, if your business is co-owned and you have established a buy-sell agreement to allow surviving owners to buy out the deceased owner's inheritors, you might have also bought a life insurance policy to provide funds for the purchase. If so, consider canceling this policy, and if you have had it for a while, pulling out its cash value, if any.

Take in More Cash

When a sharp economic downturn hits, customers, suppliers, lenders, and investors all simultaneously try to hoard cash. This can mean that even if your business is still showing a bottom-line profit, you might have an empty bank account and no funds to pay bills. And if your sales have dropped to the point where you're in the red, you can be sure your cash problems will soon be even worse.

Okay, so far we may not have told you anything you don't already know. But hopefully here are a few ways to raise cash you might not have thought of.

Get Cash Out of Inventory

Whether you are a manufacturer, wholesaler, or retailer, if your sales have dropped significantly, chances are you now have too much inventory. That means the cash you so desperately need is sitting in your store or warehouse in an illiquid form. To convert it to pieces of paper with pictures of dead presidents, take some or all of these steps:

- Begin an energetic guerilla marketing campaign to coax more customers to buy more of what you are selling. As discussed in Chapter 8, one of the most effective ways to do this is to ask for support from your long-term customers.
- Hold a blowout sale offering enticing discounts on slow-moving items. But remember that your goal is not only to reduce inventory, but also to make a profit. So be sure to surround sale items with attractive goods that you discount only slightly.

EXAMPLE: Bangkok Designs, a clothing importer, has a warehouse and retail store overloaded with women's wear. Holding a three-day warehouse sale, in which a few items of essentially unsalable merchandise are marked down as much as 90%, other hard-to-move items are discounted 50%, but the more popular intimate wear is reduced only 20%, Bangkok is able to pull in a quick $30,000.

- Consider unloading dead inventory to deep-discount resellers such as liquidators, dollar stores, or even flea market operators. Even a few cents on the dollar is better than a truckload of unsalable items.

Coax Customers to Prepay

Health clubs, movie theaters, and car washes have for years given people an incentive to pay in advance for discounted services. For example, a theater might offer ten shows for the price of seven if you buy a coupon book. A health club might give you three months free if you join for a year.

Although many types of businesses have not traditionally marketed this way, offering discounts for prepayment, it's time they thought about this highly effective way to raise quick cash. So whether you are a landscaper, a physical therapist, or a paper box company, figure out a way you can sensibly encourage your customers to give you their cash ahead of time.

EXAMPLE: In January, always its worst sales month, Sugimoto Pool and Pond, a business that maintains swimming pools and decorative ponds, offers its customers a card worth 120% of its face value, redeemable anytime during the next year. When 35% of its customers sign up, Sugimoto has enough money to pay off the debt accumulated by virtue of its poorly timed expansion.

Raise Prices

During hard times, businesses typically must lower prices in order to attract customers. But especially for businesses that offer a wide array of goods or services, there are always some items for which prices can be raised. Often this results from the fact that during prosperous years, businesses neglect to do a careful analysis of all their prices.

As a general rule, prices designed to attract customers to your shop, office, or website should be kept as low as possible. Be more aggressive when you price discretionary items customers might purchase once they're there. For example, a yarn shop might feature rock-bottom prices on basic, single-color yarns, while keeping prices up for the luminescent, multihued varieties customers gravitate to once through the door.

EXAMPLE: Koski Firewood is forced to lower prices for cords of oak after an aggressive competitor with a wood yard on a main road puts up a huge sign advertising bargain prices. As a result, profit margins all but disappear, causing Pete and Mike Koski to consider closing down. But before they do, they consult with their informal group of advisers including their retired Uncle Frank, who has successfully run several businesses. Frank spends a day at the wood yard and comes up with these recommendations, which, taken together, put the business solidly back in the black.

- Raise prices on kindling 30%. Almost everyone adds several boxes to their order, but few pay close attention to its cost.
- Raise the delivery fee 40%. The super-frugal will borrow a pickup and haul their own wood, but most others won't notice.
- Add $20 to the fee for moving wood from curb or driveway and stacking it next to the house. Most people do this themselves, but those who can't be bothered will pay more.

Another place to look to raise prices is for goods or services that, despite—or maybe even because of—the recession, are in high demand. For example, a CPA might lower rates for basic tax schedule preparation so as not to lose business to price-cutting competitors, but raise fees for helping small businesses prepare bankruptcy-related schedules or deal with IRS tax bills.

Give a Discount for Prompt Payment

Especially when times are tough, many customers will appreciate and take advantage of discounts for early payment. If you need cash, offering a discount of 5% or more can make sense for payments on the day goods are received or services rendered. Even a 2% to 3% discount for bills paid within ten days can be a substantial motivation to pay a bill PDQ.

Collect Overdue Accounts Receivable

When lots of your customers are past due in their payments, it's almost always as much your fault as it is theirs. Even in a recession, efficient account management practices should result in most customers paying you on time. Put more bluntly, canny businesspeople avoid training their customers that it's okay to pay late, by taking quick action to penalize them. If you haven't done this, it's past time you started.

Dial for dollars. If you already have lots of overdue accounts, you'll need not only to fix your long-term policies, but also get a bunch of customers to pay pronto. Especially if you are seriously short of cash, your best bet is to pick up the phone. Whether you are a consultant calling a late-paying client, a landscape architect calling a homeowner, a wholesaler calling a retailer, or a small manufacturer calling a wholesaler, demand to talk to the person who owes you the money, or in the case of a business, the person with power to write the check. Don't be bashful—the delinquent payer absolutely needs to know that you need a check (or electronic payment) now and in full, or you'll immediately take legal steps to collect. Don't be fobbed off with excuses or vague promises that you'll be paid soon.

Withhold goods or services. If, after several phone calls, the money is still not forthcoming, what are your realistic options? It depends in part on what type of business you run and whether the customer needs more of what you sell. For example, if you produce a highly popular product or provide a service your customer needs more of, your first step is to put late-payers on credit hold—that is, don't provide more goods or services until the account is fully current. The credit hold approach might not work if there are more local suppliers of the product or service you provide. For example, if yours is one of several wholesalers that delivers fish to area restaurants and you put Ahi Bill's cafe on credit hold, Bill can buy from one of the other wholesalers. In practice, however, the other wholesalers are sure to know that he is one of your longtime customers, suspect that you have put him on credit hold, and call to check his credit. In short, if Bill is to stay in business he is going to have to pay you.

Offer a one-time discount in exchange for catching up with back payments. For example, a consultant, architect, or landscaper might offer a 10% to 20% discount for immediate payment on overdue accounts receivable. To encourage participation, when providing the carrot, don't be afraid to also show the stick by threatening to file a lawsuit or to turn the account over to a collection agency.

Sue, or hire a lawyer. Especially for large overdue accounts, get the recalcitrant debtor's immediate attention by suing in small claims court. In most states, the limit on claims is $5,000 to $10,000, and you don't need a lawyer. Or hire a lawyer to collect it for you, either for an hourly fee or a percentage of the amount collected (pay by the hour if the debt is large and the debtor is solvent). If you are lucky, a frosty letter or two from an attorney will shake loose your cash without a lawsuit being filed.

Turn accounts over to a collection agency. For smaller, seriously past-due debts that you're not interested in taking to court, your best bet is to turn them over to a collection agency. These agencies normally charge about 50% of the amount they collect. Talk to local businesspeople to get a recommendation for an agency with a good reputation for both doggedness and ethical behavior.

Borrow Money

While getting a traditional loan in this economy may be next to impossible for small businesses, there are a few other financing opportunities out there.

Consider an Alternative Lender

One innovative new company, OnDeck Capital, offers loans up to $100,000 based on a business's cash flow and/or credit card transactions. OnDeck collects the loan repayments by automatically debiting your bank account for a small amount (typically $100) each day. Although there is obviously a coercive aspect of this approach, at least it assures that you won't get behind on loan payments. OnDeck's small loans are easier to qualify for than a traditional loan and more quickly processed, but interest rates aren't low— usually 18% to 20%—and you still must have sufficient cash flow to repay. OnDeck requires that business owners sign a personal guarantee, meaning your house, savings, and other assets are at risk if your business fails while you still owe them money. For more information, go to www.ondeckcapital.com.

> **TIP**
>
> **Don't count on borrowing from a bank or investor.** Even when times are good and profits are rolling in, only a small minority of small businesses owners can raise debt or equity from banks or investors outside their circle of family and close friends. And when a business begins to lose money, there is close to a zero chance of finding an arm's-length investor. However, the 2009 federal economic

stimulus package provides $730 million to the Small Business Administration's loan program to stimulate small business bank loans and nonprofit microloans to small businesses, so credit in this area may loosen up a bit.

Another alternative form of "social financing" has also developed in the past year or so: Peer-to-peer lending sites pair up borrowers who list their loan needs with private investors who are willing to offer loans at certain rates. The social lending websites getting the most press are Lending Club, Zopa, Prosper, and Loanio. With the country in such a credit crunch, these online services may be worth looking into.

Consider Borrowing From Friends and Family

Borrowing from family and friends is sometimes possible, but not often sensible unless someone you are close to personally has both deep pockets and business experience. Take into consideration that if you borrow money from a parent or other close relative, everyone in your family will know about it and a good many will disapprove, especially if the lender is elderly and other family members hope to inherit. If you really can repay the loan promptly and in full, all may be well, but if not, you are at high risk of becoming the family goat.

If, given these warnings, you still plan to pursue this approach, we recommend that you present the potential lender with a formal business plan. It should include a profit-and-loss forecast and a cash flow analysis that you have already vetted with your advisory board and that clearly demonstrate how and when your business will return to profit. Assuming your future business prospects look good, two things may help seal a deal.

First, offer an interest rate that fairly compensates the lender for taking a substantial risk. Given the rocky economy and the amount of risk involved in lending to a financially challenged small business, 12% to 16% might be reasonable (though to keep the IRS happy, the rate should not be much higher than what a bank might offer you).

TIP

Don't be casual about borrowing money. Even if you have known the lender all your life, prepare a formal promissory note setting forth how and when the money is to be paid back and at what interest rate. You can download an appropriate form from Nolo's Online Legal Form center at www.nolo.com. Or a service like Virgin Money can help you create a loan proposal, formalize the loan, and set up an electronic funds transfer. For more information about formalizing loans from friends and family, see *Business Loans from Family and Friends: How to Ask, Make It Legal, and Make It Work,* by Asheesh Advani (Nolo).

Second, for larger loans, it's routine to offer the lender the sweetener of a small equity stake in your business. Explaining how to do this (typically by organizing as a small corporation and issuing the lender warrants, which can be converted to stock at a preset price) is beyond the scope of this book, but something a small business lawyer can help you with.

TIP

Don't be a pest. Somewhat paradoxically, your best chance of success will likely be to approach friends or relatives who have lent you money in the past. Especially if you have paid some of it back, these people will already be your supporters. And your chance of hearing a "yes" will go way up if you can convince the potential lender that you won't ask yet again.

Get Money From a Factor for Your Accounts Receivable

Factoring involves selling current accounts receivable to a business (the "factor") that will pay you immediate cash and then collect the debts when they are due. In a typical transaction, the factor will promptly pay you 60% to 80% of an invoice, with the balance held in reserve. If the factor collects the debt in full, it will release the reserve, less its fee, which normally amounts to 1% to 5% of the debt.

Factoring probably sounds good so far, but there are several downsides. First, factors' fees amount to a relatively high interest rate, certainly far higher than a bank would charge for interest on a line of credit (but because factoring does allow you to show a lender a stronger cash position, it may help you retain a line of credit otherwise in jeopardy).

Second, factors normally won't advance money on overdue or otherwise dicey receivables, including receivables for goods that can be returned for credit or are perishable or receivables from risky customers. In short, a factor isn't interested in *your* credit history (as a bank would be), but in its estimate of your customers' ability to pay. For example, if you are a small clothing manufacturer who is owed money by Macy's, a factor would likely advance you most of the money due on that invoice, but would refuse to purchase a similar invoice for goods you sold to several boutiques with questionable credit histories.

Factoring transactions basically fall into two broad categories, recourse and nonrecourse. In recourse factoring, the company selling its receivables is on the hook to repay the factoring company all money advanced, plus fees, if the customer doesn't pay. In the more common (and expensive) nonrecourse factoring, the factor assumes the risk of nonpayment.

Factoring has been traditionally used in the garment and other goods businesses, but today it is also used by architects, contractors, and others in the construction industry, as well as by trucking and other transportation businesses. Even service businesses and those awaiting payment on government contracts are using factors. Simply search online for "receivable factor" to find a long list of factors and websites.

Save Your Bank Line of Credit or Promised Financing

Many small businesses have never had a bank line of credit, or if they did, lost it as soon as their business began to tank. But if yours is an exception and, despite having financial problems, you are still considered bankable, chances are you won't keep your credit line much longer unless you act quickly. That's because, as you probably know, most lines of credit have what are called covenants—loan conditions that let the lender cancel your credit line if your business is out of compliance. The most common covenants require that you meet or exceed a particular financial ratio designed to assure the bank that you'll be able to repay the loan. For example, banks typically require that a borrower maintain a two-to-one ratio of earnings (minus expenses and taxes) to loan principal. Another common covenant requires a small business to maintain a ratio of assets to liabilities of at least two to one. In addition, most banks include catch-all language that allows them to revoke your credit line if they are uncomfortable with your business prospects—for example, if there is any "material adverse change" in your business.

Most line of credit agreements require that you inform the bank as soon as you know that you might not comply with a covenant, or if your business has suffered any "material adverse change." It follows that if, for any reason, you are worried about getting your line of credit renewed, or if you see you'll have a problem meeting your covenants, your best approach is to set up a meeting with your bank as soon as possible. Along with the usual required financial reports and accounts receivable and payable schedules, you'll want to present a business plan for the next year with a convincing budget that shows your business making a profit in the near future. The more you show the bank that you are actively addressing your profitability problem, the likelier it is to keep working with you.

For instance, if your sales are down significantly, be prepared to show the bank that you are making corresponding cuts in costs, such as suspending employee benefits, making layoffs, eliminating travel and entertainment expenses, cutting the staff development budget, and so on. It will also be extremely helpful if you can show the bank that new money is coming into the business from you or another investor. So if a relative is willing to lend you $50,000, get this commitment in writing before you sit down with the loan officer.

Keep in mind that you'll need to walk a fine line when discussing your financial problems. On the one hand, you'll want to convince the bank that you would have met your covenants had your business not been blindsided by the extraordinary economic downturn, but on the other, you'll need to show that you now have a convincing plan to survive it.

What about the possibility of, instead of talking to your bank when you first realize that you'll fail to comply with a loan covenant, immediately drawing down the line and using the money to pay your creditors? If your business is a corporation or an LLC, this is usually a poor idea, because you will be substituting your personal legal obligation to repay the bank (by using the credit line) for your business entity's obligation to pay unsecured creditors. As discussed in Chapter 4, if your business fails, you are personally on the hook for all loans and accounts you have personally guaranteed, but not those exclusively in the name of your corporation or LLC.

> **TIP**
> **Protect your bank account.** If you owe money to a bank on a loan or credit line, it's often wise to keep your checking and other accounts elsewhere. This is because the fine print of your loan or credit line agreement probably gives the bank the right to grab without notice ("offset," or "setoff") funds in your checking account. True, this might violate yet another covenant that requires you to keep all funds in their bank, but if you lose your line of credit, this will be the least of your worries.

What Not to Do

Just as important as trying out the strategies discussed just above is knowing what to stay away from. You don't want to make matters worse.

Don't Use Merchant Cash Advances

Another type of financing for small businesses that make credit card sales is known as a merchant cash advance funding. It isn't appropriate when you're in financial trouble, however. It typically works like this: the cash advance company (AdvanceMe is the first and most reputable company in this field) buys your future credit card sales, advancing you a portion of the anticipated receipts. You authorize the company to automatically take a portion of your daily credit card sales through an agreement with your credit card processor.

On the plus side, if your credit sales don't end up being enough to pay back the loan, some advance companies have no recourse against you, as long as you don't switch credit card processors, because your personal guarantee is not required. The down side is that cash advance companies charge high fees, which often work out annually to as much as 25% or even 50% of the value of each advance.

Paying such high interest usually makes sense only if you're investing the money in something with a high rate of return, so that you can easily pay the fees. So you shouldn't go this route to pay regular bills, though it might make sense in an emergency. But if getting a merchant cash advance is your only hope of surviving beyond a month or two, it's probably time to think about closing your business down.

Try Not to Max Out Your Credit Cards

If you have nowhere else to get cheaper money, you may be tempted to borrow heavily against your credit cards. For three big reasons, this is usually a poor idea. First, interest rates are typically astronomical, as are late fees and an assortment of other penalties. Second, credit card debt is a personal obligation, so even if your business is organized as an LLC or corporation, if it fails, you'll be obligated to repay the credit card companies. (By contrast, unsecured business debts of a corporation or LLC are not your personal responsibility.) Third, borrowing heavily against credit cards usually means other strategies to raise cash have failed, a strong signal that your business can't be saved and you are pushing yourself closer to bankruptcy.

Weigh Borrowing Against Your House

Given the current reality of depressed house prices and tight credit, and especially if your business is losing money, you may not qualify for a second mortgage or a home equity loan. But even if you do, think at least three times before doing so.

Taking money out of a good house to put it into a questionable business makes sense only if you really have a no-nonsense plan to return your business to profitability. Especially if your business is a corporation or LLC, meaning your business and personal debts are separate (see Chapter 4 for a discussion of the legal status of debts), borrowing against your house risks taking money out of a relatively safe and legally protected personal investment to move it into an already troubled business.

If you operate as a sole proprietor or have already personally guaranteed LLC or corporate debt, you might think it makes sense to borrow against your house (at least compared to maxing out credit cards), because your personal assets are already on the hook to pay business debts and the interest rate will be far lower. But there is a very important potential downside. By borrowing against your house you are turning an unsecured debt into a secured debt, which means that, especially in states with almost unlimited "homestead" exemptions (Florida, Iowa, Kansas, Massachusetts, Oklahoma, Rhode Island, South Dakota, and Texas), you are essentially giving up your state's homeowner protections. If you can't pay the home equity debt, you could lose your house.

EXAMPLE: Bobbington Glass, a sole proprietorship owned by Tom and Emily Bobbington in Miami, runs into financial trouble. Tom and Emily take out a $25,000 home equity line of credit, reasoning that the interest rate is far lower than it would be if they maxed out their credit cards and that either way they will be personally responsible to pay the debt. However, when Bobbington Glass fails six months later and Tom and Emily file for bankruptcy, the bank initiates foreclosure proceedings against the house, which is security for the line of credit. By contrast, if Tom and Emily had borrowed the same $25,000 on their credit cards and then filed for bankruptcy, Florida's homestead exemption would prevent the bank from taking their house. (See Chapter 13 for more on how the homestead exemption works.) ●

Minimize Liability for Your Debts

"If you think nobody cares if you're alive, try missing a couple of car payments."
EARL WILSON

Once you have gotten a handle on your cash flow and devised a plan to get your business at least back to breakeven, it's time to think about the debts that have likely piled up during the period when costs were exceeding income. Here, we focus on the consequences, both immediate and long-term, of failing to pay off your debts.

To successfully steer your way to a debt-free existence and keep yourself out of future trouble, you need to fully understand your liability for debt. The most important point is that debts fall into different types of legal categories, meaning that some of your creditors have more rights to collect and a bigger ability to negatively affect you and your business than do others. Because you may be up against some lenders with sophisticated financial knowledge and legal resources, it's important for you to understand the legal status of each and every one of your debts and what each creditor's rights are.

Are You Personally Liable for Business Debts?

There is a huge difference between debts that only your business is liable for and those that you are legally responsible to pay from your personal assets, such as your personal bank account and your equity in real estate, if your business can't pay them.

Which debts are you personally liable for? Most important, every business owner, no matter whether the business is organized as a corporation, LLC, partnership, or sole proprietorship, is personally liable if the business doesn't pay the taxes it withheld from employees' paychecks. (For more about why paying these taxes is always your first priority, see "Prioritizing Debt Payments," below.)

For other types of business debts, your business structure and what kind of contract or purchase order you signed usually determines whether or not you're personally liable.

Sole Proprietorship or Partnership

If you're operating your business as a sole proprietorship (or independent contractor), you and your business are legally the same, which is another way of saying that you personally owe every penny that your business can't pay. So if there aren't enough money or assets in your business to pay its debts, creditors can, and sometimes will, take your personal assets that aren't protected by state exemption laws. (See "What Can Creditors Do If You Don't Pay?" below.)

This is also true for general partnerships, with this added twist: Each partner is personally liable for 100% of the business's debts (and any partner can usually bind the entire partnership to a business deal—a scary combination). This means that if there aren't enough business assets to pay the debts, and your partners are broke, creditors can take *your* personal assets to pay *all* of the business's debts, not just your pro rata share of the debts.

Corporation or LLC

If your business is organized as a corporation or LLC, you and your business are separate legal entities. As such, you have no personal liability for the debts of your business, meaning that creditors can't take your house or other personal assets to pay your business's debts.

EXAMPLE: Jean's Book Shoppe, Inc., orders books from 80 publishers and three wholesalers before the business tanks. Unable to pay its expenses, the corporation declares bankruptcy. The publishers' and wholesalers' bills are all unsecured debts of the corporation, and Jean, the corporation's sole shareholder, is not personally responsible for paying any of them. In the bankruptcy, the store's inventory will be sold to the highest bidder. The proceeds will be used to pay the costs of bankruptcy and the Book Shoppe's creditors, who may be fortunate to receive a few cents on the dollar.

However, because most banks, landlords, and suppliers know about limited liability, they often do not extend credit to or lend money to a small business organized as an LLC or corporation without the owner's personal guarantee. If you signed a personal guarantee for a particular loan, lease, or contract, you promised that you would pay it personally if your business did not. Put another way, every time you personally guaranteed that you would repay a debt, you deliberately gave up your limited liability for that debt. You volunteered to let the creditor sue you to take your personal assets if the business defaults on the payments.

If you have taken out a loan for a business vehicle or business equipment, or a bank line of credit, check to see if you signed a personal guarantee. The same goes if you've leased space.

You may also have given up your limited liability if you were careless about signing purchase agreements and service contracts. These agreements sometimes display the personal name of the business owner without the name of the corporation or LLC. If you signed an agreement in your personal name and not on behalf of the corporation or LLC, you're personally liable for the underlying debt, even if it was the supplier's mistake.

If you're not sure whether you have given a personal guarantee on an agreement or loan, check both the language of the agreement and the signature block to see whether you signed it in your name or in your capacity as an owner or officer.

EXAMPLE: Josephine signs a loan contract as Josephine Smith, CEO of Salt & Pepper LLC. Only her business is liable to repay the loan. But she signs her business lease as just Josephine Smith, so she is personally liable to the landlord.

In addition, you may have used credit cards or home equity loans to obtain funds for your business, which definitely means you are personally liable for those debts. (You are almost always personally responsible for making payments on your credit cards, even if they have your business name on them, under the terms of the application you signed.) Finally, if you secured a business loan or debt by pledging specific property such as a house, boat, or car, that property can usually be taken or foreclosed on to pay the debt.

After reading this, you should be able to divide your debts into those you are personally liable for and those you are not. This is crucial, because if you are short of cash and fear that your corporation or LLC may fail, you'll want to pay the debts you are personally liable for first. That will give you a far better chance to keep your house and other personal assets should your business ultimately fail owing a significant amount of debt.

EXAMPLE: Greg and Marina were avid coffee drinkers and book lovers who had always wanted to open a coffee roastery with a cozy café offering weekly poetry readings. To get their business started, they file LLC formation papers with the state and spend $35,000 on a big new roaster that can crank out a thousand pounds of coffee per day. Unable to get a small business loan, they charge the coffee roaster on their personal credit cards, figuring they will pay it off quickly with income from the business. They also sign a two-year lease on a corner building in an artsy neighborhood, for which the landlord required their personal signatures. Next they arrange for weekly deliveries of beans from a nearby wholesaler, with invoices in the name of Cozy Roast LLC. They have no money left over to spend on marketing, but hope to add it to their budget later.

Unfortunately, when they open their doors, crowds fail to appear, and their original sales forecast proves to be too optimistic by half. Five months later, still operating in the red, Greg and Marina contemplate closing down. If they do, this leaves them personally liable for their $35,000 personal credit card debt for the coffee roaster as well as the remaining months on their two-year lease (unless the landlord can rent it out again—see "Special Rules for Leases," below). Because they didn't personally guarantee or personally sign a contract for the bean deliveries, only the business is liable to pay the bean invoices (assuming Greg and Marina have properly followed LLC formalities). If their LLC fails, at least they won't personally owe any money for the beans.

Liability for Jointly Owned Debt

Debts that you share with another person—a cosigner, spouse, or partner—can raise some legal issues, especially if you eventually consider bankruptcy.

Cosigners and Guarantors

Cosigners and guarantors legally guarantee that they will make debt or loan payments if you don't. Because these are personal guarantees, it makes no difference whether your business is organized as a sole proprietorship, partnership, LLC, or corporation.

Unfortunately, even if you were to get out of paying a debt—say you file for Chapter 7 bankruptcy and get your liability wiped out by the court—your consignor or guarantor would still be legally on the hook to pay it. If this were to happen, you might not want to stick the cosigner or guarantor with the debt you just escaped (many close relationships have been ruined this way). You could legally "reaffirm" the debt in bankruptcy—basically, promise to repay it—and keep making payments after bankruptcy. Another option would be to make an informal arrangement with the cosigner or guarantor to eventually repay any amount they pay the creditor. Or you could file for Chapter 13 (repayment) bankruptcy instead; in that case, the cosigner would not be called to account until you completed your repayment plan, three to five years down the road.

Spouses

One spouse's liability for the other spouse's debts depends mostly on where you live.

Community Property States

In "community property" states, generally any debt incurred by one spouse during marriage (but before separation) is owed by both spouses. Likewise, in these community property states, all income made by either spouse during marriage, as well as property bought with that income, is community property, owned equally by husband and wife. This means that creditors of one spouse can go after the assets and income of the community (the married couple) to make good on that spouse's debt. It follows that if that if only one spouse files for Chapter 7 bankruptcy in a community property state, all of the eligible debts of both spouses will be discharged.

Community and Common Law Property States		
Community Property		**Common Law**
Alaska*	Nevada	Everywhere else
Arizona	New Mexico	
California**	Texas	
Idaho	Washington	
Louisiana	Wisconsin	

*In Alaska, couples can elect to treat their property as community property.
**In California, community property laws also apply to registered domestic partners.

EXAMPLE: Linda runs a fabric store in Houston, Texas; her husband is a local bank executive. Over the last few years, Linda's store has been suffering from poor sales, but the recession is the final nail in the coffin, as people all but stop spending money on customizing their houses. Linda closes her doors owing $35,000 to suppliers, $15,000 to her landlord, and $10,000 in other invoices.

Because Linda and her husband live in a community property state, these creditors can sue both Linda and her husband personally to collect the money owed. Linda no longer has an income to take, but her husband's is significant, and her creditors are able to garnish $5,000 of her husband's income per month until the debts are paid off.

TIP

You can agree to keep property separate. Couples in community property states can sign an agreement with each other to have their debts and income treated separately. This can prevent your spouse from being liable for your business debts. Signing an agreement now won't help your spouse escape personal liability for business debts that you already owe, but if you believe your business is viable in the long term, signing an agreement now (and then scrupulously keeping your assets separate) can protect your spouse from future business debts. See a lawyer with experience in postnuptial agreements for help in drafting this type of agreement.

Common Law States

In "common law" property states, debts incurred by one spouse are that spouse's debts alone. Debts are jointly owed only if they were jointly undertaken—for example, if both spouses signed a contract requiring them to make payments—or if the debt benefits the marriage (for example, the debt was for food, clothing, child care, or necessary household items). Otherwise, creditors of one spouse cannot legally reach the other spouse's money, property, or wages to repay a spouse's separate debt. However, if both spouses' income has been put into one joint account, a creditor may have the right to take at least 50% of the money from the joint account to pay a separate debt. The law of some common law states also provides that if you and your spouse jointly own property, such as a house, but a debt is yours alone, the creditor cannot force a sale of the property by attaching a lien to it. As to bankruptcy, if you, but not your spouse, file for Chapter 7 bankruptcy in a common law state, only your joint and separate debts will be discharged; your spouse's separate debts would not be discharged.

EXAMPLE: Will Horton, the sole owner of Horton Rental, rents construction equipment and party furniture and supplies in Albany, New York. His wife Amanda is an independent jewelry appraiser who makes a good living. After a few years of strong construction rentals, Will's business drops off steeply as housing starts disappear. Will markets his party rentals heavily to help tide him over and tries to lower his debt costs by selling some of the construction equipment that is sitting idle. But after not being able to pay some of his bills for several months, a creditor is threatening to sue the Hortons.

Fortunately, because the Hortons live in a common law property state, the creditor can't sue Amanda and garnish her income. And because the Hortons hold title to their house in "tenancy by the entirety" and live in New York, a creditor cannot put a lien on the house and force its sale as long as Amanda is alive. If Amanda and Will were to sell the house, however, the creditor would have to be paid off with Will's half of the proceeds.

> **TIP**
>
> **Keep what's separate, separate.** If you live in a common law state, you absolutely don't want to have your spouse personally guarantee your business debts. Unless your spouse cosigns a loan or personal guarantee, your spouse can never be liable for your business debts in a common law state if you keep your income separate.

Business Partners

All partners are personally responsible for all of the partnership's debts. And because each partner has the legal power to obligate the partnership, creditors can come after your personal assets to collect on a debt even if another partner signed the deal and you did not. If you were to file for individual Chapter 7 bankruptcy, you could get rid of your personal liability for the partnership debts, but the remaining partners would still be on the hook for 100% of the partnership's debts, unless they too filed for bankruptcy.

EXAMPLE: Adam and Steve, acquaintances from a Master's program in geology, form a partnership to assess and repair damage to California streams. They take out a $40,000 equipment loan, which Steve's parents cosign. Over a few years, they build a successful business by getting contracts from state and federal agencies.

But when the state suffers economic woes, payouts are frozen for three months, and 75% of Adam and Steve's jobs are cancelled. They try to continue business as usual, fearing they'll lose great employees forever if they lay them off. But after the money isn't unfrozen in month four, they begin to cut payroll, sell equipment, and sublet unused office space. Unfortunately, they are so far in the red by now that they can't make their loan payments or pay suppliers. With their backs to the wall, they decide to lay off their entire workforce and hibernate the company (see Chapter 1) until the government is paying again.

As business partners, Adam and Steve are personally liable for all business debts. Their main supplier sues over a $40,000 debt, and because there is no money left in the business, goes after Adam and Steve (and Pam, Steve's wife) personally to pay the debt. Steve has no income now, but Pam does, and the supplier can go after it because they live in a community property state and Pam is equally liable for the debt. After getting a court judgment against Adam, Steve, and Pam, the supplier garnishes 25% of Pam's paycheck. Steve and Pam decide to file for Chapter 7 bankruptcy, meaning both spouses' debts will be discharged and Pam's paycheck will no longer be garnished. Most important, they can keep their house, since they have only $75,000 in equity in it, the amount exempt from creditors in their state. (See "What Can Creditors Do If You Don't Pay?" below.)

After Steve and Pam's bankruptcy, Adam is still 100% liable for the supplier's debt. Because he owns assets that are not exempt and that creditors may take, such as a vacation house, he takes out a second mortgage on the vacation house and pays the supplier. The partners also default on the $40,000 equipment loan, but Steve's liability for it was discharged in bankruptcy, making Adam 100% liable for it (along with Steve's parents, who cosigned the loan). Adam refuses to pay, claiming that since he made good on the supplier's debt, he considers his half of the partnership debt paid. Eventually Steve's parents, the cosigners, pay off the loan rather than risk being sued and losing their house.

What Can Creditors Do If You Don't Pay?

First, know that you can't be thrown in jail for not paying your debts (with the exception of back child support if you could pay but don't). And a creditor can't just take money from your bank account or grab your tax refund—unless you owe back taxes or you've defaulted on a student loan. To collect a debt, the general rule is that most commercial creditors must first sue you and win a money judgment (a court award) against you. But there is a big exception to this rule: Creditors don't have to sue first if the debt is guaranteed by collateral. Common examples are a car loan where the car you bought is security (collateral) for the loan, or a mortgage or home equity loan where the house itself is pledged as collateral (though in about half of the states, a lender has to go to court before foreclosing).

Secured Debts

Many businesses owe secured debts—businesses typically pledge collateral for credit lines, and business owners often pledge their personal property for business debts. Let's take a look at how quickly lenders can call in or foreclose on collateral when a secured debt is not paid.

Secured vs. Unsecured Creditors

A secured creditor is any creditor to whom you or your business has pledged collateral in exchange for a loan, line of credit, or purchase. Collateral might be business property, such as inventory and equipment, or your own property, such as your house, car, or boat.

There are also "involuntary secured creditors"—those who have filed a lien (legal claim) against your property because they have a judgment against you or you owe a tax debt. Either way, if you or the business can't pay back the debt, a secured creditor can repossess or foreclose on the secured property, or order it to be sold, to satisfy the debt.

An unsecured creditor is one to whom no collateral has been pledged and who hasn't filed a lien. Typically, unsecured debts include credit card charges and amounts your business owes for inventory, office supplies, furnishings, rent, and advertising, as well as what's owed for services such as maintenance, equipment repair, or professional advice.

Repossessions

As you probably know, if you miss a payment or two on your car loan (and, as is typical, the loan was used to buy the car and is secured by the car), the lender has the legal right to physically repossess the car and sell it to recover the money you owe, plus the costs of the sale and attorney's fees. To do this, the lender doesn't have to get permission or a court judgment. Under the terms of the contract you signed with the lender, a repo man can simply reclaim the lender's property. (In many states, the lender doesn't have to give you notice of the repossession; you will just wake up and find your car gone.) When all is said and done, you will still owe the difference between what the lender sells the car for and what you owed on the loan, called a "deficiency." Also, the repossession will appear on your credit report for seven years.

Cars are the most commonly repossessed type of property, but if you borrowed money to buy business equipment or machines and used the purchased equipment as security, the creditor will have the same repossession rights. Also, some department store credit cards provide that the creditor automatically takes a security interest in the property you buy, so if you don't pay the bill, the creditor might try to repossess the property. However, because creditors must get a court order to enter your house or business, repossession of property other than vehicles is rare.

Similarly, with leased vehicles or business equipment, if you miss a lease payment, the leased property can usually be immediately reclaimed without a court order.

Foreclosures

If you have a mortgage or deed of trust on your house, or an open home equity line of credit, you must make payments on time to keep the house. If you don't, the lender can and probably will foreclose on your house, because it is collateral for your debt. But foreclosures are not as quick as vehicle repossessions. In half of the states a lender has to go to court before foreclosing, and in the other half, advance notice is required from the lender.

Similarly, if you pledge your house as collateral for a business loan or line of credit and you default on that loan, the lender can foreclose on your house. (In this situation, the lender must always file a foreclosure action in court, no matter what state you're in.) To avoid having the lender foreclose, you must either repay the debt or, if the debt is more than your equity in the house, at least pay the lender that amount so that it no longer has a reason to foreclose.

The foreclosure process works differently in different states. In some states, the lender must file a lawsuit to foreclose on a house (called judicial foreclosure). In others, it can foreclose on property without going to court (nonjudicial foreclosure). A judicial foreclosure typically takes several months longer than a nonjudicial foreclosure (though in California a nonjudicial foreclosure can take a year or more), giving you time to save some money and, if necessary, find a new place to live.

If you're behind on your mortgage, you might be able to negotiate a loan modification with your lender. For example, the lender might agree to add your missed payments to your loan balance, to stretch out your loan over a longer term, or to convert an adjustable rate mortgage to a fixed-rate one.

Your other options are selling your home for less than you owe (called a short sale), returning the deed to the lender (called a deed in lieu of foreclosure), or refinancing through the Federal Housing Administration (FHA) or the Homeowner Affordability and Stability Plan, a plan created in 2009 to help families restructure or refinance mortgages and avoid foreclosure.

RESOURCE

Foreclosure information. For up-to-date information about your options if you are facing foreclosure, see *The Foreclosure Survival Guide*, by Stephen Elias (Nolo).

TIP

Filing for bankruptcy can delay foreclosure. When you file for bankruptcy, all creditors, including mortgage lenders, must cease collection activities and foreclosures. However, the lender can ask the bankruptcy court for permission to proceed with a foreclosure if you're behind on your payments, so a bankruptcy may delay a foreclosure only a couple of months. (For more on bankruptcy, see Chapter 13.)

Unsecured Debts

Unsecured creditors such as credit card companies and most trade creditors must first sue you and win a money judgment against you before they grab your income and property. This is true whether you are personally liable for the debt (as is the case for sole proprietors and partners, or because you signed a personal guarantee for your corporation or LLC) or whether only your corporation or LLC is liable for the debt.

Typically, however, before seriously considering a lawsuit, a creditor will try to collect the debt for several months and then turn it over to a collection attorney or agency, which will restart the process. In some instances the creditor will conclude that you don't have enough property that can easily be grabbed to pay off the judgment, and won't bother suing.

For instance, say your house is worth less than you owe on your mortgage, and your sole proprietorship consignment shop has few business assets and is doing so poorly that you don't anticipate having more than a few dollars of steady income that a creditor could grab by ordering the sheriff or marshal to take money from the business premises (called a "till tap"). Your creditors, or any collection attorney or agency your debt is turned over to, may not sue you because they know it's unlikely they could collect the money judgment. That's called being "judgment proof."

Instead, the creditor may simply write off your debt and treat it as a deductible business loss for income tax purposes. Typically, in five or six years, depending on your state's statute of limitations, the debt will become legally uncollectible. (Only a few states, such as Kentucky, Louisiana, Ohio, and Rhode Island, have longer statutes of limitation, up to ten or 15 years.)

However, you can expect to be sued if there is significant money at stake and you have valuable personal or business assets (or just business assets if your business is a corporation or LLC)—or if the creditor expects you to acquire significant assets in the future. For instance, if you are a sole proprietor and have an advanced degree, your creditor might assume you'll eventually get a decent job and sue you now—and just wait for you to make some income. (In many states, a court judgment can be collected for at least ten years.) What might a creditor think is worth suing for? Significant amounts of cash or accounts receivable, valuable business equipment and property, and, if you're personally liable for a debt, valuable personal assets such as jewelry, fine art, collectibles, antiques, motorcycles, expensive bicycles, boats, or a vacation house.

How a Creditor Must Collect a Judgment

Collecting a judgment is harder than winning it. If a creditor has gone to court and won a judgment for collection of an unsecured debt, theoretically the creditor (now called a judgment creditor) will be able to take any cash in your business's bank account, your business income, and your business assets to pay off the debt. If you're a sole proprietor or partner, or signed a personal guarantee for a debt, the judgment creditor could also garnish your wages and take money from your personal bank account, as well as your nonexempt personal property, to pay off the debt. However, the creditor must first locate the property and then get a court order and pay the sheriff to take it.

Probably the most common collection method is for a creditor to obtain a writ of garnishment, under which a sheriff could garnish 25% of your wages to pay the debt (except in Pennsylvania, South Carolina, and Texas, where garnishments are not allowed). But assuming you are still a self-employed business owner, garnishing your wages will be pretty difficult since you don't get a paycheck (unless you're an employee of your corporation). However, your spouse's wages could be garnished to pay your business debts if you live in a community property state (Arizona, California, Idaho, Louisiana, Nevada, New Mexico, Texas, Washington, or Wisconsin), assuming your spouse is named in the judgment.

Often a more effective collection technique (if your business sells goods or services for cash) is for the sheriff to come to your business and take any money he can find there—in the cash register (a till tap) or on your person. Or a sheriff could be authorized to take business vehicles, equipment, or tools of the trade to pay your debts, something that will happen only if those items are clearly worth more than you owe on them. It's also possible that the creditor could get a court to order customers and clients to pay any money they owe you directly to the court.

However, most creditors won't go to these lengths to get your property. Instead, many will simply attach a "judgment lien" to any real estate or assets the business owns (or valuable personal property or real estate that you own, if you are personally liable for the debt). The lien will allow the creditor to collect when you sell or refinance the property.

TIP

Check to see what liens are recorded against your business. The Secretary of State's office in every state maintains a registry of liens, listing judgment liens, tax liens, or security interests that creditors claim in your property. You can do a Uniform Commercial Code (UCC) records search online at your Secretary of State's website to search for your personal and business names to see what liens have been recorded against you. If you find any incorrect information—say you have paid off a debt but it hasn't been reflected—ask the lender in question for a UCC release, something that is required by law.

Wage Garnishment

If you do have regular wages coming in, perhaps from a side job or because you are an employee of your corporation, your wages can be garnished to enforce a court judgment. The total amount your creditors can take from your wages is 25% of your net pay. That limit applies whether you have one creditor or many. And if your wages are low, there are additional protections—you must be left with weekly income equal to 30 times the federal hourly minimum wage. (A few states have lower limits.) But if you owe back child support or back taxes, expect to lose a much larger percentage of your wages—50% or more, depending on whether you are supporting others. Social Security checks, retirement plan proceeds, unemployment and disability benefits, or workers' compensation awards cannot be garnished, except to pay federal taxes or child support (or unless they have accumulated in your bank account).

Exempt Property—What a Judgment Creditor Can't Take

Though a judgment creditor can usually grab cash from your bank account or force the sale of most business assets, a judgment creditor can't take personal property that is legally exempt from creditors. Most states provide that a certain amount of your personal assets, such as food, furniture, clothing, cannot be taken by creditors or by the bankruptcy trustee in bankruptcy court. In addition, most states exempt from creditors:

- the equity you own in one vehicle, up to a certain amount—commonly from $1,000 to $5,000, and
- a significant amount of the equity in your house—often between $10,000 and $50,000, depending on the state.

RESOURCE

Find your state's exemptions. For a complete list of exempt property, go to www.legalconsumer.com/bankruptcy/exemptions and enter your zip code.

Most states also let you keep a couple of thousand dollars' worth of business equipment and tools of the trade, as well as money in tax-deferred retirement plans. Also, in most states (except community property states, discussed above), a creditor can't take property that belongs to you and your spouse if the debt is in your name only. The practical effect of these exemptions is that no matter how many debts you have and no matter how many judgments are entered against you, creditors can't grab much essential property.

EXAMPLE: For years, Dax's hobby has been restoring classic cars; he owns two himself, a '64 Shelby Cobra and a '59 Cadillac Eldorado. After being urged by his friends to quit his day job to do what he loves, Dax opens his own shop, which offers custom auto detailing, paintless dent repair, auto painting, and classic car restoration. He applies for a business license, rents a small warehouse in an industrial area, buys two auto lifts, and increases his cache of tools, which was already sizable. To pay for everything, he takes a personal equity line of credit out on his house, after striking out in his attempts to get a bank line of credit for the business. Unfortunately, almost as soon as Dax opens his doors, the economy declines, and people cut back on luxury services, such as regular car detailing, and even dent and ding repair. At the same time, many classic car enthusiasts are forced to put their hobbies on hold. As a result, Dax doesn't bring in enough money to cover his costs, can't pay his rent, and goes out of business, leaving a mountain of debts.

If he is sued or has to file for bankruptcy, here is what he has to lose and what he should be able to hold on to:

Since Dax lives in California, is married, and has only $60,000 equity in his house (he owes $300,000 and the house is worth $360,000), he will get to keep his house (California law exempts $75,000 of equity for families). He will also get to hold on to his clothing, furnishings, and appliances. He will also be able to keep up to $6,750 in business assets, if he has fully paid for them and if he continues to use them to make a living, including tools, equipment, and a commercial vehicle, but the rest of his business assets will likely be taken. He will be able keep only $2,550 in equity in personal vehicles, so he is likely to lose his classic cars. He also stands to lose the money in his business bank account, as well as his personal bank account, because he was a sole proprietor. If he gets a new job, up to 25% of his wages could be garnished. If Dax's wife brings home an income, 25% of that income can be garnished to pay the business's debts, if his wife is listed in the judgment. (If Dax files for bankruptcy, however, the wage garnishments will stop.) Dax's IRA is safe from creditors.

TIP

Bankruptcy can get rid of unsecured debts. If you have been sued or have been threatened with a lawsuit, you're at risk of losing cash or property. If the majority of your debt is unsecured and you have little chance of paying it off, you might consider bankruptcy, which can get rid of most, if not all, of your unsecured debt. For more information on bankruptcy and alternatives, see Chapter 13.

Special Rules for Leases

Back rent is treated like any other unsecured debt, but you are subject to streamlined eviction procedures if you don't pay. If you're behind on residential rent payments, the landlord is likely to start an eviction lawsuit against you within a few weeks. Unless the building is found to be uninhabitable (substandard or unsafe), chances are you'll be ordered to vacate within about six weeks. A commercial eviction is quicker than a residential eviction—it can be over in just a few weeks.

You can try to negotiate with the landlord to make up unpaid rent over the next several months, but unless you do this before the landlord files an eviction lawsuit, normally you'll have little chance of success. Your landlord may be likely to negotiate if lots of properties are vacant in your area. If you can show that, while your business is short on cash, you have a believable long-term survival plan, you may be able to get a new lease with lower rent. Your chances will improve if you can possibly show that you or a private lender will invest new capital in the business if the lease and other obligations are reduced. (For more on negotiating your rent down, see Chapter 3.)

If you have to move out when you have time remaining on a lease—residential or commercial—your landlord can sue you for the remaining months' rent. However, in most states the landlord is obligated to try to rerent the space first to minimize the loss. This is called "mitigating the damages." Chapter 12 has more information on how to get out of a lease early with the fewest consequences.

> **TIP**
>
> **Find a new tenant yourself.** A landlord who expects to eventually collect from you all of the rent you owe under the broken lease may move slowly to find a new tenant. If you help find a new tenant and get the space filled faster, you'll limit your future liability under the lease.

Prioritizing Debt Payments

Now that you have an overview of the legal status of your various debts and the consequences of not paying them, you'll understand why you'll definitely want to pay some debts before others. Yes, ignoring any debt comes with consequences, but paying some debts is vital to protecting your business and personal assets. Here's what to pay first.

Payroll Taxes

If you have employees and withhold taxes from their paychecks, get those withheld amounts to the government on time, every time. It may be tempting to borrow from these funds, because after you collect the taxes, you usually have a few weeks before you must deposit them. Don't ever do it, no matter how behind you are on your bills or how angry your suppliers, landlord, or other creditors are getting. Here's why.

As an employer, you withhold money from your employees' pay to pay payroll taxes (Social Security and Medicare) and your employees' income tax withholding. If you don't pay withheld Social Security and Medicare taxes and federal income withholding taxes (called the "trust fund" portion of these taxes), you will owe a penalty equal to the entire amount of the unpaid trust fund taxes, plus interest. Some states impose similar penalties for failing to deposit state income tax withholding and sales taxes that you have collected.

The trust fund penalty can be imposed on any and every person who fails to see that the taxes are paid, including all owners and officers of the company, whether or not they normally pay the bills or monitor finances.

Even directors and minority shareholders can be held personally liable if they were responsible or partially responsible for deciding to pay other pressing bills in lieu of the trust fund taxes. Even if your company is a corporation or LLC, you and your co-owners can be held personally liable for the trust fund taxes and the resulting penalty.

And that's not the worst part. To pay these trust fund taxes and the resulting penalty and interest, the feds can seize business equipment, money your creditors owe to you, *and* any property you own personally. The IRS can also garnish your wages (if you receive a paycheck) or pension plan payments and seize the assets in your individual retirement accounts. Filing for bankruptcy will not protect you. Finally, the IRS can charge you with a crime for failing to deposit your payroll taxes. If your business is in such poor financial condition that you can't pay your payroll taxes, you should turn to Chapter 12 for information about closing down.

Payroll

Even if you make layoffs, there will no doubt be some employees you need to keep on to keep the business going. Make sure you continue to pay these employees' wages on time. There are hefty state law penalties for not paying wages on the day they are due—some states charge a penalty of $1,000 per employee, per pay period; others charge a penalty of 30 days' wages per employee. And if you fail to pay wages for even a few weeks, the state labor commissioner can padlock your business. Unpaid wages cannot be fully wiped out in bankruptcy.

Independent contractors' fees do not fall in the same category as wages (unless the contractors can successfully argue they were employees). Instead, a contractor has the same legal status as any other unsecured creditor, meaning that a contractor who didn't get paid would have to sue you to get a judgment before being able to seize your assets. And if you're organized as an LLC or corporation, the contractor couldn't grab your personal property.

Utility Bills

You obviously can't run a business without electricity and water. If you're behind on these bills, your utility provider probably has the legal right to cut you off without going to court. So if you're going to stay in business, try to negotiate a payment plan promptly. If you wait until your service is cut off, you'll have to pay a fee to get it turned back on, including, possibly, a large deposit.

Business Phone

Assuming you use a land line for business and plan to stay in business, this is another bill that should have priority, so customers can continue to reach you.

Child Support

Failing to pay child support can land you in jail if a court finds you are not destitute. Your wages or business income can also be grabbed by the state to pay it, without a court judgment. What's more, a child support debt never goes away—it is always collectible, and you can't wipe it out in bankruptcy. (If you truly can't make your payments, go to court and ask the judge to reduce your obligation. That's the only way you can change it.)

Loans for Which You're Personally Liable

If your business is a sole proprietorship or partnership, you're personally liable for all debts. But if your business is a corporation or LLC, you'll be personally liable only for loans or agreements that you personally guaranteed. (See "Cosigners and Guarantors," above.) It follows that, to protect your personal assets, you'll want to pay the debts you personally guaranteed before other unsecured debts, which are obligations of your business only.

Court Judgments

If a creditor has already gone to court and won a judgment against you, the creditor can pay to have a sheriff seize your property or garnish your wages (and in some circumstances, those of your spouse—see "Liability for Jointly Owned Debt," above). Obviously it makes sense to make arrangements to pay court judgments before unsecured debts that you haven't yet been sued over.

Secured Loans

As discussed above, a debt is secured if a specific item of property (called collateral or security) is used to guarantee repayment of that debt. If you don't repay the debt, most states let the creditor take personal property without first suing you and getting a court judgment. If the property is something you or your business cannot live without, such as a forklift, truck, or cash register, stay current on your payments or expect the company to promptly repossess the property.

Your Mortgage

If you want to keep your house, you'll need to keep paying your mortgage (and second mortgage, if you have one). If you don't, the lender can foreclose on the house, because it is collateral for your mortgage. And if you pledged equity in your house as collateral for a home equity loan or line of credit, you'll need to keep current on those payments as well. (However, if there isn't enough equity in the house to cover the home equity loan, line of credit, or other second mortgage—meaning that the second mortgage is no longer secured—it might make sense to continue paying only the first mortgage, because the second mortgagor is unlikely to sue.)

However, if you know you can't afford your mortgage payments, in the medium term you might be better off selling your home (if you can), renting a moderately priced place, and using any money left over to pay your debts.

On the other hand, if you can't sell your house for more than you owe and you can't make the payments, your best bet may be to stay in it for as long as possible without making payments and use the money you save to pay other critical bills. Eventually, the house will be foreclosed on.

RESOURCE

Help with foreclosure. For information on the intricacies of foreclosure, see *The Foreclosure Survival Guide,* by Stephen Elias (Nolo).

Vehicle Payments

If you need a vehicle to continue your business or keep your job, do what you can to make the payments. Otherwise your vehicle will be quickly repossessed. But if you're paying for a more expensive car than you need, consider selling it and buying a cheaper one. This will save you a bundle in the long run—even if it costs you a few dollars to pay off the difference between what you owe and what you sell your car for. If your car is leased, websites like swapalease.com and leasetrader.com may be able to get you out of your lease and into something cheaper.

If you're already late on loan payments, consider voluntarily turning the vehicle over to avoid repossession—even though you will legally owe any difference between what the lender can sell the car for and what you owed on the loan. If the deficiency is not too large, try to negotiate with the lender before you surrender the property, to get the lender to cancel the entire debt—in writing—in exchange for your cooperation. But understand that a voluntary surrender might still show up as a repossession on your credit report.

Accounts Sent to Collection

After several months of trying and failing to collect a debt, many creditors turn their debts over to a collection agency, which will immediately launch a steady stream of scary letters and phone calls. (If you write to the agency and demand that it stop contacting you, under federal law the collection agency can no longer contact you, except to tell you if you are being sued.) The next step could be a letter from a collection attorney or a lawsuit, if the creditor or collection agency believes you have enough assets to make it worthwhile to sue you.

Collection agencies often collect a percentage of whatever they recover, so they are often willing to agree to a cash settlement for less than the amount owed—especially if they believe that you otherwise plan to file for bankruptcy. (See Chapter 3 for more information on negotiating debt settlements.)

Business Rent

If you plan to keep your current commercial space, pay your rent. If you don't, the landlord is sure to start eviction proceedings against you fairly promptly. But if you can survive without your commercial space or office by moving to a much smaller space or even into a spare room in your house, consider the strategies to get out of your lease discussed in Chapter 12.

Also, remember that, as discussed above, if you move out when you have time remaining on a lease, your landlord can sue you in court for the remaining months' rent if the landlord is not able to rerent the space.

Insurance Premiums

Premiums should be further down on your list, but you don't want to pile a liability claim on top of all your other financial problems because your premises liability or auto insurance ran out and you're not covered for a slip-and-fall lawsuit or a car accident. (And remember, if you are operating as a sole proprietor or partnership, the costs of any mishap not covered by insurance will be a personal debt.) Instead of letting coverage lapse, try to reduce your premiums by trimming unneeded insurance coverage and raising deductibles (See Chapter 3.)

Suppliers' Bills

If you're a sole proprietor or partner, you're personally liable for supplier's bills, but a creditor must sue you and get a judgment before threatening your personal assets. For this reason, suppliers' bills generally have a fairly low priority, unless of course you need to order more goods or supplies from the same supplier. If your business is a corporation or LLC and you haven't guaranteed suppliers' debts with your personal signature, these bills are an even lower priority unless, again, you need to order from the same supplier.

If you do need to keep ordering goods from a supplier, try to make payment arrangements with the supplier. If you don't, you risk having them cut you off, or at the very least require you to pay COD (There's more on how to negotiate with suppliers to lower or postpone bills in Chapter 3.)

Credit Cards

Credit card balances are normally unsecured, personal debts, even if the card is in the name of a business organized as a corporation or an LLC. But because the creditor can't grab your property without first suing and getting a judgment against you, and because credit card debt is easily dischargeable in bankruptcy, credit card balances are a lower legal priority. But remember that penalties and interest on credit cards add up fast, so unless you're considering bankruptcy, failing to make at least the minimum payments will quickly put you in a big debt hole that it will be hard to get out of.

Estimated Taxes

If your business is in the toilet, chances are you can decrease or eliminate your usual estimated tax payments, if you haven't already. How? Most people base their estimated tax payments on their previous year's net income, but in a financially troubled year, your income is sure to be much lower. As long as you end up making estimated payments equal to 90% of your income tax liability for each quarter, you won't be assessed a penalty. If you do underpay your estimated tax liability, there will be a small penalty, but if skimping on estimated tax payments allows you to pay other more critical bills, it may be worth it.

> **RESOURCE**
> **More information on estimated taxes.** Go to www.irs.gov and get IRS Publication 505, *Tax Withholding and Estimated Tax.*

Other Business Debts

Your lowest payment priority is for run-of-the-mill bills for things like advertising, entertainment, dues and subscriptions, repairs and maintenance —and, on the personal side, medical bills. Though you may get hit with late fees if you don't pay, these unsecured creditors have to sue you and get a court judgment to be able to take your business or personal assets. (See "What Can Creditors Do If You Don't Pay?" above.) Plus, most unsecured debts can be discharged in bankruptcy, if things take a turn for the worse. Do keep in mind that if you are 30 or more days late on a bill, the information can go on your business or personal (if you're a sole proprietor or partner) credit report.

Staying Out of Deeper Trouble

When your business is sliding down and the bills are piling up, it's natural to try to come up with creative methods for paying down your debt, to stay in business as long as you can. Unfortunately, some of the most creative ways to pay your bills are also the ones most likely to get you into further trouble. Here's what to avoid.

Don't Try to Hide Assets

Sometimes, out of desperation, a business owner tries to protect personal or business assets by giving them to friends and relatives or otherwise trying to hide them from creditors. Although few small business people have the knowledge necessary to move cash to an offshore bank account, many try to hide it in the name of a parent, child, coworker, or friend. Don't do this. Creditors' attorneys are experienced in ferreting out such hidden assets, and in extreme cases, these tactics can even give rise to civil and criminal charges of fraud.

In judging whether a particular transaction or transfer was fraudulent, a court will look at whether the new owner of the property paid a fair price for it. If you transfer two trucks and a $25,000 bulldozer to your cousin for $1,000, you are likely to regret it.

Many states' fraudulent transfer laws allow creditors to look back four years to see if you transferred any property to relatives or close business associates for less than full value. And in case you later file for bankruptcy, the bankruptcy trustee (the person who will be handling your case at bankruptcy court) can scrutinize transfers made in the past two years or use the state's longer look-back period.

Don't Lie on Loan Applications

If your business is in serious trouble, you may find yourself frantically trying to borrow money, and in the process may be tempted to misrepresent your financial condition. Don't. If, in applying for a loan, you overstate the value of your assets, inflate your income, or fail to disclose all of your existing debts, you can be guilty of fraud. And fraudulent debts can haunt you for years, especially if you later file for bankruptcy. A bankruptcy creditor will be able to easily compare the assets and income you listed on your loan application to those on your bankruptcy petition to see whether your loan application was fraudulent. If the bankruptcy court decides that a loan was obtained by fraud, it could refuse to discharge that debt. And even if your business is a corporation or LLC (which would normally protect your personal assets), you could be held personally liable to repay a loan obtained fraudulently.

> **CAUTION**
>
> **There are other don'ts if you're considering bankruptcy.** If you think you might end up filing bankruptcy, you also will want to avoid missteps such as paying creditors who are related to you before others, borrowing money from family and friends, or taking a credit card cash advance to pay your bills. For more information, see Chapter 13.

How to Protect Yourself From Further Personal Liability

So far, we've talked about what you can to do to deal with debts that you already owe. Now let's consider what you can do in the future to limit your personal legal liability for debt.

Sole Proprietors and Partnerships

As discussed earlier, if you are operating as a sole proprietorship or a partnership, you are forever personally liable for all business debts. In contrast, owners of LLCs or corporations are not liable personally for business debts unless they guarantee them with their personal signature. Because of this advantage, you may be interested in forming an LLC or corporation.

If, despite your current business problems, you believe your business is viable in the long term, quickly forming an LLC or corporation will protect your personal assets, such as your house or your car, from being taken to pay off new business debts. If you are able to pay off to pay off your old debts—the ones that you incurred while you were a sole proprietor or partner—and you convert to an LLC or corporation, you'll be protected from personal liability for most new debts.

You can't, however, get rid of personal liability for those old debts. So if you are considering converting to a corporation or LLC, keep in mind that doing so won't allow you to escape your personal liability for current business debts. That means that your past business creditors could still come after your house, car, and other personal assets if you don't pay your old debts. In addition, in most states, if you don't pay or settle your old debts before you form a new corporation or LLC—or have the LLC or corporation take over the debts and pay them in a timely fashion—the creditors of your old business can get a judgment against the new corporation or LLC and seize assets of the corporation or LLC to sell to pay the old debts.

RESOURCE

How to incorporate or form an LLC. You can form an LLC or corporation almost immediately online. Nolo.com is one of several affordable LLC and corporation formation services. But first, for more information on the basics of corporations and LLCs, and which business structure might be best for your business, visit the section on LLCs, Corporations, and Partnerships in Nolo's free online legal encyclopedia at www.nolo.com/legal-encyclopedia/llc-corporations-partnerships/index.html.

Once you form a corporation or LLC, you need to notify all of your suppliers, customers, and clients that your company is now a corporation or an LLC. It is essential that you send a letter to them saying that you have changed your business structure and giving your new name (which can be the same but must include "LLC" or "Inc."). And then you should make a clear request that they do business with you in your new name from here on. A sample letter is below.

Letter Announcing a Business's New Legal Structure

June 14, 20xx

Dear Ms. Tranchez:

Torchlight Productions has recently changed its legal structure from a sole proprietorship to a limited liability company. The name of the business has changed to Torchlight Productions, LLC.

The new business has taken over all assets and liabilities of our previous business, including contracts, orders, debts, and other accounts payable. There has been no change in the ownership of the company, and there will be no change in policies or delay in payments. We will be providing the same fine products and services on which we built our reputation.

Please be sure to pass the word to your accounts payable department and other relevant departments that we will now do business exclusively under our new name and that cannot recognize orders, invoices, bills, or any other business communications that use our former name. Please note that our address has not changed.

Thank you for being one of our most valued clients. We look forward to a long and healthy business relationship with you.

Very truly yours,
Emme Lorenz
Torchlight Productions, LLC

Follow Notification and Publication Rules in Your State

California, Georgia, Maryland, Virginia, Wisconsin, and the District of Columbia have a "bulk sales law," which applies to companies that manufacture or sell inventory from stock (and in California, to restaurants). Bulk sales laws are designed to prevent business owners from evading creditors by transferring their business assets to another company.

The bulk sales law requires you to give your creditors notice that you have transferred the assets of a sole proprietorship or partnership to a new corporation or LLC under a new name, and that the new entity assumes the debts of the prior company. In some states, this notice also must be published in a local newspaper, recorded in the county land records office, or sent to the Secretary of State. Your local newspaper or recorder's office should be able to help you with this notice.

To fully establish your new limited liability status, you should now sign all paperwork, invoices, checks, and contracts in your new capacity—for example, President of Sidewinder LLC. Also make sure to change all letterhead, invoices, and marketing material to reflect your new corporate or LLC name. Keep all new personal and business financial transactions totally separate, as an essential step to preserving the limited liability that your new LLC or corporation affords you. For example, all checks should be written from your LLC account and clearly state you are an LLC or corporation, and no personal bills should be paid from this account. (Transfer funds from the business account to your personal account first.)

You should also change the name on your business license, tax registration certificate, or seller's permit to reflect the new corporate or LLC name. Depending on your locality, you may be required to apply for other new licenses and permits under the corporation's or LLC's name as well.

> (!) **CAUTION**
> **Partnerships, beware of tax implications.** If you plan to convert a
> partnership into an LLC or corporation, things can quickly get tricky from a tax point
> of view. While some states provide straightforward partnership conversion forms,
> these don't take into consideration the legal and tax ramifications to closing down
> an existing co-owned business and starting a new one. As a result, you will probably
> need an attorney's help, or at least a consultation with a business accountant or tax
> expert, before you convert your partnership. (If you're looking for a lawyer, Nolo.
> com features a lawyer directory as a free resource to our customers. You can find
> comprehensive profiles of attorneys who handle business, tax, bankruptcy, and debt
> issues in your state at http://lawyers.nolo.com.)

Corporations and LLCs

To avoid any possibility that a creditor could later claim your corporation
or LLC is a legal sham and your business is merely a sole proprietorship or
partnership, it's crucial to act like your business is now an entity separate
from you.

Follow Corporate and LLC Formalities

The most important rule to follow is to hold and document regular meetings
as required by your corporate bylaws or LLC operating agreement, giving
proper notice to all owners of the meetings. Also be sure to follow proper
procedures on electing officers and voting on other matters.

If you don't follow these formalities, it will make it easier for a creditor to
say that you did not have a real corporation or LLC—that the corporation or
LLC was just a sham to help you defraud creditors and that it was really just
you running the business. (When a creditor makes this claim successfully, it's
called "piercing the veil.")

For example, if you are having financial difficulties and want to sell off
significant assets or lay off a significant portion of your workforce, you
should call a special meeting of your board of directors, at which you
communicate the details of your financial situation to request approval for

the sale or layoff. Document the directors' approval in a resolution and insert it in the minutes of the meeting.

RESOURCE

Information and forms for recording minutes and resolutions. See *The Corporate Records Handbook: Meetings, Minutes & Resolutions* or *Your Limited Liability Company: An Operating Manual*, both by Anthony Mancuso (Nolo).

Avoid Personal Guarantees

Whether you've just formed your corporation or LLC or you've operated one for years, remember that to protect your personal assets you must also refuse to personally sign business contracts or make personal guarantees on leases, loans, or contracts. If a particular vendor balks at supplying you under these terms, you can usually find someone else who will work with you, especially if you establish business credit by paying up front for the first order or two.

To get a bank loan or line of credit, you may not be able to avoid giving a personal guarantee—unless you can convince the bank that there are enough corporate or LLC assets to secure the debt. Think twice before taking on this serious legal burden.

How can you expect suppliers to give you credit terms without a personal guarantee? You can establish a good business credit record for your corporation or LLC just as you can establish good personal credit. To start, get a trade line of credit from several suppliers and a couple of business credit cards.

RESOURCE

Building a track record for your LLC or corporation. Dun & Bradstreet offers a program called CreditBuilder that, for a few hundred dollars, helps you report your payment history to establish good business credit. For more information, go to http://smallbusiness.dnb.com and search for CreditBuilder.

Concentrate on What's Really Profitable

"Business is a good game—lots of competition and a minimum of rules. You keep score with money."

NOLAN BUSHWELL

You should be able to state in just a few sentences how your business makes—or hopes to make—money. The fact that so many entrepreneurs can't do this goes far to explain both why few small companies are profitable in good times and why so many are subject to quick collapse when times are bad.

People still in the start-up phase or even those with a business that has been open for a while and is losing money, tend to be so excited about their entrepreneurial dreams that they ignore the core question of how they'll turn a profit. They happily chatter about their ideas, but can't provide income and expense projections that show how the business will make money. (Ask them for a dollars-and-cents explanation and they'll think you just haven't been listening, and start all over again to explain their entrepreneurial vision.)

Even in good times, just opening the doors of a shop or service business and hoping you'll sell or repair enough Fiddlyhumps to make a decent living is almost always a prescription for failure. For starters, you need to know your costs: how much you'll spend purchasing inventory, marketing your goods or services, paying rent, making service calls, compensating staff, plus what is likely to be a surprisingly long list of other costs. Only then you can begin to figure out exactly how many Fiddlyhumps you'll need to sell or fix each month and for how many dollars, so as to cover these expenses and earn an adequate profit besides.

When an economic meltdown happens, it's even more crucial to understand exactly how you make money, because otherwise you are almost sure to make the wrong cutback and marketing decisions. Flying blind, you're far more likely to hit a mountain than a runway.

EXAMPLE: Leili is a hair stylist who pays $1,200 per month to rent her station in a nice shop. Before the downturn, she worked 35 hours per week and netted $1,975 before taxes, meaning that she was earning about $56 per hour. But once hard times hit and people started to cancel and delay their appointments, her sales fell 25%. In an effort to fill up her chair, Leili considered cutting prices across the board.

But her marketing guru sister Resa suggested she break down how much she made for cutting and coloring hair, on an hourly basis. When Leili did the math, it turned out that she earned just $50 per hour on cutting, which was time-intensive, but $90 an hour on coloring because she could work on other clients while the color set. Armed with this information, Leili told her sister that since she made so much more on coloring, she planned to hold a 20%-off color sale for the rest of the year.

Instead, Resa suggested that Leili first do an experiment. For the next month she should notify her customers that she was discounting color 20%. Then, the following month she should return color to its normal price while mailing and emailing everyone a "recession special" of 20% off haircuts. Based on her results, she should then adopt the better long-term strategy.

In the first month, the 20% color discount produced only a tiny uptick in appointments, meaning that Leili actually worked harder for less total income. But when she discounted cuts 20%, her volume increased 30% for cuts and 20% for color, meaning that her income went up substantially.

Leili soon realized that her second plan worked so well because when older women took advantage of her cut discount, it brought attention to their graying hair, which they then wanted covered. But when they received an email telling them they could get a discount on color, they had time to consider that they could do it themselves for far less.

Getting a Quick Profits Plan on Paper

By now you should have completed your profit-and-loss forecast and cash flow analysis, which together should give you a good overall view of whether your business is solvent. In this chapter we want you to adjust your focus by asking you to grab a paper and pen (or your computer) and on one page describe which parts of your business still make money, or could make money if you cut overhead and made some marketing changes.

This will probably turn out to be tougher than you expect, especially if your business is losing money. To help you, next are some examples of brief profit statements written by people with small businesses. Don't worry if you don't fully grasp every detail of each business—these are back-of-the-envelope profit forecasts for internal use, not formal business plans to present to a stranger. And once the profits information is set out, we'll show you how each entrepreneur used it to make sensible business decisions.

There's No Substitute for Doing the Math

Ralph learned this lesson the hard way more than 30 years ago, when then-tiny Nolo was invited to participate in a Fourth of July flea market sponsored by a local consumer-owned grocery store. Nolo set up a booth and sold damaged and slightly out-of-date books for a dollar or two each, and raked in money.

That evening, his pockets bulging with bills, Ralph stopped by a friend's house for dinner and described his new vision to increase Nolo profits by selling books at similar flea markets. One of the other guests, who had considerable retail experience, started to chuckle. "I bet if you added up all your costs," he said, "you worked a long, hot holiday for practically nothing."

To show him exactly how wrong he was, Ralph got out pen and paper and went to work. In addition to $30 to rent a booth, $10 for supplies to make signs, and $25 to be included in the flea market's ads and flyers, the largest cost was paying two Nolo employees (who traded working on July 4 for time off on another day) to help Ralph set up, stock, and run the booth. And then there were a few hours of employee time before the flea market to pack up the books and afterward to unpack the ones that hadn't sold. Add a couple of dollars for gas and $15 to treat workers to lunch, and it turned out that Nolo netted only $70. Ralph had traded his holiday for $7 per hour.

Nolo did eventually find a way to get a few bucks out of distressed merchandise by selling it to "remainder" outfits, which buy large quantities of publishers' overstock for a few cents on the dollar. (The books end up on bookstores' bargain tables.) Although this approach yields far less per individual book, selling in bulk with minimal overhead costs means not only a profit, but also getting to sleep in on July 4.

Making Money in a Service Business

The dollars and cents of service businesses, especially those that don't operate from expensive commercial space, tend to be easy to explain. When your overhead is low and the main thing you're selling is time, it's not hard to understand what you need to do to make money.

For example, to earn a good income, an accountant needs only to sell a reasonable number of hours each year while getting paid promptly and keeping overhead expenditures under control. And if an accountant does poorly, the problem can usually be summed up in nine words: not enough clients buying and paying for enough hours. It follows that to fix things, the accountant will first want to improve marketing to bring in more work, and secondarily look at cutting overhead. Similarly, other service providers without high overhead, whether they are consultants, plumbers, music teachers, SAT tutors, exterminators, or massage therapists, should quickly be able to state how many hours of time they must sell at any given hourly rate to operate a financially successful enterprise.

In some fields, such as making emergency house calls to unplug sinks or toilets or plucking ducks for hunters, it's common to charge by the unit or job, not the hour. Fortunately, the math is no harder. For example, if a successful duck plucker cleans and wraps 10,000 ducks per season at $4 each (before moving on to cleaning salmon for a similar fee), it won't be hard to subtract the costs of doing business to arrive at a profits figure.

Even if you expand your business by renting more space or buying additional equipment, the math needed to figure out how the business will make a profit usually won't be much more complicated. And if you hire people to help, as long as the employees' cost can be marked up three to five times, all should be well.

Here are two quick and dirty—but nevertheless effective—profits statements for service businesses. As you'll see, each of these entrepreneurs has a good handle on the dollars-and-cents side of their operations, which allows them to make sensible cutback decisions when hard times require it.

Able, a House Painter

Here is Able's statement based on what he regards as his normal business over several good years.

I'm a house painter with a three-man crew that I sometimes expand to as many as eight when I'm working two or three jobs at once. My wife Sid works as part-time bookkeeper and scheduler. To pay her and the crew and cover other expenses, such as the cost of my truck and equipment, and net at least $120,000 to support our family, I need to gross close to $300,000 per year. I accomplish this by charging customers $60 per hour for my crew members and $70 for me. I pay my less-skilled employees $15 per hour and my highly experienced foreman $24 per hour.

I spend time doing things that don't produce income, such as bidding jobs, maintaining equipment, and taking a vacation, so I bill only about 800 hours of my own time each year. So, to meet my income goal I need to charge at least 4,500 hours for my crew. When the weather and the economy are both good, I can do better, meaning Sid and I can earn the $120,000 we need to live on and put money aside as well.

Doing the Numbers in a Good Year	
Revenue	
Crew (4,500 hrs × $60)	$270,000
Able (800 hrs × $70)	56,000
Total Revenue	**$326,000**
Expenses	
New Truck	$30,000
Gas	600
Paint and Materials	10,600
Office	18,000
Marketing	5,000
Wages & benefits (bookkeeper)	30,000
Wages & benefits (crew)	105,300
Miscellaneous	2,000
Total Expenses	**$201,500**
Net Profit (before taxes)	**$124,500**

Now let's fast forward to the economic downturn. Able's volume falls by 50%, and to get this much work, he has to lower his bids by at least 20%, meaning that he now charges his time at only $50 per hour and his crew's at $40 per hour. What can Able do to survive? He starts by determining that he can't solve the shortfall by simply doing more painting himself. Since he is by far the best salesperson, Able needs to put time into marketing, including bidding on as many jobs as possible. He also knows he can't afford to cut the hours of his foreman, even though his hourly rate is higher, because doing so risks losing his most skilled painter, something that before long would surely damage his reputation for top quality work. Based on these assumptions, here is Able's hard-times amendment to his first statement.

To cut overhead, I moved the office into the basement. In addition, I decided not to replace my truck, and of course I hired less labor because I had fewer jobs.

Doing the Numbers in a Bad Year	
Revenue	
Crew (2,250 hrs × $40)	$90,000
Able (800 hrs × $50)	40,000
Total Revenue	**$130,000**
Expenses	
Truck maintenance	$2,000
Gas	450
Paint/Miscellaneous Materials	6,000
Marketing	8,000
Bookkeeper	30,000
Wages & benefits (crew)	51,480
Miscellaneous	2,000
Total Expenses	**$99,930**
Net Profit (before taxes)	**$30,070**

Even counting Sid's pay for bookkeeping, it's obvious that Able and Sid are now in financial hot water. They have some high personal expenses that are important to them: Their two children go to Catholic school, and when times were bright two years ago, they bought a new house with a pricey mortgage. They realize more changes are necessary.

To try to put our business back on its feet, my first step was to ask my crew whether they would temporarily work for 25% less. Because they would otherwise be unemployed they agreed, as did my foreman. This let me mail a flyer to my old customers offering a super deal if they would commit to repainting now. I picked up six new jobs and put my foreman and two painters back to work full time. This meant Sid and I now have an income of over $90,000, just enough to pay the school bills and mortgage if we scrimp on everything else.

Going forward, Sid plants to take a course in color theory and help me with estimating, including leafleting neighborhoods close to where we have a job, offering a free consultation and estimate. If this works out, I can spend more time painting and further increase our income.

TIP

Employees cost more than you think. If you hire even a few people, otherwise productive time and energy must be diverted to communication, coordination, and other management tasks, none of which makes the cash register ring. Recognizing this, it's important that each new employee you hire make a substantial contribution to your bottom line. If they do, great—your management efforts will more than pay for themselves. But especially in bad times, when profits fall or disappear, you'll want to reassess. If an employee doesn't make your business substantially more profitable, you would do better to stop wasting your own precious productive hours on managing that person. Better to look at contracting the task out to someone who does nothing else or concentrate on getting the maximum possible return for your own time.

Scott, an Attorney for Small Businesses

Scott is a lawyer who specializes in new business start-ups and helping existing businesses do the legal paperwork necessary to raise money to expand. He also handles other problems for his business clients, including bankruptcy.

During normal times I try to work a 35-hour week, not counting hours I spend keeping up on my field through reading and attending legal education classes. With five weeks off each year, this means I have 1,645 hours to sell. I share a nice office with two other lawyers; my portion of office rent, my one-third share of the salaries for our one full-time secretary and one part-time paralegal, and my other expenses are about $100,000. In addition, I spend about $25,000 entertaining clients, taking classes in continuing legal education, travel, and professional publications (books and online materials). Obviously, I have to cover this $125,000 expense nut before I pocket anything.

My goal has been to bill at least 80% of my 1,645 working hours (or 1,316 hours) at $250 per hour, bringing in just under $329,000. This leaves me with a net of about $194,000 after covering expenses and any bad debts, which are usually about $10,000. But because I have a couple of clients with continuing legal needs who pay up front for my time whether or not they use all of it, these deals net me substantially more than $250 per hour, so my net is actually closer to $224,000.

Doing the Numbers in a Good Year	
Revenue	
Billable hours/Retainers	$359,000
Total Revenue	**$359,000**
Expenses	
Office rent and secretarial services	$100,000
Entertaining	15,000
Publications, professional dues, classes	5,000
Business travel	5,000
Bad debts	10,000
Total Expenses	**$135,000**
Net Profit (before taxes)	**$224,000**

Now let's look at what happened when the recession hit. The first indication that Scott faced trouble came in the form of a large increase in his accounts receivables. Many clients who usually paid their bills upon receipt now paid in 60 to 90 days, and about 15% had stopped paying altogether. In addition, new or expanding businesses were hard to find, so a good portion of his business dried up. Suddenly he was billing only 980 hours per year.

When you figured in the bad debts, his expenses had risen, and his net had fallen to less than $60,000.

Doing the Numbers in a Bad Year	
Revenue	
Billable hours/Retainers	$210,000
Total Revenue	**$210,000**
Expenses	
Office rent and secretarial services	$100,000
Entertaining	15,000
Publications, professional dues, classes	5,000
Business travel	5,000
Bad debts	27,000
Total Expenses	**$152,000**
Net Profit (before taxes)	**$58,000**

Studying these numbers, Scott decided that his major problems, in order of severity, were not getting paid for hours he had worked, not working enough hours, and unless he solved the first two problems, too much overhead. To put his business back on track, he devised this plan:

Send clients a strong signal that bills have to be paid on time, every time. To kick off his new policy, Scott politely gave all clients whose accounts were overdue the opportunity to pay promptly in full at a 10% discount (or to call and arrange a mutually agreeable installment plan). In addition, he began accepting credit cards, giving clients another convenient way to pay. Next, for clients who were still in arrears more than 60 days, he began a campaign of friendly but firm letters and phone calls (and also adopted a policy of providing no additional services, except as required by bar association rules). The result was a substantial influx of cash. Finally, when two clients simply ignored his requests to pay, Scott sent them a letter threatening a lawsuit (and explaining their right to first go to fee arbitration under bar association rules). One client paid; the other went bankrupt. Going forward, Scott also decided that clients who habitually paid late would be asked to pay an up-front retainer for substantial jobs (a policy that would be sweetened by offering a 10% discount), with Scott putting the retainer money in a client trust account until he billed for the work.

Reduce fees 25% for all new work, as a practical way to share his clients' economic pain. To qualify for this "recession rate," bills had to be paid within a week of receipt. In the same letter, he told his clients that he was now handling business debt problems for clients, including lease renegotiations, advice on layoffs, debt collection, assignment for benefit of creditor plans, and business bankruptcy. The combination of these new services and his lower prices resulted in a 30% increase in Scott's business. In addition, he joined several online lawyer directories, listing business bankruptcy as one of his services. This resulted in a steady stream of new clients.

Reduce rent and entertainment expenses. With bad debts reduced and business on the upswing, Scott felt less need to radically reduce overhead. But he and the lawyers with whom he shared office space did decide to squeeze in one more attorney to share the rent and salaries. That reduced expenses by $25,000. In addition, he cut his annual entertainment budget by $8,000 and reduced his vacation to three weeks.

Making Money in Retail or Manufacturing

Businesses that carry inventory, such as a retail store, or that buy new materials or components, such as a manufacturer or publisher, face a tougher task than do service businesses in understanding how to make money, especially in a tough economy. It follows that your back-of-the-envelope profit statement will necessarily look more like the formal profit-and-loss statement and cash flow analysis we discuss in the appendix. But it should still be possible to demonstrate that you understand how to return your business to profitability by producing a straightforward, albeit slightly longer, profit-and-loss statement.

Unfortunately, most shop owners and small manufacturers are not sure what it will take to make their enterprises sufficiently profitable. This helps explain why so many seemingly popular small retailers and manufacturers come and go, especially in tough economic times. Their owners, it turns out, never quite understood business basics, such as how much they needed to mark up their goods at a given sales volume and inventory level to cover their expenses (rent, salaries, the cost of carrying inventory, and marketing expenditures to mention a few) and still make a decent profit. When the economy turns sour, they simply don't know what to do to survive.

Here's one business owner who has a good handle on what's needed to do to make a reasonable profit: Felice, who publishes regional guidebooks.

My goal is to gross $1 million a year and net a 9% profit, or $90,000. To do this, I need to develop and maintain a list of 20 core titles that annually sell 5,000 or more copies each at an average cover price of at least $20.

If I meet that sales goal, my gross is $1 million after wholesalers and retailers take their 50% cut. The cost to manufacture each book is about $2, or $200,000 per year, all told. I pay my authors a royalty of 10% of net receipts (10% of $1 million, or $100,000). This leaves $700,000.

Doing the Numbers	
Revenue	
Gross sales at retail	$2,000,000
Net receipts	1,000,000
Cost of Goods	
Manufacturing ($2 per book)	$200,000
Author royalties (10% of net)	100,000
Total cost of goods	300,000
Gross profit	700,000
Expenses	
Rent and utilities	$30,000
Equipment (lease and purchase)	40,000
Book storage and shipping	50,000
Salaries and benefits for 6½ employees	350,000
Payments to freelancers	130,000
Miscellaneous	10,000
Total Expenses	$610,000
Profit	**$90,000**

> ### TIP
>
> **Good will doesn't count.** Often when naïve businesspeople pencil out the dollars and cents of a business, profit turns out to be thin or even nonexistent. Instead of just facing the truth that without adjustment the business won't work, it is common to argue that although startup or marketing costs are high, exposing the business to lots of customers will eventually pay off. Sorry, but business doesn't work that way. Each business endeavor should make economic sense on its own. And if it doesn't now, there is little chance things will improve in the future.

If something goes wrong with one part of your retail or manufacturing business—for example, sales of new products are disappointing—you'll have a tougher job reducing expenditures than would a service provider. Of all business expenses, the substantial cost of keeping an inventory of merchandise is usually the least well understood and accounted for. For instance, if you typically carry $200,000 in inventory, your profits must be large enough to cover the cost of tying up this investment, as well as all the other expenditures necessary to keep the doors open. If you use a bank line of credit to cover some or all of your inventory investment, the cost just to finance the inventory might be $10,000 to $20,000 per year, depending on how fast things sell.

EXAMPLE: Tamara opened a shop specializing in handmade Southwestern furniture. She located in a large, bright space near the affluent residential area that she expected to produce the bulk of her customers. Business was good, and for a few months she believed she was going to be a big success. But then, just about the time the economy began to turn sour, she looked more closely at her profit-and-loss statement and found that the cost of buying and maintaining a large display floor of furniture was gobbling up most of her cash. She was going into the red for several months of the year. Scared and disappointed, Tamara considered closing the store.

But then one of her advisers had a suggestion. If the cost of keeping a big inventory was the problem, why not sublease two-thirds of the store and embrace a different sales model? This time, Tamara would work with just a few high-end furniture makers who were willing to supply her with floor samples of their tables, chests, chairs, and other items. Customers would then place orders and pay in advance. Free of the need to pay rent on a large retail space and to tie up cash in inventory, Tamara began to have continuous, positive cash flow.

> **TIP**
>
> **Add a service component to a retail business.** A struggling low-profit retail enterprise might be able to save itself by adding a higher-margin services component. For example, a bookstore specializing in building and design books could make referrals to highly regarded local architects, contractors, and builders, for which it would receive commissions. In this business model, the low-margin retail business would be reinvented to provide a steady stream of customers to the much higher-profit service business. (For more ideas on creating profits, see Chapter 6.) ●

Innovate on a Shoestring

"Even if you're on the right track, you'll get run over if you just sit there."
WILL ROGERS

Look at a ten-year-old snapshot of Main Street in any American town or big city and compare it to what you see today. Many of the old businesses probably no longer exist, and many of the survivors have no doubt expanded or updated their appearance. Look again after the current recession has finally ended and you are sure to see that more of the old-timers have either updated their style and offerings or gone out of business. The same sort of winnowing will occur on the directory board in the lobby of any office building.

Where are the missing businesses? A few will have moved, but, especially when economic headwinds are stiff, the majority will be kaput. Even in normal economic times, 80% of business start-ups don't reach their fifth birthday. During dicey economic times, one big reason so many enterprises stagnate or even flatline can be summed up this way: lack of innovation. Enterprises that build creative change into their structure are far more likely to survive a recession than those that look for a recipe for success and then hope to endlessly repeat it.

The reason innovation is crucial to long-term success in both good and bad times is simple. To establish and maintain a profit margin robust enough to survive a business-killing downturn, you need a true competitive advantage. And if you are smart or lucky enough to accomplish this, you must keep your competitive edge in the face of rivals who will inevitably try to copy it and customers whose thirst for the new and trendy will turn yesterday's brilliant innovation into tomorrow's big yawn.

When a small business does well and its product or service is temporarily in short supply, it will attract competitors. Unless the profitable business quickly smartens up and finds a way to distinguish itself, these competitors will quickly find a way to siphon off customers. This is just what happened in the last few decades to many pioneering video stores, quick oil changers, and photocopy shops. Businesses that entered these fields early, when the new service was in demand, often did very well in the short run. But because their business formulas were so easy to copy and few outlets took steps to distinguish themselves, only a minority survived when deep-pocketed chains flooded in.

Competition doesn't always come from big chains. For example, if you establish a small graphic design business to help businesses lay out advertising copy, you'll be competing with dozens, if not hundreds, of others who do much the same thing. And especially during a recession, all of you will be selling your services to business customers, most of whom are very price-sensitive. So to bring in business and charge the prices you'll need in order to support yourself, your design work must clearly be more desirable than your customers can buy down the street (or increasingly, on the Web). For instance, if you are the first local graphics shop to offer a library of popular art deco design elements, chances are your competitors will quickly offer similar motifs. To keep your edge, you'll need to be ready with fresh work, perhaps by turning the clock back to the creative design motifs of the 1930s when WPA artists and architects created a unique body of work. Or maybe you'll seek inspiration in wonderful 18th-century Japanese art. Either way, you'll have to constantly innovate.

You might think that the value of building a competitive edge would be obvious in good times and even more so when customers have a death grip on their wallets. Think again. It never seems to occur to many entrepreneurs to look for ways to aggressively outthink their competitors, which is a huge reason so many never become solidly profitable even in the best of times. For example, all over America, independent coffee shops, not savvy enough to give people a good reason to prefer them, struggle for survival in the shadow of mediocre chain outlets. Similarly, the typical pet food outlet, chiropractor, sandwich shop, or freelance bookkeeping service doesn't have the know-how to create and keep a competitive edge over the ever-present herd of similar businesses. True, because pets and people need to eat, and the IRS and sore feet are always with us, when times are good these look-alike businesses may make enough money to survive. But when the hammer of a deep recession falls, only those that offer customers something extra are likely to prosper.

Fortunately, there are lots of low-cost ways to distinguish your business in customers' minds. Depending on the business, that something extra might be high quality at a reasonable price, a clear technological edge, an accessible location, a superior website, or just really friendly, caring service.

The need to innovate never goes away. When you consider how to reconfigure your business so it will be best positioned to survive, think about not only whether a particular innovative new direction will be substantial enough to set you apart from the competition, but also about how you will be able to extend your advantage over time. And it should go without saying that it won't be enough to come up with a couple of clever ideas and then go back to business as usual. Especially if your profits have melted down to the point where you're not sure your little enterprise will survive, you'll need to build a culture that supports innovation, now and forever.

In my experience, innovation in the small business world occurs in three ways: invention, copying, and serendipity. Let's examine each to see how it might help your business.

Invention

It's hardly a secret that Americans love new things. From iPhones and water-miser toilets to plasma 1080p Blu-ray compatible HDTVs and plug-in hybrid cars, much of our time is spent using tools and toys that didn't exist a generation or two ago. It's not only big inventions, however, that change lives and make fortunes. Think about the equipment in today's dental offices and compare it to what was in use a decade ago. Virtually every tool has been substantially improved or changed. Interestingly, many of these state-of-the-art gizmos were thought up by dentists themselves who thought it was more fun to invent things than fill another bicuspid.

Similarly, many of the services we now take for granted are either relatively new or are packaged or delivered in innovative ways. For example, in contrast to the way they operated a generation ago, most small businesses now outsource payroll preparation, equipment maintenance, graphic design, and many other tasks to specialists whose work is better, cheaper, and faster than could be done in-house. Similarly, 21st-century electricians, plumbers, contractors, and most other service providers use many tools and techniques that didn't exist when Bill Clinton was president. A generation or two ago, hiring a housepainter usually meant living through a month of having a couple of men hang off heavy wooden ladders, swabbing away with short-handled brushes. Today the combination of lightweight ladders and scaffolding, power sanders, fast-drying wood-fillers, and paint sprayers means the same job can be done in a week.

When goods or services are improved or replaced, someone always makes money. Much of the profit usually falls to those who quickly figure out a way to market the new product, service, or business method. For example, when easy-to-customize modular storage systems were first developed to organize closets and garages, interior designers who quickly embraced these exciting new tools charged hefty fees to customers determined to improve on closet designs that had changed little for several centuries.

Like art or poetry, "eureka" breakthroughs either occur or they don't—there is little most of us can do to turn ourselves into an Edison, Bell, or Shockley. But fortunately, to prosper in the small business world, you don't have to invent a palm-size camcorder or underwater telephone. In fact, most profitable innovations consist of combining or connecting two or more fairly mundane things. For example, in the early 1990s, a tiny website dedicated to buying and selling used items figured out how to combine the fun of a local swap meet or garage sale with the global connectivity of the Internet. Starting with the sale of a broken laser pointer for $13, eBay, now one of the world's most valuable corporations, was born. Similarly, Amazon.com's patented "one-click shopping" helped it create a hugely successful business selling a huge variety of merchandise.

In your own neighborhood, many service businesses probably now provide traditional services in ways so efficient and attractive that even in recessionary times, their customers stick by them instead of going to their price-cutting competitors. For example, several independent optometrists and eyeglass shops now work together, so in one stop you can have your eyes checked, order new high-quality and high-fashion glasses or contacts, and have them ready in 24 hours, with the further assurance that adjustments and minor repairs are free forever. An estate planning lawyer we know has given up her traditional office-based practice and switched to making house calls, an old-fashioned service that her clients, many of whom are elderly, find highly desirable.

Businesses are especially likely to profit from innovations that are congruent with powerful long-term trends, such as renewable energy sources, organic food, health-enhancing exercise, and recyclable packaging, to mention just a few. If your plumbing business goes green, in the sense that you emphasize low-flow toilets, showerheads, and more efficient hot water systems, you should easily set yourself apart from the half-dozen Roto-Rooter, Mr. Rooter, Zap Rooter, and AAA Rooter businesses in your area.

EXAMPLE: Poster Compliance is a California company that provides attractive state-specific laminated posters to employers, who are required by law to post certain information about wages and hours, health and safety law, workers' compensation, and so on. Faced with lots of competitors, Poster Compliance set itself apart by developing a line of posters using recycled paper and soy ink. In just a year, the "green" posters increased Poster Compliance's market share by a hefty percentage.

Many new enterprises turn in a profitable new direction when someone gets mad at how traditional enterprises operate and decides there must be a better way. It might be as simple as becoming disgusted with the quality of the coffee in local restaurants and figuring how to serve a tastier brew. As you sip your morning latté at Starbucks, Peet's, or an independently owned purveyor of excellent coffee, it may seem like this hugely profitable innovation was a no-brainer. Not so. If you are old enough to remember how bad most American coffee tasted 20 years ago, you'll understand just how much insight and determination was necessary to create businesses that really can serve a great cup. A local tile shop, which sells beautifully designed, handcrafted tile, got started in large part because its owners were frustrated with the unimaginative selection available at local building supply outfits.

EXAMPLE: The partners in a small architectural firm, BT Associates, are fed up with competing with dozens of other firms for every residential and small commercial job. To learn about a hot new field, they volunteer to design an emergency response center for their county, at no cost. When the center, which combines lightweight design with the strength and flexibility to withstand almost any conceivable disaster, as well as a NASA-like dedication to the optimum use of the latest communication techniques, wins several design prizes, BT Associates is quickly able to parlay its experience into a national leadership role in this specialized but growing field. They begin to land a substantial percentage of the jobs they bid on all over the country. Even when a local firm can use its political connections to beat them out, it often contracts with BT Associates for lucrative behind-the-scenes design help.

Copying

In big-business doublespeak, copying the ideas of other businesses is called "benchmarking," something that all major corporations routinely practice. For example, the owners of virtually every large entertainment and sports complex in America have for decades sent managers to Disney World to look for people-handling practices they can beg, borrow, or benchmark. Because most of Disney's business practices are right out in the open, learning from and even copying them is not only smart and cheap but, as long as competitors don't try to borrow the Mouse, Duck, or other copyrighted characters or patented inventions, is perfectly legal. It should come as no surprise that Disney itself has borrowed innovative ideas from many other entertainment venues.

Copying is a particularly great way to innovate in the world of small business, especially when times are tough and you need to change or die. America is a big place, and in many fields there are so many small operations that it can take years for best practices to permeate a whole business segment. For example, if you run a struggling children's clothing store in Omaha, you may be able to check out a dozen similar operations in California and come away with several innovative business ideas no one in Nebraska has yet stumbled onto. Similarly, if you own several bagel shops in Seattle, you would be nuts not to check out the New York bagel scene when visiting the East Coast. And if you pick up a couple of good ideas, you would really be *meshugeh* if you didn't quickly adopt them.

EXAMPLE: Trina owns a small teashop on the outskirts of Austin, Texas. The recession has tightened the pocketbooks of her largely retirement-aged clientele, and her once-popular gathering place is barely hanging on. While visiting a cousin who has a toddler in Oakland, California, she is taken to Tot'nTalk, a combination daycare-coffee shop where harried mothers have a place to meet friends and socialize while their offspring happily play in a play area overseen by a friendly teenage babysitter. The lightbulb goes on over Trina's head as she sees a way to convert her dying teashop into a popular gathering place for the many growing families in her area.

Borrowing the best practices of others should be a part of every business's ongoing innovation plan. Because it's free and easy, you may already do it on an informal basis. But to improve your chances of success, start a systematic study of excellent businesses in your field, particularly those that are not in your immediate area. Staying clear of local competitors will avoid unnecessarily angering them and at the same time force you to explore beyond the familiar, increasing your chances of discovering a breakthrough business model.

To find businesses good enough to serve as role models, talk to suppliers and other knowledgeable people who work in a different geographical area. For example, if you run a small ad agency in Bangor, Maine, that is struggling to survive because many of your customers are cutting their ad budgets, you might call several business acquaintances who use similar agencies in the mid-Atlantic states. Ask them for the names of three excellent local ad shops in their area. If they can't help, maybe they know someone who can. Once you get a preliminary list, do some more checking (looking at websites can tell you a lot) to shorten it to a few successful businesses that are most like yours.

At this point, you'll need to decide whether it makes more sense to call the other business, explain what you are doing, and suggest sharing best practice information, or to anonymously study their operations. Depending on a number of factors, including whether you can arrange an introduction and how transparent the business is, either approach can work. Obviously, it's a lot easier to learn a lot about a deli by walking in the front door a few times than it is to figure out what makes an ad agency tick by schmoozing with the receptionist.

Establish a separate notebook or computer file for every business you study, dedicating a section for each key business area you want to study. Depending on the business, this might include signage, marketing, staffing, website design, key products, and delivery methods. For example, if a business you study apparently gets lots of calls because of a super-clever yellow pages ad, you want to capture that information in your notebook so that you can design an equally compelling ad.

EXAMPLE: After working several years as an electrician, Maureen, who is excited by the aesthetic and energy-saving possibilities of new lighting systems, opens Maureen's Full-Service Lighting with an electrician's business built in. Her idea is to give do-it-yourself remodelers a one-stop way to buy new lighting systems and get them installed. Although in her city there are plenty of lighting retailers and electricians, no other business has efficiently merged the two. In large part, this is because lighting stores are afraid to offend electricians, who are themselves wholesale customers as well as a source of customer referrals.

Maureen is convinced that given time, her customers will be so enthusiastic about her operation that they will refer others. She concedes that she may alienate some independent electricians, but believes most of them already buy cheaper generic products at big box stores. Maureen reasons she will gain far more than she loses by funneling lighting purchasers directly into her own installation business. And she hopes that once she gives these customers quality service, they will call her when they have future electrical needs.

But just a few months after Maureen opens, local businesses announce major layoffs, and sales are far slower than her business plan predicted. She begins to worry that, despite her innovative approach, she won't have the financial wherewithal to survive until her new concept has a chance to prove itself. To help her decide what to do, Maureen recruits an advisory committee chaired by her Uncle Jimmy, an investor who retired early with a big nest egg. Although Jimmy and the others are impressed with Maureen's business plan, their concern is that it's not innovative enough in these bad economic times. Jimmy wants Maureen to take the time to study some highly successful lighting shops to get ideas. Jimmy gets on the phone, calling lamp manufacturers and wholesalers who do business across the country.

He learns that the hottest lighting retailers all have one thing in common: they have fully embraced "green" lighting. Jimmy buys Maureen a plane ticket, and in a week they visit five lighting stores in four states, all of which concentrate on energy-efficient fixtures. Convincing Maureen's advisory committee, Jimmy proposes that

Maureen start featuring green products that will save big on the cost of electricity. Maureen enthusiastically agrees and immediately sets about remaking her shop to emphasize energy-saving products plus educational materials on using them. When all this is in place, she installs a bright green awning with her new name, "Maureen's Energy-Saving Lighting" and in smaller print, "Electrician on Duty." Because Jimmy believes Maureen now has a concept that will thrive during hard times as well as good, he lends enough money to bring her dream to reality.

Serendipity

Way back in the 1950s, in his groundbreaking book *Innovation and Entrepreneurship*, legendary business thinker Peter Drucker pointed out that many profitable innovations result from accidental or unexpected breakthroughs. He meant the kind of thing that occurs when you set out to develop a better variety of easy-to-remove packaging tape and end up inventing a revolutionary kind of wallpaper that both sticks tight and is easy to peel off the moment you get sick of it. What's so special about Drucker's insight? After all, from the discoveries of penicillin and saccharin to the inventions of nylon and Velcro, it's obvious that chance plays a significant role in finding new ways to do things.

Drucker really gets interesting with a second and more telling point: When businesses accidentally stumble onto a hot new product or service, even one that could give them a more competitive advantage, they often fail to recognize it or even actively suppress it. That is, they keep fooling around with the tape and stick the wallpaper in the trash.

EXAMPLE: Leo and Stan are longtime partners in the Arrow Glass Co., a nothing-special glass supplier. It sells hundreds of types of glass to contractors for use in residential and small commercial construction projects, and also caters to do-it-your-selfers. A few years ago, more and more people began asking Arrow for several types of plastic, particularly for newer, unbreakable burglar-deterring types that could be substituted for window glass. At first, Arrow sent these people elsewhere. Finally, after turning away more and more business, Leo and Stan began stocking a few of the most commonly requested types of window plastic, keeping them in an unused area behind the stairs they not-so-privately referred to as the Plastic Hole.

When plastic sales immediately turned out to be solidly profitable, helping Arrow to have its best ever year, Leo and Stan were delighted that they finally had the financial wherewithal to expand and improve their facility. They bought and remodeled the next-door warehouse, which let them more than double their selection of glass. Despite the huge increase in floor space, they left the Plastic Hole in its same dingy spot.

Were Leo and Stan obtuse? No question. Unfortunately, they were also typical. Like most business owners, they were slow to recognize and even slower to embrace an accidental business breakthrough. Doing so would have meant fundamentally changing their original mindset, which is never easy.

Think about the small enterprises you patronize. How often does your drycleaner, plant nursery, or hair salon change the way it does business? If the answer is somewhere between "rarely" and "never," you can safely bet that the business is guilty of ignoring and probably even suppressing new information, and as a result is sailing so aimlessly through the recessionary storm it is in danger of sinking. A more nimble competitor will surely appear, embrace the new concepts, and quickly grab market share.

Here are several more examples of businesses that are ignoring information they should be embracing to improve their competitive position:

- A struggling small-animal veterinarian who frequently gets calls from concerned pet owners after regular business hours, but doesn't look into hiring another vet to run an evening clinic.

- A certified public accountant specializing in income taxes, who, despite being asked questions almost daily about planning to limit estate tax, never reorganizes his business to provide customers helpful information and nonlegal services on this topic.

- A copy shop on a congested street that doesn't institute a free pickup and delivery service or otherwise improve access despite the fact its high-volume customers constantly complain about parking and ticket hassles.

- A consultant who helps city and county governments plan police, fire, and other public safety buildings but turns down requests to help plan newly popular disaster-response centers because they are outside her area of expertise.

- A haircutting salon, in a city that is fast becoming the home for thousands of Southeast Asian immigrants, that doesn't seek out haircutters who speak one or more of the newly common languages.
- A store selling teak garden furniture and expensive knickknacks for house and garden that is repeatedly asked where tools can be sharpened, but fails to start a sharpening service.

Poor babies. By not gathering and acting on the information their customers are thrusting upon them, these businesses—all of which surely have lots of competitors—are turning their backs on ways to improve their profitability.

But if a successful business you know has recently made positive changes to the way it looks, what it sells, or how it interacts with its customers, chances are its owner has learned to make smart use of new information—and to constantly improve the company's competitive position.

EXAMPLE: Madge opened a gift shop, Something Special, in a small university city in the Midwest. Selling a wide variety of items, she barely broke even her first year. Then when the economy tanked and sales dropped, Madge, a single mother with two teenagers to raise, decided to put up a going-out-of-business sign. But while the sign was on order, a customer came in and bought almost $1,000 worth of Native American crafts that were displayed on a couple of shelves at the back of the store. When the customer also asked to be alerted when the next shipment came in, Madge reflected that sales of such artwork had been fairly profitable from the start and other people had made similar requests.

After checking to be sure no one else in the area had captured this niche, Madge decided to store her going-out-of-business sign for a few months while she converted half of the store to North American Indian arts and crafts. She helped her new emphasis along with a marketing campaign featuring programs and workshops hosted by many of the Native American artists and a website built by her tech-savvy son. Soon, Something Special was special enough to succeed despite the recession.

In the big business world, innovation is often the product of many years of expensive research—that's what it takes to produce new drugs, computer chips, and more powerful, longer-lasting batteries. Fortunately, the information necessary to innovate in the small business world is usually far more available. Indeed, for the business owner with an open mind, good ideas that can be implemented at a reasonable cost are available everywhere.

A great example of how to improve a business by paying attention to unexpected information involves the Holiday Inn in Cumberland, Maryland. As reported by Associated Press writer David Dishman, for years this motel bore the heavy burden of being built hard against a railroad line. When the hotel wasn't full, desk clerks, fearing that guests would be bothered by the 65 noisy trains that clattered past each day, assigned guests to the quieter rooms closer to the unpleasant highway. Then one day a train enthusiast contacted Sales Director Karen Twigg to ask how much extra it would cost to book a room facing the tracks. Twigg could have politely said they were the same price, accommodated the man's request and gone on with her routine. Instead, she quizzed the caller about why he wanted to overlook the trains and found out that he was a train freak. Realizing that he wasn't the world's only train enthusiast, Twigg decided to see whether the Holiday Inn could profit from her new knowledge. She did this by starting a promotional campaign aimed at train buffs: "Make tracks to stay with us." This message was a big hit, and train-loving travelers from all over the world booked track-side rooms with a view of all those locomotives pulling their loads in and out of the CSX switching yard and maintenance shops.

Now take a moment to think about your business. Especially at a time when every sale is precious, do you have the innovative mindset to recognize and profit from valuable new information? Tempted to answer "Yes"? No problem, as long as you can name three trends in your field and what you are doing to raise your profits (or stem your losses) by taking full advantage of them.

Making Innovation a Continuous Process

If the innovative ideas you introduce turn out to be on target, and you run your business competently, chances are you'll survive tough times. Your long-term task is to keep innovation happening, so that aggressive (or even desperate) competitors don't figure out a way to catch up to or leapfrog your new approaches.

This isn't easy. As the owner of a small business, you will be pulled in many directions every day. Customers must be satisfied, employees organized, supplies ordered, and bills paid, to mention just a few necessities. And in the midst of all this, you must still plan to improve your business at a time that sales are hard to come by and profits are meager. You might think the biggest problem is having time to come up with creative ideas, but the opposite can just as often be true. For some entrepreneurs, ideas are as plentiful as pumpkins in October; it's picking the best ones and carving them to perfection that's difficult. And once each is implemented, you also need to be able to track its success or failure. You'll never have time to nurture the best ones if you aren't equipped to recognize and shuck off the losers.

When thinking about how to improve your business, start with three key principles. First, if your business has been successful in the past, and especially if it is still at least slightly profitable, you'll want to improve it incrementally, not fundamentally try to reinvent it. This way, you both minimize the possibility of jeopardizing your success while at the same time take steps to extend your entrepreneurial edge and protect your profit margins. For example, suppose your small software company has had a profitable specialty in designing database software for lumberyards. When the recession hits, orders decline 15%. It probably doesn't make sense for you to try to apply your innovative inventory-tracking ideas to retail stores or other businesses you don't fully understand. Better to focus on new features that will make a new release of your software so essential to your struggling lumber industry customers that they will buy it even when money is tight.

If your bottom line is in the red, you'll want to innovate more boldly; if the business you have now is failing, your best hope is to quickly and fundamentally change it. If you are right, your new ventures will produce the added income you need to survive. And if your idea doesn't work, you won't be any worse off.

Third, whether you decide to make incremental or fundamental changes, focus on the real needs of your target market, not on your own hopes and dreams. When asked—and it's always wise to ask—customers often request the most basic improvements, not clever breakthroughs. For example, a lawyer, house remodeler, or landscaper who adopts a policy of returning all phone calls within three hours may do more to please customers and clients than they would if they developed a laundry list of new services. Similarly, a coffee shop that serves better grades of coffee and tea may score more points with breakfasters than if it went to far more trouble to create a whole new menu.

EXAMPLE: Madge, the woman who was smart enough to turn her failing gift shop into a successful purveyor of Native American arts and crafts, distributed a questionnaire to a number of her best customers requesting feedback as to how she could better serve them. Several suggested she add folk art from other parts of the world, including Nepal, Tibet, South East Asia, and Central America. Worrying about spreading herself too thin, Madge nevertheless decided to expand her inventory to include folk art from all the Americas. Although doing this required renting a small adjoining space, Madge's new initiative was profitable from the start.

Fortunately, most innovative ideas are free—so you should be gathering as many as possible. And because business-changing ideas rarely show up on schedule or in easy-to-recognize ways, bringing as many as possible to the surface will take both creativity and stubbornness. For example, if you operate an organic grocery, you'll want to encourage the high school kid who uses your cute little wheelbarrow to move heavy orders to customers' cars to tell you if customers frequently ask where they can buy one. This doesn't mean you'll ultimately decide to sell wheelbarrows—just that you want to capture this information.

Here are some suggestions that may help you design an information-gathering system.

Brainstorm

Brainstorming sessions with people who are worried about your short-term prospects and care about your long-term success can be very useful. Depending on the size and sophistication of your business, participants might include the members of your advisory board, an investor, family members, key employees, and contractors. You might possibly include a supplier you need to reassure about the business's viability. Most of these people will have ideas to improve your business. Some will be wildly impractical, others far too costly, and one or two just plain kooky, but there are likely to be at least a few excellent ones.

Groups of from six to eight people—ten at most—work best. Arrange to get the participants together in a quiet place for several hours. To make sure everyone is well informed about your business, provide in advance financial projections, marketing information, and other helpful background materials.

Prepare by placing an easel holding a big pad of white paper at the front of the room with an important question written at the top using a dark marker. Something like "How can ABC Ventures quickly increase profitable sales?" works well. Designate as facilitator someone who can write clearly, has a good sense of humor, and is comfortable in front of people. It's often best if you don't assume this role. Your presence at the front of the room might intimidate some participants and keep them from offering suggestions they're afraid might be seen as criticism.

The facilitator, acting as master of ceremonies, should begin by making it clear all ideas are welcome and that there is no such thing as a stupid suggestion. It's also a good idea if the facilitator coaches people to be brief, explaining that the exercise works best if you first collect as many ideas as possible *without evaluating them.* Later, you can discuss the most viable ones. For example, if you operate a suddenly lagging solar hot water and photovoltaic cell company, the first person might say "Advertise in the PennySaver," the second "Offer summer discounts," the third "Pay salespeople bigger commissions for larger orders," and the fourth "Work with lenders to make it easier for homeowners to finance installations."

No matter how seemingly silly, boring, or counterproductive an idea may at first sound, the facilitator should record it without argument or editing (except to summarize long-winded statements). Again, a big key to freeing people up to tap into their creativity is to convince them there really are no bad ideas. For example, if someone who works at one of your money-losing greeting card shops starts to explain why she thinks it would make sense to also run a takeout coffee bar, don't laugh and ask for a more serious suggestion. Just write on your white board "sell coffee." Who knows—if there isn't a place in the neighborhood where customers can get a decent latte, a card and coffee shop might just work. Once participants trust that all contributions really are welcome, it's likely that suggestions will come fast and furiously. After half an hour, your sheet might look something like the one below.

How Can ABC Ventures Become Profitable?

- Sell goods at cost—mark up services.
- Pay employees sales commissions.
- Provide free customer parking.
- Raise starting pay—retain worker loyalty.
- Deliver on Sunday.
- Target marketing to affluent young adults.
- Improve the website.
- Sell coffee.
- Provide a money-back guarantee.
- Deliver in the evening.
- Stay open Sunday.
- Buy XYC Inc.
- Advertise in Spanish.
- Search for strategic partners with money to invest.
- Open two more locations.
- Sponsor kids' sports teams.
- Recruit workers of all racial backgrounds.
- Create a clever yellow pages ad.

It usually takes less than an hour—and sometimes less than 30 minutes—to extract all of a group's good ideas on a particular subject. Especially if things are going well, you'll want to give people a short break and then ask them to consider a second question. This time you'll probably want to focus on a narrower issue, again giving the group as much useful data as possible. For example, if your spa offers a number of different massage and exercise packages, and you want ideas on how you can better market the most profitable ones, you'll want each participant to have information about your sales volume by spa package, profit margins for each, hours of peak usage, and so on.

Depending on your business, here are some areas you might want to probe:

- How can we identify our best potential customers?
- Once identified, how can we find more of them?
- How can we encourage our satisfied customers to tell others about us?
- How can we encourage customers who have disappeared to reappear?
- What additional products or services can we introduce?
- How can we better distinguish ourselves from our competitors and let their customers know what's special about us?
- How can we increase sales at popular times?

EXAMPLE: Mark quit his job as a psychologist to open Bright Spot, a plant nursery specializing in roses and Japanese maples, a narrow focus he believed would give him a competitive edge over his generalist competitors. But after 18 months, it was clear that Bright Spot was in serious financial trouble. In tough economic times, not enough people were willing to pay a premium for its specialty products.

On a Monday at the end of the summer, when the business was closed, Mark convened a meeting of his family, his business advisers, and his three key employees. He asked for honest feedback as to whether Bright Spot had a future or whether he should put it out of its misery and go back to talking to depressed 18 year olds.

After a half an hour, in which the participants searched for something positive to say about Bright Spot, Mark's scrawny 15-year-old son put a positive spin on his sum-mer, saying "Dad, I know we're losing money, but I've gained ten pounds and really bulked up carrying all those bags of dirt."

Sara, one of Mark's advisers, asked about the dirt. It transpired that customers in the big new subdivision north of town couldn't seem to buy enough dirt to mix with their hard-as-rock clay soil. When the group looked into the profits of dirt and other soil amendments, they concluded that Bright Spot might have a future if it turned the large fenced area behind the nursery into a dirt yard. To accomplish this, Mark ordered truckloads of different types of soil and piled them high and made a deal with Fred, a guy with a dump truck, to do deliveries. When the new service immediately proved popular, Mark added various types of mulches and landscaping products, such as ornamental rock, and even oversized iron garden sculptures. In a few months, Bright Spot was profitable.

Chances are your brainstorming sessions will produce at least several excellent ideas you haven't already thought of. If you are lucky, you'll get one that truly improves your business. But it's also possible that your brainstorming group won't produce ideas that are likely to substantially improve your prospects. If you assembled an able, energetic group, this might be a signal that the foundational concept behind your struggling business needs rethinking.

Get Employees Involved

Your employees undoubtedly know a great deal about your business. And many of them probably care nearly as much about its success as you do. In addition to including key employees in your brainstorming sessions, here are some efficient ways to solicit their good ideas.

"5/15" reports. Periodically ask everyone in your company to spend no more than 15 minutes writing down their suggestions for improving the business. You, in turn, should be able to read each report in five minutes. Reports can be kept confidential if the writers want it that way—otherwise, share the ideas with everyone.

Notebooks. Give every employee who deals with the public a notebook (paper or electronic—it makes no difference) and ask them to keep track of all customer requests and suggestions.

Email conferences. If your business has an internal email system, establish a new-idea conference where employees can post and read suggestions. To keep things fresh, it's best to time-limit each conference. For example, on April 1, you might ask employees for their ideas on improving customer service, giving them a week or two to respond. On May 1, you could ask for ideas about new products and services.

How to Encourage and Reward Employees' Good Ideas

To encourage employees to stay interested in generating ideas to improve your business, and at the same time avoid jealousy or the feeling that one employee may be claiming too much credit, it's a good idea to do three things:

- Publicly recognize the person (or people) who contribute a good idea. Make sure everyone in the company knows, by making an announcement at a company meeting or sending a company-wide email.

- Spread the credit around as widely as possible. For example, if someone in your warehouse figures out a better way to track inventory, you might celebrate by taking the hero of the day and a group of coworkers to lunch. Of course, you will also want to remember the clever employee when it's time for raises or promotions.

- If your budget permits, establish a bonus pool. Make appropriate awards monthly or quarterly. For example, if your monthly bonus pool were $500, one month you might award all of it to the two employees who developed a plan to cut $15,000 in costs. The next month, you might make three different awards to people who suggested innovative ways to market a new service.

For good ideas on how and why to establish a bonus pool, grab a copy of *Ideas Are Free: How the Idea Revolution Is Liberating People and Transforming Organizations*, by Alan Robinson and Dean Schroeder (Barrett-Kohler).

Involve Customers

If yours is an established business with repeat customers or clients, these folks almost surely want to tell you things. Too bad that so few businesses encourage them to do so. Many businesses actually find ways to resist or reject customers' good ideas.

EXAMPLE: Craig, a long-time member of a local gym, overheard the manager talking with a contractor about the layout of a new stretching room. The conversation was in a public space, so Craig politely asked if the new room could contain wider mats. When the manager didn't seem very responsive, Craig pointed out that big men like himself who didn't easily fit on the existing mats used two mats so as not to bump neighboring stretchers. Craig's point that small mats actually resulted in fewer—not more—people using the stretching space was so right-on that several other members immediately spoke up to agree. After listening for a very short time, the manager interrupted to say that the size of the mats wasn't his decision, but he was pretty sure the owner would buy more of the small ones.

"No big deal," you may be thinking. After all, most people won't switch health clubs based on the size of their mats. Don't be so sure. If a competing exercise facility advertised a new yoga, Pilates, and stretching area, it might siphon off a fair number of customers who were tired of being ignored.

Not only is it wise to listen to good ideas your customers bring to you, it also makes sense to solicit them. Depending on your business, there are a variety of appropriate ways to ask for feedback. Traditional methods, such as asking interested customers to submit a brief questionnaire online, by dropping it in a box, or by mailing it back in a postage-paid envelope, often work well. But you'll want to reach out to customers who don't normally volunteer suggestions. One way to do this is to give them a little advance thank-you present. A home repair contractor who sends a measuring tape along with the feedback form is sure to receive more forms back.

It's a mistake to ask for suggestions unless you are prepared both to implement the best ones and tell your customers you acted on their feedback. If you take those two steps, you'll not only increase customer satisfaction (the exercise mats really are wider), but will also reinforce the trust you want them to place in your business (customers will feel greater involvement with and loyalty to a business that pays attention to them).

One good way to let people know that their suggestions aren't being ignored is to periodically list ones you have implemented. For example, when the customers of Pam's independent drugstore stuffed her new suggestion box with requests that she carry more naturopathic remedies, she not only established such an area, but created a small display area next to the suggestion box listing this suggestion and a number of others she had implemented. She also put this information on her website.

Take Time to Think About Your Business

Although it's always rewarding to get your employees and customers involved in suggesting ways to improve your business, it's at least as important to engage the creative juices of your single most important worker. That's you—just in case you have been too busy lately to remember.

Your first thought may be, "Oh, no. I already obsess about my business. The last thing I need is to spend more time worrying about it, especially now that the bad economy threatens to strangle it." The truth is that even if your business is a mighty success, you do need to think about how you can apply new and innovative information to keep your edge and stay ahead of competitors. Fortunately, done right, this is very different from lying awake at night replaying familiar problems and hassles for the 200th time. Just the opposite; to open your mind to fresh ideas, you need to put day-to-day hassles aside.

You may already have your own favorite method of brainstorming. Whether it involves going for a jog or a bike ride, listening to music, or picking the brain of a creative relative or mentor, the key is to make enough time to do it on a regular basis. Allowing yourself to be too busy or too tired to think creatively is always a mistake.

Although it's particularly hard to step back when business is bad and you are almost frantic to reverse the slide, taking a few days or even a week off is an excellent way to make time and energy to think about strategic issues. You may be thinking, "I haven't had a decent vacation in years—there is just no way I have the luxury of taking time off during hard times." Think again. A person too busy to take a couple of days off is almost always so overextended that turning around a poorly performing business will be impossible.

Choose the Best Ideas to Implement

Especially when a business is in financial jeopardy, choosing the best from a basketful of innovative ideas is no easy task. But in a world where ideas are cheap, time short, and implementation often expensive, you might have only one chance to get it right.

One good way to start is to systematically rank ideas by awarding points, on a one-to-five scale, to the ones that best fulfill your key criteria. For example, if your primary goal is to reach out to more customers, you would give the most points to ideas calculated to do that. The second step is to adjust your rankings based on how much each idea costs. One excellent way to do this is to double the point total of ideas that can be implemented at the lowest comparative cost while halving the points of the most expensive ones. Because you never really know which ideas will work until you try them, it's usually wise to try as many of the top scorers as possible.

Let's take as an example Amos, who was laid off from his job maintaining computers at a large corporation. He decides to accept his father's offer to take over the family's barely profitable Reliable TV Repair business to see whether he can breathe some life into it. He uses several methods, including a brainstorming session with employees, a supplier, and his dad, to come up with new ways to achieve his four big goals: increase sales, improve marketing, improve customer access, and introduce new services. To decide which to implement first, Amos creates the following grid:

Idea	Increase Sales	Improve Marketing	Improve Customer Access	Introduce new services	Total
Change name to emphasize big-screen TVs & computers	2	2	1	0	4
Paint the truck	1	3	0	0	4
Stay open longer hours	2	0	4	0	6
Make weekend house calls	4	4	4	0	12
Fix and troubleshoot computers	5	3	0	4	12

His final step is to factor in how much each idea will cost to implement. Realizing that painting the truck will cost very little, and that adding the words "Big Screen" and "Computers" to the Reliable name will also be cheap and easy, he decides to double the points for these. And although he'll obviously have to pay employees to make house calls on the weekends, he concludes that even with cutting the total points on this one from 12 to 6, going forward with it makes sense. After all, if new business doesn't justify the added costs, he can pull back. Now the totals look like this:

Change name	8
Paint truck	8
Stay open longer hours	3
Make weekend house calls	6
Fix computers	6

Not surprisingly, based on these results, Amos decides to add computer repair services, make weekend house calls, repaint his truck and change the name to Reliable Big-Screen TV and Computer Troubleshooting. But until he can make a decent profit, he'll have to put keeping the shop open longer hours on hold.

Identify Your Customers

"I don't know the key to success, but the key to failure is trying to please everybody."
BILL COSBY

When business slows precipitously, lots of entrepreneurs spring into action, trying to drum up more business. They run a print ad here, buy a radio spot there, and distribute leaflets everywhere. This sort of frantic marketing probably won't work for at least three reasons. First, it costs too much. Second, a scattershot approach won't reach enough of your core customers. And third, it will divert you from following the low-cost focused marketing initiatives that can succeed.

Before you can develop a sensible marketing plan, or plan what products and services to offer, you first must take the time to identify your most likely customers. Too many entrepreneurs overlook this step, at their peril. This chapter will help you do it. (After you've done this, check out Chapter 8 for ways to develop low-cost marketing strategies to reach these customers.)

Aiming at the Bull's-Eye

Some businesses start the process of identifying their best customers by hanging an oversized target on the wall at a brainstorming session. In a process that is well described by Cheryl Woodard in her book, *Starting & Running a Successful Newsletter or Magazine* (Nolo), publishers typically begin by listing their most likely subscriber groups near the center of the bull's-eye. Pretty good prospects go into the middle rings. Those who just might subscribe are relegated to the outer circles. For example, the publishers of a home furnishings magazine might list people shopping for a new house near the bull's-eye, the soon-to-be-married in the next ring, and those whose kids have just graduated from college—and may have a few extra dollars to refurbish the house—in an outer circle. Similarly, the publisher of a consumer product guide might be eager to reach reference librarians who are regularly consulted about how to find consumer information, and less eager to market to college students, many of whom are still trying to perfect the art of asking their parents for more money.

Targeting your best customer prospects in this way makes great sense, especially when times are tough and you desperately need to reach more customers at an affordable cost. For instance, if your small dental lab is struggling to make ends meet, you would want to list near the center of your target the specific dentists or groups of dentists you believe are most likely to patronize you. Only then does it make sense to take the next step of reaching out to explain to them why your business offers a superior value.

Especially if you market to different customers for different reasons, filling in your target can be more difficult than you might first imagine. For example, if classes at your aerobics and dance studio are half empty, you will want to identify more folks who you are pretty sure will enthusiastically don their leotards for your master classes, as well as those you hope to coax into your early morning weight-loss sessions and the hopeful parents who will bring their budding ballerinas to your after-school session.

Unfortunately, many businesses have only a hazy idea of who their customers are and how best to reach them. They follow the open-the-doors-and-hope-for-the-best marketing approach, which of course goes far to explain why so many underperform in good economic times and fail during bad ones.

For example, a new restaurant might place a few ads in free local newspapers, do some leafleting in neighborhood office buildings, place an early-bird special sign in the window, and buy into several two-for-one coupon books. A couple of these initiatives might make sense if they were part of a coherent marketing plan aimed at budget-conscious diners who live or work close to the restaurant. But in the absence of such a focused plan, this approach is likely to do more harm than good. For example, if the restaurant owner hopes to attract a more affluent dinner crowd later in the evening, two-for-one deals and cut rates to early diners are likely to amount to a kiss of death, because many upmarket customers equate low prices with poor quality. Given the fierce competition in the restaurant business during times when people cut back on eating out, only establishments that first clearly identify their prime customer base and then develop affordable marketing strategies to reach them will have much chance of success.

It might sound easy to identify your most likely customers, but many small business owners—even those desperately motivated to increase sales—don't do it well. Take a look at Hillary, the owner of Happy Pup, a day care service for dogs. When asked to identify her marketing target, she says:

"We market to busy working people with dogs."

Sound pretty good? In fact, this statement is so vague as to be all but useless as a marketing tool, because:

- The great majority of working people can't possibly afford Happy Pup's rate of $25 to $40 a day.

- Just because a dog owner works doesn't mean someone else in the family isn't available to care for Bingo.

- Old dogs (or just plain mellow ones) may be content to stay home alone.

- Other dog-sitting services are available—why should dog owners choose Happy Pup?

Asked to try again, Hillary comes up with this more detailed profile:

"Happy Pup concentrates on affluent working people who want to provide the highest quality of care for their active dogs."

Because this statement takes into account the owners' ability to pay and their desire to give their dogs excellent day care, it's a big improvement. But several crucial targeting factors are still missing. As you may have guessed, Hillary's biggest omission is her failure to consider location. Assuming most people won't drive more than five to ten miles out of their way to drop off Sassafrass, it's obvious that Happy Pup should concentrate its marketing efforts on affluent owners of younger dogs who live or work fairly close to its facility.

And what about owners who are highly focused on their dog's well-being? If Happy Pup really does offer superior care, shouldn't Hillary also look for owners who care about things like the amount of staff attention, exercise, and playtime their dogs will receive?

After thinking about these additional factors, Hillary's third effort goes like this:

"Happy Pup markets to affluent working people who live or work within five miles of Rose & Vine streets in Kansas City, and who want to provide their active dogs a clean, nurturing environment emphasizing play and exercise."

Hillary had little chance of creating a coherent marketing plan before she figured out who to aim it at. After a little disciplined thinking, her chances of success went way up.

EXAMPLE: Here is a marketing target for an accountant who specializes in providing services to authors, musicians, inventors, and others who make their livings selling intellectual property.

Filling in Your Target

Now it's your turn to identify your most likely customers—the groups near the center of your business's bull's-eye. Take a deep breath and be ready to focus on this exercise for as long as it takes.

To start, get out a big piece of paper, draw a bull's-eye, and list your most likely customers closest to the center. If possible, get help from your advisory board and employees. At this stage, don't complicate the exercise by simultaneously trying to figure out how you'll market to them. No question, as discussed in the next chapter, that's crucial—but for now, just identify the groups or individuals who are the most likely to buy what your business sells, and be ready to explain why each of these groups should prefer your products and services.

Start With Your Current Customers

No matter what your field, when you create a marketing target for your business, the words "current customers" should almost always be listed near the bull's-eye. That's because with very few exceptions, such as businesses that market to tourists or help people with one-time problems (divorce and tubal ligation come to mind), your existing customers are the easiest to reach. It might seem obvious that the customer list of a successful business is a golden asset, but many if not most small businesses all but ignore it. Instead of extending great offers to existing customers and developing additional products and services they'll appreciate, they concentrate their marketing efforts on the more difficult task of finding new customers.

What's the best way to determine whether your current customers are interested in additional products or services? Simple: Ask. If you stay in close communication with your customers and make it easy and fun for them to tell you about their needs and concerns, they will. Business owners like accountants, architects, or Web designers who work with a relatively few customers can often best do this in person. Businesses with larger customer rosters will find it more convenient to periodically email customers a short, easy-to-fill-out form asking for suggestions about new and improved services. (To say thanks in advance, always include a small present such as a coupon for a free or discounted product or service.)

EXAMPLE: When her "jack-of-all-trades" dad died, Mandy stepped in and took over his business, which did snow removal, yard maintenance, and even pumped out vacation-home septic tanks in a resort area. One day she got a call from Janet, a customer whose main home was in a city several hours distant. When she next cut the lawn, could Mandy please take some cat food with her and feed the feral cat that was living under the porch, Janet asked?

Not only was Mandy happy to do this, she was even happier to prepare a questionnaire to all her customers, asking them whether there were additional things she could do when she visited their properties. When quite a few responded yes, Mandy developed a service she called Property Check. For a modest fee, she would work with the homeowner to develop a list of things for her to check on regularly.

Each time Mandy visited the property, she promptly emailed to the owner a list of all items checked and any problems discovered. Before long, Property Check became so successful that Mandy hired an assistant to drive the honey wagon and concentrated on developing more new services for absentee owners.

Here are just a few examples of businesses that profitably target existing customers with new goods or services:

- A dentist who, after fielding a number of questions from patients with snoring and other sleep problems, sends an email to all patients asking if they are interested in solutions to sleep-related problems. When 30% say yes, he pursues the continuing education programs necessary to provide the service.

- A used bookstore whose business has sagged since Amazon and other websites began selling used books creates a marketing target with existing customers near the center. Then, after doing in-depth interviews with a number of them, the bookstore decides to carry about 750 new books, including bestselling biography, science fiction, mystery, and cookbooks. Displayed in the window and on attractive racks near the front of the store, these new books are immediately popular with existing customers who occasionally splurge on a new title or purchase them as gifts. And they do wonders to bring passersby—a market that retailers always want to target—into the store.

- A restaurant in a popular vacation area identifies tourists as one of its three key types of customers, along with middle-income local residents and police, fire, and medical workers from a nearby public security and hospital complex who live and work within three miles. Reasoning that it has only a short time window to sell more to tourists, the owner fills an underused space near the cash register with locally produced mustards, jams, hot sauces, and other gourmet specialty items. The products are sold individually and also in boxed collections ready for mailing. Just produce your credit card and the recipient's address, and the restaurant will do the rest. The program is so popular with visitors who want to send something home from the area that the restaurant sets up a website to handle repeat orders.

Need

People who have a pressing need for your goods or services, even if that need is occasional or intermittent, are obviously more likely to patronize your business than those who don't. For example, when a tooth hurts you need a dentist, but when your car is dusty you can either leave it in the rain, wash it yourself, or patronize a car wash.

It's important to approach the concept of need through the eyes of your customers. For people with disposable income, need can be a subjective concept: I *need* the latest iPhone. I *need* to have my hair highlighted every six to eight weeks. I *need* to play golf at least once a week. Of course, when thinking about need, price can dictate whether that need is negotiable— whether it falls into the "must have" or "really want" category. One segment of the population "needs" luxury goods only if they believe they are getting a relative bargain.

EXAMPLE: Jan and Lance operate Rose Beauty Supply, a big-city shop that special-izes in selling high-end beauty supplies at discount prices. Identifying middle- and upper-income women who feel a need to be well-coiffed on a daily basis as their broad customer base, Jan and Lance decide to aim new marketing at women who work in their area's several museums and many nonprofits, reasoning that many of these women have upscale tastes, but limited budgets.

Price

Who will be attracted to your price point? In some markets—discount haircutting or fast food, for example)—people often make purchasing decisions based on a "low" price. And in every market segment, there are lots of bargain shoppers.

However, in some areas, people are more likely to patronize the business they believe provides the best value, regardless of price. In an affluent neighborhood, for example, a shoe store that sells well-made but higher-priced shoes will do better than a low-cost competitor, and the dry cleaner considered the most trustworthy in town is typically seen as providing a better value, though it charges more than its competitors. Even in hard economic times, plenty of people have money. But to part with it, especially for upmarket products and services, they need to be sold on qualities such as reliability, durability, and lasting value.

Are you targeting bargain shoppers or affluent customers? It's hard to do both. It just might save your business to improve the quality of your goods or services and to target more upscale customers who have more discretionary income, especially in tough times. Sophisticated customers who perceive that you offer a more valuable product or service are far more likely to stick with you and to sing your praises to others.

Access

If cost and quality are equal, customers usually follow the path of least resistance, patronizing easy-to-access businesses and avoiding those that are tough to get to. That's why many customers can be targeted around convenience factors like free parking, home delivery, and evening hours. Online shopping also provides quick, easy access to goods, especially for people who work on a computer much of the day. The success of Amazon and other online retailers should offer all the proof you need.

EXAMPLE: Catch & Release, a retailer of fly fishing gear located in a small city near several famous fishing rivers, decides to target customers outside the area who they hope will buy online and pay premium prices for top-end, often handcrafted equipment. To offset the inconvenience of shipping time, they offer free two-day shipping on every order over $100. To the owner's surprise, 30% of website orders come from people who live within 30 miles of their shop, many of whom had not previously been customers.

Experience

As you develop your marketing target, it's often useful to think about potential customers in two broad categories: people who have had experience with businesses like yours (sometimes lots of it), and those who are new to the field. In some fields, this doesn't apply; for example, if you operate a mid-priced shoe store, all of your potential customers will have patronized similar businesses and will have a pretty good idea of what to expect. By contrast, if you recently started an upscale vintage clothing boutique in an area where shopping for used clothes has always meant going to Goodwill or the church jumble sale, many of the people you hope to attract will never have shopped at a store like yours.

You'll have a different job targeting and satisfying newbies as opposed to experienced customers. For example, if you recently opened the third Indian restaurant in your area, obviously you want to target people who already know and like Indian cuisine. But if yours is the first Indian restaurant in town, you'll want to target people who have experienced Indian food elsewhere as well as adventurous diners.

If you haven't thought about potential customers in this way, you may wonder whether it is easier to convince the uninitiated to try something new or to market to a group of experienced—and possibly jaded—consumers. There is no one answer that applies to all businesses, although in a recession when people become more cautious, you'll probably do better trying to attract more customers who are already knowledgeable about what you sell. Even so, in some instances it may make sense to target groups of experienced and novice customers as long as you understand that doing so will require different marketing strategies.

Coffee is a field where this has been famously done. Thirty-plus years ago, Americans drank uniformly terrible coffee, whether they bought it in cans and made it themselves or ordered it at restaurants. Only a few coffee drinkers who had spent time in Europe and the Middle East, where coffee quality was far higher, even knew what they were missing. Then, specialty coffee stores that sold richer, more varied coffee and coffee drinks in European-style shops began to pop up. One of the first was Peet's, a tiny Berkeley, California, company. Like Peet's, many of these shops started in college towns, where they were supported by people who had experienced quality coffee while traveling. At first, they didn't reach much beyond their small audience of coffee aficionados. But then, Starbucks and other large chains entered the market, successfully targeting and reaching out to the broad middle class.

Rounding Out the Target

Sandy, a fast-pitch softball coach, opens a batting cage to teach hitting to pre-teen and teenage players. With softball's growing popularity, Sandy believes she will soon be able to quit her day job. And sure enough, during the prime spring months, more girls try to book lessons than she can accommodate. But as families cut back on spending and many of her students change their focus to soccer, the flood of students slows to a trickle. On a Tuesday evening in October, she is lucky to give two half-hour lessons.

To attract more off-season students, Sandy decides to engage in a marketing campaign, a subject about which she knows next to nothing. When she first tries to describe her target audience, the best she can come up with is "girls and young women age eight to 18 who want to play better softball and who live within 20 to 30 minutes' driving distance of my facility." Realizing that she has merely described her existing market—the one she already knew wasn't producing enough year-round business—she resolves to do better.

After much thought and consulting a college softball coach friend, she enters the following in her target's inner circle: "serious players age 12 to 18 who play tournament softball on club teams, who live within an hour of my facility, and who play, or hope to play, high school or college ball." This is a narrower focus, but Sandy concludes that these young women are so motivated to improve their skills that if she can reach them and their parents with the message that she can help polish their skills to "college scholarship" level, she will fill up her cage year round.

Sandy also makes several other entries close to her bull's-eye. One is for high school and club softball coaches who may want to rent her cage—or the extra space in the back of her facility—by the hour during bad-weather months to run their own hitting clinics. Although renting space is primarily a strategy to reduce overhead, Sandy realizes that it is also a great way to meet and work with people who might refer her new students. Finally, Sandy lists young baseball players in one of the outer rings of her target. She isn't sure high school boys will take hitting lessons from a woman, but she thinks younger ones with slugging older sisters might. And if they do, and noticeably improve their performance, their friends will follow.

Don't Waste Money on Ineffective Marketing

"If you hype something and it succeeds, you're a genius; it wasn't a hype. If you hype something and it fails, then it's just a hype."
NEIL BOGART

When hard times cause widespread unemployment, millions of financially pressed Americans look for less expensive goods because they have to. Bargain hunting also becomes fashionable for the affluent. Fashionistas who have never walked through the door of a consignment store suddenly become "recessionistas" who think it's cool to shop there. This means that retailers who sell luxury goods need to hype their goods in terms of long-term value, practicality, and durability. It's not enough to just be cool and expensive.

While this national penny-pinching mood lasts, your business has little choice but to embrace it. Get in tune with tough times by offering customers a steady stream of good deals. But do it in a way that still lets you make a decent profit. The best way is to embrace clever but cheap marketing campaigns designed to attract both existing and new customers.

Market the Right Products or Services to the Right People

No matter what high-energy, low-cost methods you select to promote your business, to succeed you must point them at those most likely to patronize your business. (Chapter 7 discusses how to identify your best potential customers.) Once you identify your target audiences, you can think about the goods or services they will be most likely to buy.

Go with your winners—your most popular and profitable products or services. Too many inexperienced entrepreneurs crush their hopes for survival by pushing less desirable products they are simply trying to get rid of. They feature the wrong goods or services—items that used to sell well, but are now fading, items someone mistakenly ordered too many of, or a service that has such low mark-up that selling lots more of it won't produce enough profit to justify the effort. They seem to believe that discounting things no one wants to buy will somehow make them money. It's a little like a baseball team that uses its best giveaway to put more fannies in the seats of a mostly empty stadium on a Tuesday night to see a lousy team. Far better to use the collectors' item baseball cap to try to add 10,000 people to an already three-quarters full stadium for a Saturday game against the Yankees.

For some types of businesses—for example, a hardware store that sells to casual consumers, serious do-it-yourself remodelers, and contractors—targeting and ranking customers and the products each group is most likely to buy will require engaging in a fairly complicated, data-heavy process. For others, including consultants and other businesspeople who provide a niche service to a relatively small clientele, it will be as easy as listing the names of a relatively few customer prospects and the services or products that are popular with them.

Once you have identified your target groups of customers and what they are most likely to buy (and are sure you'll make a profit if they do), you are ready to adopt a marketing plan designed to quickly reach more of them.

If your potential customer universe is relatively small—for example, you're an accountant who specializes in helping authors and musicians—your best approach is probably a personal marketing effort. If half a dozen literary agents represent most of the well-known authors in your area, getting to know the agents and educating them about your expertise would be a good start. After all, a prominent literary agent who appreciates that you are fully current on the tax ramifications of the ways royalty deals are being structured in a recessionary environment (and even better, if you are available to advise the agent on structuring deals) is in a great position to recommend you to others. Similarly, local publishers and support groups for inventors, musicians, and writers are excellent venues through which to get the word out to many potential clients.

If your potential customer universe is bigger and more diverse, consider broader and less personal ways to market your goods or services. Because in a recession, businesses typically need to raise cash fast as well as secure more long-term customers, here are suggestions for both short- and long-term initiatives.

Short-Term Money-Makers

There's nothing wrong with trying the staples of business: sales and special offers. Everybody likes a good deal.

A weekly sale featuring an item that will bring in customers likely to buy other more profitable services.

EXAMPLE 1: A struggling dry cleaner institutes a series of weekly specials—sleeping bags, formal wear, quilts, and drapes. Many of the people who respond to these offers also bring along the rest of their accumulated dry cleaning, and the cash register begins to sing.

EXAMPLE 2: A jeweler offers to replace two watch batteries for the price of one. A fair number of customers who show up with a handful of stopped watches also bring along jewelry in need of repair, something the jeweler makes a good profit doing.

A reciprocal discounting program conducted in partnership with nearby high-quality businesses. This can also help build community among neighborhood businesses, something that may lead to other benefits down the road.

EXAMPLE: Seven neighboring stores on University Avenue (a book shop, a bakery, a shoe store, a print and framing shop, a wine bar, and a clothing store) print up an attractive flyer featuring 20% off discount coupons for all seven stores. Buy something at one of the stores and you get a coupon redeemable within 24 hours at any of the others.

A letter to long-term customers asking for support at a difficult time, including a discount coupon (see "Ask Long-Term Customers for Support," below, for a sample letter). There's no shame in letting loyal customers know that your business needs more support to survive.

A "recession special" to reconnect with customers or clients. If you can email your customers, your costs will be very low.

EXAMPLE: A lawyer, architect, electrician, hair stylist, or other service provider offers one-third off normal hourly rates for 90 days as a thank-you for support during tough times.

A leaflet program, featuring an attractive offer, left at homes, businesses, or under the windshield wipers. But be sure your flyer is well designed and easy to read, and presents your business as reliable, established, and dedicated to providing quality goods or services. You want your flyer to stand out from the many cheap leaflets that don't inspire confidence.

EXAMPLE: Jackson Plumbing, a relatively new company in need of customers, leaflets 300 houses offering to fix one leaky faucet for $40 and each additional one for $20. Twenty homeowners immediately call, delighted that Jackson is not charging the usual $90 just to show up. And once the faucets are fixed, half a dozen hire Jackson to do larger jobs. The next week Jackson leaflets 300 more houses with similar positive results.

A free class or a series of classes designed to quickly expose your business to many potential customers.

EXAMPLE: Chloe's Yarn Shop offers free knitting classes three mornings per week. When the classes immediately fill up with people wanting to learn how to make low-cost gifts, Chloe expands to a five-day schedule and gives every novice a 10%-off coupon redeemable on any purchase of $50 or more.

Long-Term Outreach

Don't forget, in your understandable desire to drum up some quick profits, that you need a strategy to help your business do well over the long haul. Here are some ideas for establishing your business's identity.

Sponsor an event to get your name out in the community. For example, a sporting goods store sponsors a 50K bike ride, providing hand pumps and water bottles with its name on them, donating the entry fees to a local food bank, or a fish restaurant cosponsors a "Sustainable Seafood Day," providing food samples in exchange for great press coverage. Especially when money is short, you'll want to look for events where your business's positive energy can make a substantial impact at low cost. Because sponsoring and organizing an event can take more money and time than you have to offer, your best bet is to take part in an event someone else is organizing.

RESOURCE

Headlining your own event. For good advice, see *Event Marketing & How to Successfully Promote Events, Festivals, Conventions & Expositions,* by Leonard Hoyle (Wiley).

Help nonprofit causes to bring goodwill to your business. For example, a landscape architect leads a nonprofit effort to restore the town's neglected rose garden. A plant nursery sells vegetable seeds and baby plants for 20% off to anyone who promises to donate at least one third of their garden crop to a homeless center.

Support the arts. A downtown restaurant might offer to display local artists' works on its windows and walls, to help sell them. The art is chosen by a group of judges headed by the curator of the nearby university art gallery, at a well-attended competition. In the process, the restaurant cements its reputation as a cultural hangout.

Get the media to publicize your business for free. Setting yourself up as an expert in your field can bring mentions in the media for you and your business. For example, a general contractor who runs a house inspection business self-publishes a small book covering the 20 most likely hidden problems, how not to get ripped off on repairs, and how to make technically easy but labor-intensive repairs on a self-help basis. Widely distributing his book for free through real estate offices, lenders, and at several annual homebuyers' fairs, it helps establish his expertise with local media outlets, where he is regularly interviewed and quoted. Or he might offer to write a monthly column for the local paper, featuring tips for homeowners.

Don't Spend Big Dollars on Advertising

When sales drop, lots of business gurus urge small business owners to increase advertising. And when advertising often turns out to cost more than it brings in, many actually recommend increasing it again. Bad idea.

There are two huge drawbacks to spending money on conventional advertising, including radio and TV spots and scattershot newspaper ads. First, your recession-battered small business desperately needs to hoard its cash for more immediate needs. Second, but just as important, relying on advertising as your main way to attract business risks stifling more imaginative initiatives that can attract more long-term customers at a far lower cost. Much like giving a teenager a big allowance and then wondering why she doesn't get a job, once the monthly ad buy is made, too many business owners fail to work hard to get the word out in other ways. Why should they bother? Their ads are already out there attracting all the customers they need, right?

Unfortunately, it's rarely that easy, even for large businesses with huge ad budgets. And it's virtually never a winning strategy for small outfits with very limited marketing budgets, especially in tough times, when the media is already overloaded with the big guys' 40%-off deals.

EXAMPLE 1: Ted is an early retiree lucky enough to have received a generous severance package from his former employer. With money in his pocket and his kids grown, Ted fulfills his lifetime dream of opening a small bookstore, Academy Books. After two years of barely breaking even, the local economy nosedives, and Academy begins to lose money. In an effort to attract more customers, Ted signs a contract with a weekly newspaper to run a display ad in the next 12 issues. When he writes the check and hands over the simple ad copy, Ted feels good—he's taken a big step toward turning his failing shop around.

After two months, as the economy further weakens and Academy's sales continue to drop, it becomes clear that the ad isn't producing enough customers even to pay for itself, let alone help Academy sell enough books to earn a profit. But when Ted calls the newspaper to express his concern, Joy, the salesperson, says that ads work best when they run for an extended period and that she also thinks Ted's copy needs "more zip." So with Joy's help, Ted designs a flashier ad, signs a second contract, and continues to hope for the best. When sales improve only slightly, Ted begins to worry that he'll soon need to close Academy's doors for the last time.

Now let's give Ted another chance.

EXAMPLE 2: This time, instead of buying advertising, Ted adopts a number of low-cost marketing techniques designed first to bring in badly needed cash as fast as possible and, second, to build Academy's long-term roster of loyal customers. Ted, after doing the customer targeting exercise in Chapter 7, defines his customer base as truly dedicated readers who live within five miles of his shop. Here are the marketing initiatives that Ted adopts:

- **Save Academy Books.** Ted gathers a group of regular customers (a librarian, teacher, two authors, a readaholic business owner, and the deputy mayor) who have deep roots in the community and who will commit time to seeing that Academy survives. Forming Save Academy Books, this group sends letters and emails to all past customers telling them that Academy needs their immediate support to avoid closing. In addition, the volunteers hold a well-promoted press conference to get this message out to the wider community via the media. Fortunately, because many media people are readers, the story runs in more places than Ted expected. When book buyers flood in, Ted realizes Academy has the cash to implement the rest of his plan.

- **Weekly readings.** Academy starts a weekly series of readings with local authors. In addition to announcements in Academy's regular email newsletter and in-store signs, Ted sends invitations to each author's one hundred nearest and dearest friends, relatives, and workplace colleagues. This guarantees that the events are successful and that lots of potential new customers visit Academy. The readings prove so popular that Ted arranges for the local public radio station to tape them and replay them on Sunday evenings.

- **Discount coupons.** Academy works with neighborhood businesses (a coffee shop, restaurant, hair salon, and others) to displays Academy's bestsellers in their shops and to give customers a 15% off coupon redeemable at Academy that same day. (Ted first planned a 10% off coupon good for a week, but decided that impulse shoppers would probably buy promptly, or not at all.) Ted gives everyone who buys a book at Academy a discount coupon for the other businesses.

- **Lending library.** Ted borrows an idea from the 1930s and starts a fee-based lending library focusing on bestsellers, for which there is always a long waiting list at the library. He charges $3 per week. Ted rents the typical $25 hardcover book 15 times and then puts it on his discount table for $7.50, meaning he eventually takes in $52.50 for a book that cost him about $12.50. More important, the program brings more people into Academy, many of whom eventually buy books.

Obviously, there are lots of differences between the marketing approaches in these examples. But most importantly, in Example 2, Ted uses his energy and common sense to design low-cost ways to let readers in his target group know about his business, while in Example 1, he simply pays the local newspaper to put his ad in front of a big audience—many of whom simply aren't interested in buying books.

> **TIP**
>
> **Advertising can boomerang.** Because most consumers quite sensibly have a negative attitude toward advertising, ads may discourage—or even drive away—customers. Imagine you spot a new restaurant that looks so inviting that you consider booking a table when your in-laws are in town. A few days later you receive a card deck in the mail that includes discount coupons for rural home sites, a backyard spa, a car repainting service, and two-for-one meal offers from several restaurants, including the one you just discovered. Is your first thought "Hooray, I can get a great deal at a terrific restaurant"? Or are you more likely to decide to pick a different eating place?

Ask Long-Term Customers for Support

It's far easier to get existing customers to purchase more than it is to find new ones. If you can motivate your long-term customers to both increase their purchases and recommend your business to others, you'll be well on your way to survival.

So in a recession, when everyone spends less and even many longtime customers disappear, your first marketing task is to recover them. The simplest and most effective way to do this is by a personal communication. Although it's tempting to ask for support via a low-cost email, most community-based businesses will get better results from a personally addressed letter (or if your customer or client list is short, a phone call). Using the mail also allows you to include an attention-grabbing discount coupon, something that might not work as well when part of an email.

Asking for Support? You're Not Alone

As reported in *The San Francisco Chronicle* (October 16, 2008) here is a letter written by Wilkes Bashford, owner of an upscale clothing store (oops, haberdashery), to his longstanding customers. Bashford included a "Friends of Wilkes certificate"—in other words, a discount coupon.

Dear Friends,

Many people currently greet me with the question: "How's business?" My honest answer has to be "challenging." In 42 years in business, the current situation is unique, hence the purpose of my corresponding with you. I am taking this unorthodox approach because we need your support.

While a number of you have continued to shop in your normal manner, others have withdrawn. Obviously for some this is a necessity. My appeal is to those folks who are in a position to continue to shop with confidence, and I urge each of you to do so.

The fall 2008 clothing for both men and women is exceptional. Our very professional sales staff would love to work with you on your wardrobe in any manner that meets your needs and desires.

Having been part of the San Francisco business and cultural scene for 41 years, with a dedicated and loyal staff, I feel a strong responsibility for their security. Your continued enthusiastic patronage is essential to this goal and deeply appreciated.

Please use the "Friends of Wilkes" certificate below and visit us soon and often.

With warm wishes,

Wilkes

EXAMPLE: John and Phillip run J&P Mobile Dog Grooming in an outer suburb. Having recently expanded to two vans and a small office in town, John and Phillip are stunned when the recession hits, business drops 40%, and they lose a small bank line of credit. To try to prevent their business ship from sinking, they send a hand-addressed, first-class letter to the 200 people who have used their services, frankly explaining that they are in short-term financial peril and asking for support. They include 33%-off pet grooming coupon. The response is fast and positive, bringing enough money to allow John and Phillip to downsize their business, which includes selling their new van at a slight loss (but still being able to pay off the loan) and negotiating their way out of the office lease by paying three months' additional rent. Now back working out of their house and driving their five-year-old van, John and Phillip generate a decent profit. They write a second letter thanking everyone who supported them and including another discount coupon, many of which are also redeemed.

Encourage Customers to Recommend Your Business

Think about how you and your family decide where to buy goods and services. For example, what process did you go through the last time you chose a house painter, gardener, lawyer, or dentist? Also recall the last few times you went out to eat or attended a movie. We'll wager that in many, if not most, of these instances, the recommendation of a trusted friend or acquaintance, not an ad, helped inform your decision.

We'll also bet that another source of the information you used to make at least some of these purchasing decisions came from media people you trust. For example, you might have picked a movie or restaurant in part because it got high marks from a critic you respect, or called a contractor whose name appeared on a respected local consumer group's "approved" list.

It should help reinforce this point if you make a mental list of five local small businesses you respect and regularly do business with, and then ask yourself how often you recommend each, or at least tell someone that you patronize them? If your answer is "regularly," it's obvious that these businesses are doing so many things right that you, and probably many other satisfied customers, promote them for free.

How to Get Positive Word of Mouth

Because positive word-of-mouth is such an important source of new customers, let's review the short list of key business attributes that reliably generate it.

Quality. Providing truly excellent goods or services that are at least a cut above those provided by competitors.

Easy access. With today's busy, almost frantic lifestyles, customers still seek out convenience over price.

EXAMPLE 1: Claire, whose New Dawn dry cleaning shop is located on a crowded city street with inadequate parking, suffers a 30% decline in business when local unemployment spikes. But despite this setback, when an old gas station a few blocks away comes up for sale, Claire taps her savings, gets a loan from her uncle and buys the property cheap. Redesigning New Dawn around easy customer access, Claire sets up a drive-through system that lets customers pull within a few feet of the front door. Backed by her well-staffed service counter, this means a typical customer is in and out in less than three minutes. When another local dry cleaner with poor customer access closes, Claire's sales return to and then exceed historical levels.

EXAMPLE 2: Ivan, a mobile knife sharpener who brings a large, fully equipped van to businesses and other venues where people can conveniently get their knives sharpened, has a big competitive advantage over shop-based competitors. Reasoning that when times are tough, people eat at home more often and need his services more, Ivan hires high school kids to leaflet local neighborhoods offering to make house calls whenever neighbors can gather ten or more knives for sharpening. The result is that people who want a few knives sharpened call their neighbors to collect enough to schedule Ivan.

Cleanliness. A small, but nevertheless significant, slice of the public makes purchasing decisions primarily on how clean a business is. For example, we have several friends who won't patronize a good-sized list of local restaurants because they aren't spotless. Similarly, a member of one of our families always buys gas from the company she believes has the cleanest restrooms. Fortunately, insisting on the highest standards of cleanliness doesn't cost much, and immediately distinguishes your business from its many sloppier competitors. It's an easy way to create a marketing edge.

EXAMPLE: Ramon inherits the Snack Shack, one of a dozen look-alike take-out restaurants along a slightly seedy commercial strip next to a popular beach resort. With tourism down, the Snack Shack is barely breaking even. Relying on his business-savvy sister for help, Ramon closes the business for two weeks while he paints, polishes, and refurnishes, so that now everything from the building, to the sign, to the chairs and umbrellas out front, to the immaculate uniforms of the servers, is white with red trim. Changing the name to Dog-On-a-Stick, the business reopens with just ten items, including corndogs, fresh lemonade, fruit smoothies, and fresh vegetarian chili. Ramon's business quickly improves, driven mostly by locals, who are pleased to see a clean and fun, kid-oriented new business in their area. They not only try it, but talk about it in very positive terms.

Stylishness. We humans are a fickle bunch, easily and endlessly impressed by the "new and improved." From store windows, waiting areas, and conference rooms to signs, stationery, and websites, update your business's displays, logo, and décor on a regular basis. Don't put this off because business is poor. Instead, if, in the middle of a recession you surprise customers with a bright new look (that doesn't cost too much), you'll stand out.

Helpfulness. Customers want to know how to use your goods and services efficiently. The more honest, easy-to-understand information and handholding you provide, the more likely they are to recommend your business to friends and acquaintances.

EXAMPLE: John's Plant Nursery offers free Saturday morning classes on how to grow abundant vegetables. Sally's otherwise similar nursery doesn't. Virtually everyone who comes to one of John's classes tells someone else about it. As a result, John sells three times as many vegetable plants as Sally.

Unique knowledge. Knowing more than your competitors—and convincing customers and potential customers that this is true—is an excellent way to get your business positively talked about.

EXAMPLE: Jen, a Korean American, opens a website, Seoul Now, aimed at providing up-to-date information about Korea's capital city to Western business travelers and tourists. Relying on relatives, friends, and a network of young commentators in Seoul to post up-to-the-minute information, Jen is able to make her site fresher, more exciting, and hipper than her competitors, something that is noted and talked about on a number of travel-oriented websites and is even noted in several Korean guide books. The happy result is that Korean hotels, restaurants, and other businesses that cater to Western visitors buy enough advertising space on her website to make it profitable.

Extras. Make yourself stand out by doing a little something special for your customers every now and then. For example, an insurance agent who sends clients a birthday card might also enclose a free smoke alarm battery.

Customer recourse. Customers want to know that they are in good hands. Telling them early and often that should anything ever go wrong, they can rely on your no-hassle money-back guarantee is one excellent way to accomplish this. For example, we have friends who will buy electronics only at Costco because Costco is known for accepting returns of products that break, even years down the road.

Asking Customers to Recommend You

If your business does all or most of the things on the above list pretty well, chances are you have earned a good reputation with your customers. Now that times are tough and you need every bit of help you can get, you are in a great position to ask your customers to help you gain new ones. In the section above, we discussed how to ask customers for their own support. Fortunately, it's only a small additional step to ask them to send their friends. Here are some suggestions.

Let customers help their friends. Send a letter or email to all your customers, not only asking them for support, but also to recommend you to friends. And of course include discount coupons.

EXAMPLE: John and Phillip, the mobile dog groomers we met earlier, not only send a discount coupon along with their letter requesting support from their existing clients, but include three more coupons with the added request that they be passed along to the recipient's dog-owning friends.

Ask for prospects. Personally ask your truly enthusiastic customers if they will supply a list of their friends and give you permission to write or email them using the customer's name. And again, don't forget to enclose a discount coupon.

Be generous. Especially when times are tough, customers appreciate and talk about a good deal. For example, if your garage provides a free oil change or car wash as part of every service appointment, your customers will tell others.

Be appreciative. Acknowledge your customers' recommendations and referrals. A personal thank-you is best, but if that's not practical, a note or email will suffice. Consider adopting a system to reward customers for recommending others. Depending on your field, this could be a thank-you gift, a discount on future services, or even cash.

> **RESOURCE**
>
> **More on advertising and marketing.** Nolo publishes an inspirational little book called *Marketing Without Advertising,* by Michael Phillips and Salli Rasberry, that has an expanded discussion of advertising and its alternatives. Like all Nolo publications, it's available at Nolo.com. Or check it out of your library—that way your marketing efforts will be off to a truly cost-effective start. Also check out the Guerrilla Marketing series written by Jay Levinson and others, especially *Guerrilla Marketing* (Mariner Books), *Start-Up Guide to Guerrilla Marketing* (Entrepreneur Press), and *Guerrilla Marketing on the Internet* (Entrepreneur Press).

Use Paid Listings Effectively

Some types of paid listings, including those in the yellow pages, in the services section of a penny-saver newspaper, and in special-interest media, such as publications and websites aimed at parents, sports enthusiasts, or dog lovers, can be effective at letting people know about your business. The thing that distinguishes paid listings from conventional ads is that listings are "narrowcast" to people already looking for your product or service, not broadcast to a general audience, as is the case with most newspaper, radio, or TV ads. Listings work precisely because, unlike conventional ads, they don't try to reach a broad audience, but instead aim for placement where motivated customers are most likely to discover them.

EXAMPLE: For a fee, lawyers can post profiles on Nolo's online lawyer directory. Lawyers do it because they know that more than a million monthly visitors come to Nolo.com for free legal information. It stands to reason that many of those visitors will be interested in professional help.

Here are some places where listing-type ads may work:

- **Single-interest websites** where goods and services are listed by category or keyword.

- **Publications or websites of nonprofit organizations** or other groups popular with people you want to reach. For example, if you're a child care provider, it would make sense to place an inexpensive notice in the monthly newsletter published by a working moms' support organization.

- **Publications aimed at tourists,** if your business caters to visitors. Sometimes this involves buying a small listing or ad in a specialized publication distributed at airports, hotels, and tourist attractions, but often it's possible to get your message distributed to a wide audience for free as would be the case if, for example, you are able to get your gay-oriented club listed in the gay/lesbian section of a popular travel guide.

- **Special interest journals.** For example, an architect who specializes in designing fire stations might place a small monthly ad in journals read by city, county, and state planning officials.

- **A yellow pages ad.** Although yellow pages use is in fast decline as people increasingly search for goods and services online, it's still a good idea for local service businesses to buy a small ad. But keep it small. Costs are high, and some potential customers instinctively distrust businesses that buy big ads, believing that money spent on hype won't be available to provide superior goods or services at reasonable cost.

Dos and Don'ts of Writing a "Listing" Ad

If you're writing a small ad to appear in a penny-saver publication, one approach is to promote your business primarily on the basis of cost, featuring a bargain price and further sweetening the deal by offering a "dollars off" coupon.

There is no question that in hard economic times, many consumers look first at cost, so this approach will probably attract some new business. But in both bad and good times, most consumers understand that you get what you pay for. So it's generally better to list a fair price and emphasize reliability, high quality, and trust. You'll make a decent profit, and you won't have to cut corners. Here are some suggestions on what you might want to include:

- How long you have been in the business.
- Your relevant education and experience.
- That you provide references on request.
- That your business is family or locally owned.
- That you guarantee your work.
- That you can respond to customers' needs on a priority or emergency basis.

Market on Your Own Website

Whether you sell fishing charters in San Diego, cater weddings in Brooklyn, or sell baby gear in Peoria, you absolutely need to market your services or goods online. Existing customers should be able to find your well-designed and informative website with just a couple of clicks. And ideally, people who are looking for the service or goods you offer—but have never heard of your business—should be able to find it.

At a minimum, your website should do three things:

Give an accurate description of your business and how to best access it via phone, fax, email, and in person. If appropriate, include hours of operation, driving directions, and parking information.

Tell people what's special about your business. Provide enough well-presented information (including photos) about who you are and what you do that potential new customers will prefer your business to your competitors.

Give helpful, consumer-oriented information about your field. The goal here is to provide potential consumers with helpful, objective information so that they'll understand that they are in good hands and go forward with a purchase.

EXAMPLE: Terry operates Terry's Appliance Repair Center in Harrisburg, Pennsylvania. When business drops during the recession, Terry's first thought is to increase the size of her yellow pages ad. But then, on the advice of her tech-savvy son, she decides to spend a smaller amount creating a simple but easy-to-find website, listing access, price, and warranty of service information. When, within weeks of publication, Terry's incoming calls increase 20%, she adds a "Troubleshooting Your Problem" section to the website, focusing on the most common appliance defects and how much it's likely to cost to fix them. This results in another significant jump in calls and emails.

When Terry asks new customers how they found her, their typical response goes something like this: "When my washing machine broke, I googled 'washing machine repair Harrisburg' and found your site. The fact that your website had lots of material about washing machine problems, and when it makes sense to just buy a new one, impressed me. I also liked that you have been in business for 12 years, return all calls the same day, and guarantee your work."

If you're new to the world of online marketing, here are the basics of creating a website. First, you'll need a domain name (your address on the Web—for example, www.nolo.com) and a hosting company (also known as an ISP) to broadcast your website from its servers. A number of Web hosting companies provide both of these services for $10 to $30 per month. (Google "web hosting" to see a long list.)

Second, you need to create your website, which consists of putting relevant information about your business onto your Web pages. One approach is to buy website development software, such as *CoffeeCup*, *FrontPage*, or *Dreamweaver*, and do the job yourself. (For a great book on developing a website yourself, see *Create Your Own Website*, by Scott Mitchell (Sams).) But since this involves a time-consuming learning curve, you may find it makes more sense to concentrate on your business and hire a reasonably priced local developer to create a website for you. A third alternative is to create a simple site by using the site builder service offered by a Web hosting company, such as homestead.com or web.com.

Once you get your site up and running, you want customers to be able to find it. With so many websites out there, it's easy to get lost in the sea of results that Google spits out. If your business is unique in your area (for example, the only riding stable in town), you may not need to worry about customers being able to find you with Google, but most companies should take steps to bring customers to their site.

There are a number of things you can do to improve your site's findability and the amount of traffic that comes to your site. This process is called "search engine optimization," or "SEO" for short. The main things any SEO consultant will tell you are that to bring people to your site, you need to use the phrases that people use to search for your products and services (these are called "keywords"). For example, if you fix cars, you want to make sure that you use the words "auto repair" in the title of each of your Web pages and several times on each page. (You can use Google's "keyword tool" to find the most searched for keywords for your business.)

A good way to make your business stand out is to include relevant content—that is, information about your products or services—on your website. For instance, if you run a bed-and-breakfast in Vermont, you might write an article or two on what to look for in a B&B, the best places to see Vermont foliage, how to dress for winter weather (including an automatically updated weather widget—which you can get for free on the Internet), and so on. If you have extra time and energy, consider starting a blog to write daily or weekly posts on relevant topics, or open a Twitter account to microblog about interesting tidbits.

This just scratches the surface of SEO, which has become a burgeoning industry in the last few years. If you want help, a local website developer should be able to do a decent job. If you are in a highly competitive field, such as a dentist or veterinarian, also look at joining a directory—usually a cost-effective approach to improving your Google ranking.

RESOURCE

More information on effective websites. Especially if you want to create a full-blown e-commerce site designed to attract more than local traffic, see *The Small Business Start-Up Kit,* by Peri Pakroo (Nolo). It has an excellent chapter on building a website, optimizing it so that search engines list your site first, and driving traffic to your site.

Use Email Marketing

Whether or not your business has a website, you can use email to stay in contact with your customers. For example, you can easily and cheaply send out valuable information to customers who have signed up for your emails (post a simple sign-up sheet at your business, and let visitors sign up on your website). News about sales, schedules of events, and helpful tips about your area of expertise are all excellent ways to remind customers that you exist. For example, a tax accountant might inform clients about likely changes in the tax code and things they may want to do now to minimize next year's taxes.

To get started, you'll probably want to hire an email marketing service provider to help manage your email lists (you'll need to maintain a list of email addresses and allow people to change their email address or unsubscribe by sending you an email or clicking a link). An email marketing company can also help you develop a marketing campaign by providing HTML templates and actually sending out your messages. For more on this, see *Permission Based E-mail Marketing,* by Kim MacPherson (Kaplan Business).

Hold a "Trying to Stay in Business" Sale

If, despite all your cutbacks and seat-of-the-pants marketing efforts, your business is sinking to the point that you are considering closing down, your last best marketing hope may be a Trying to Stay in Business Sale. That's right, instead of a Going Out of Business Sale, reverse the order. That way, if it turns out that you have more loyal customers than you thought, you'll let them help save your business instead of mourn with you over its death.

Obviously, how you conduct your sale will depend on your business, but the most important element—spreading the word as far and wide as possible—will always be the same. If you can, put off your close-down date long enough to allow for distributing signs, flyers, and mailings and, if your business is well-known in the community, media outreach to let customers know that this is their last chance to support you.

As always, be sure you know how you make money and don't deeply discount so many items that you don't make a profit. For example, a lingerie store that makes 70% of its profit on bras, including sports bras popular with the patrons of two nearby fitness centers, might fill its windows with deeply discounted negligees but lower bra prices only 10%.

EXAMPLE: Emily runs a neighborhood toy store called Mrs. McKeever's that, because of its convenience and responsiveness, has managed to survive in the shadow of the big box retailers for three years. But now, with customers' budgets stretched, sales are down 30%, and Emily is about to close the door for the last time. But she decides to make a last huge effort and announces a two-week "Trying to Save Mrs. McKeever's" sale. She puts signs in every window, sends her teenage kids up and down in front of the store wearing "Save Mrs. McKeever's" sandwich boards, and mails a postcard to everyone on her mailing list. Helped by front-page coverage in the local free newspaper, the response is enormous, as hundreds of people realize that the entire community will be weakened if the store closes.

With enough cash in her checking account to make it through the next few months, Emily asks several of her most enthusiastic and locally well-connected supporters to serve on a "Save Mrs. McKeever's" committee to help her come up with a long-term survival plan.

Handle Layoffs Fairly—And Keep Your Best People

"I not only use all the brains I have, but all I can borrow."
WOODROW WILSON

Especially if payroll is your biggest expense, when your business is struggling you may find yourself looking at laying off employees—a dark day for any small business owner. Letting people go is always hard. Keep in mind, though, that your employees understand that layoffs may be necessary when times are tough. After all, they read the newspapers and see the stories of layoffs in businesses that range from small local factories to multinational companies.

If you have been in business some time, it may help to remember that over the years you've provided employment for lots of people, some of whom moved on when they found a better opportunity. The fact that forces outside your control are now causing your business to contract doesn't make you a bad employer or a bad person. The longer you resist or delay necessary layoffs, the more you put at risk your business and its ability to provide jobs in the future.

Employees don't ask for lifetime employment. What they do have a right to expect is to be treated fairly and respectfully. You can't make layoffs easy, but you avoid making them unnecessarily painful. This chapter talks about how to let people go in as fair and humane a way as possible.

When you're focusing on employees you are going to lay off, it's easy to neglect the rest of the crew. But morale suffers from a layoff, so it's extra important to acknowledge and appreciate the employees who stick with you. You don't want to lose your best people, especially when your business is struggling and you need every advantage you can get. To ensure their loyalty, you need to make sure you conduct yourself as a team player—cut your own perks and salary first, demonstrate respect for the judgment of coworkers, and lead by example. Owners who rule by edict, reward themselves excessively, and don't pull a fair share of the load end up squandering their most valuable resources.

> **TIP**
>
> **Cut pay and hours first.** Before you lay anybody off, you—and your spouse if he or she is on the payroll—should cut your own pay. If you can afford to, cut at least 25%. Also look at cutting the salary of higher-paid employees and reducing everybody's work week. Salary and hour cuts rarely reduce overhead enough to cope with a precipitous drop in income, but they might reduce the number of painful layoffs you must make. (For more on making wage and hour cuts, see Chapter 3.)

Making a Wise Layoff Plan

Unfortunately, it's easy to mishandle the layoff process so thoroughly that you all but assure your business will continue to decline. The most common mistake is to initiate layoffs without first adopting a systematic plan to shrink the business.

Don't hand out pink slips in a panic. If you do, you'll create chaos, with employees being laid off or kept based on all sorts of faulty criteria, including family relationship, friendship, how needy you think a particular employee is, and on and on. Fortunately, the right approach to making essential layoffs is not difficult, but it does require you to put aside emotion and follow a logical step-by-step process.

Come Up With a Plan to Shrink Your Business

You need to cut your expenses until they match your reduced income projections. This might mean cuts across the board or severing an unprofitable part of the business. For example, if you are running both a wholesale and retail operation and both are suddenly operating in the red, you may decide to jettison the less successful one and put all energy and resources into the other. However you focus your cuts, come up with a dollar amount that you need to trim from payroll.

Decide How Much to Cut

Your layoffs must eliminate the positions not needed to achieve your new slimmed down financial plan. For instance, if you are suspending new software research and development, you can eliminate a certain number of programmers and project managers.

That's the (relatively) easy part. If you still need to cut more expenses, and those cuts must come in the form of jobs, you'll have to figure out what jobs your company can live without.

The conventional advice is that it's less demoralizing to employees to have one big layoff than a series of small ones. In other words, toss away your rose-colored glasses and cut heavily, so that you're sure you won't have to do it again. You don't want employees constantly nervous about their jobs as they watch coworkers leave one by one. There's obviously much truth in this. But knowing and caring about your employees as you do, your instinct is probably to cut the minimum number of jobs required by your new tough-minded recession business plan. Fine, as long as employees understand that although you hope to avoid more job cuts, they might be needed. Show them how the business is doing and how much revenue you need to bring in each month, and let them know that if the revenue targets aren't hit, more jobs might have to go.

Eliminate Jobs You Don't Need or Can't Afford

Although your focus should be on eliminating jobs, you may want to do some shifting of job responsibilities. If you find that an employee in a position slated to be cut is more efficient and qualified than someone occupying a position you plan to keep, make the substitution.

Don't Discriminate Illegally

It is illegal to make employment decisions based on age, gender, race, disability, religion, national origin, or any other legally protected category. So make sure you don't discriminate (or that it appears you are discriminating) for an illegal reason. Normally in layoff situations, where you first identify job slots that you can eliminate and then cut the people occupying those slots, you'll have little to worry about, because you'll likely end up laying off people of different ages, genders, race, and so on. But if after making your list, you find that most people on it are, say, women over 40, rethink your plan or talk to an employment lawyer. Otherwise you may open yourself to an age discrimination claim.

EXAMPLE: Because sales have dropped, Acme Lumber decides to cut ten of its 30 employees: three from the office, four from the lumber shed, and two drivers. Three of the employees—two men and one woman—are over 50, two are African American, and one long-term employee uses a wheelchair. There are seven men and three women in the group, and their average age is 40, which more or less mirrors Acme's overall gender and age makeup. If Acme acts based on a logical plan to cut tasks and retain people with the most needed skills, it should have no concerns that any of these employees can succeed with a discrimination claim.

The Logistics of a Layoff

If you are laying off just a couple of employees, you'll want to do it yourself, as informally and kindly as possible. The same is true if you are laying off a relative, friend, or someone who has been with your company for many years. But no matter how low-key your approach, be sure to have the final paycheck ready, including accrued vacation pay. And don't forget to ask for keys and company credit cards to be returned, to turn off employee email (and disable passwords), and to change the building alarm codes.

If you'll be laying off more than about five people, you'll want to follow a more structured approach. Here is an outline of a sound layoff protocol you can modify to your needs.

Get Senior People on Board and Pick a Day for the Layoffs

Meet with any senior managers to make sure they are fully in the picture and understand (even better, fully agree with) your plans. Include your human resources person or bookkeeper who will handle the necessary paperwork, if you have one. All these people must commit to 100% confidentiality.

Choose a day where all senior managers will be in the office to break the news to the laid-off employees. Contrary to advice you may read elsewhere, we don't believe that there is a magic best day. Pick a day when the maximum number of people you'll be letting go will be in the office. Choose a time that lets you give departing employees a couple of hours to leave the building, and still leaves you time to gather remaining staff for a company meeting to help restore morale.

> **CAUTION**
>
> **If you're laying off a large number of people, check into notice requirements.** If you have only a few employees, you aren't required to give employees any notice before closing. But in some states, such as New York, when 25 or more employees are laid off, 90 days' notice is required, in some circumstances. And in any state, under federal law, employers with 100 or more employees are required by law, in some circumstances, to provide 60 days' notice. Check with your state's labor or employment development department to find out if your state requires a certain amount of notice.

Prepare Final Paychecks, Recommendations, and Severance

Have your bookkeeper prepare final paychecks, which should include pay for the entire final day plus all accrued vacation. Some states require you to pay employees their final paychecks on their last day; others on the next scheduled payday or within 72 hours. To be sure you comply with your state's law, it makes sense to give employees their paychecks on their last day. In addition, some states require you to pay out accrued but unused vacation days on the last day, something that is more efficient than trying to do it later. Almost all states have penalties for not paying wages when due—with some charging $1,000 per employee, per pay period, and others exacting a penalty of 30 days' wages per employee not paid on time.

Also prepare a polite letter of recommendation for each departing employee, giving dates of employment, duties, and a general statement of approbation. Your employees will appreciate your courtesy, and it may make the day go more easily for all. Even if you are laying off a worker who fell far short of the ideal, don't include anything negative—just limit this letter to dates of employment and duties.

If you plan to grant severance pay (see "Pay Modest Severance If You Can," below), prepare a separate check to be given to the employee in exchange for agreeing not to sue you over the termination. You'll need to prepare an appropriate release to have the departing employee sign. State law requirements differ somewhat in this area, so you should consult an employment lawyer about the release, especially if you suspect an employee might sue.

Pay Modest Severance If You Can

No law requires you to pay laid-off severance to employees, unless you've promised it (in your employee handbook or an employee contract, for example). But if you can pay modest severance without putting the survival of your business at serious risk, it's a good idea for several reasons:

- Departing employees will feel more respected and be far less likely to badmouth you to others.

- Continuing employees will see that even when your business is in the dumps, you are going the extra mile to be fair. As a result, they are more likely to put their shoulders to the wheel.

- When times eventually improve, you may want to rehire some of the people you have laid off, which will be far easier to do if they see you as a fair employer.

- You'll feel better about yourself.

How much severance you pay is up to you. Obviously, you can't absorb a hefty hit to your bottom line. Typically, small businesses already in severe economic distress can't afford to pay more than a week's pay for each year served, with possibly an extra week for people who have worked one year or less. But to avoid claims of discrimination, be sure to be consistent in how you pay severance, using an objective formula to calculate it.

Break the News All at Once

On the appointed day, if you have enough managers, have them meet with each departing employee at, say, 9:45 a.m. to give them the news personally. Then at 10 a.m., have the managers escort the employees to a private meeting room or, if necessary, your office. If you fear an employee might become violent, arrange for appropriate help to be standing by, as unobtrusively as possible.

> **TIP**
>
> **Take care with off-site employees.** If any employees who are on the layoff list are working remotely or are out of the building for some other reason, come up with the most efficient and sensitive plan to notify them. Do it personally if possible and by phone if absolutely necessary. Don't use email.

Start the meeting by briefly explaining the economic necessity that requires the layoff. Because people will likely be shellshocked and unable to absorb lots of information, keep it brief. For example, if your business just lost a $200,000 contract and the bank is threatening to pull your line of credit if you don't quickly cut expenses, it's enough to say just that. Don't forget to thank the departing employees for their hard work and, if you feel it's appropriate, apologize for the fact that economic necessity has forced you to cut such loyal people. Then tell people that in the envelope in front of them, they'll find their pay through today plus accrued vacation. At this stage, if you have a human resources manager, or failing that, an office manager, you may feel that it's less embarrassing to all to step out of the room, leaving the details of collecting keys, signing releases, and answering practical questions, such as eligibility for health coverage under COBRA, to someone else.

While the departing employees are still in the conference room, send a short email (or otherwise notify) all continuing employees of what's going on and ask them to attend a company meeting later the same day. Your email should simply say that the difficult economic times have forced you to reduce overhead and cut the number of employees. It should include all employees on the layoff list, thanking them for their hard work and dedication. That's it—leave the longer explanation for the company meeting.

Secure Your Computer System Before Employees Pack Up

While laid-off employees are in the meeting room, have whoever handles your computer system disable the computers of any laid-off employee who has enough knowledge to destroy or steal data or crash your network. If a departing employee wants to remove personal files from their computer while packing up, you can have someone sit with them while they do so.

Departing employees should be given an hour or so to pack up and be out of the building. It's polite to have boxes at the ready and to allow coworkers to help them pack. But in a couple of hours, everyone should have left. If you haven't already done it, make sure all computer access passwords and codes have been disabled.

Hold a Company Meeting

The same day, if possible, convene a company meeting and explain what happened and why. The more honest and up front you are, the more you'll be respected. This is not a time for an in-depth *PowerPoint* about financial details, but a few slides illustrating your business's financial situation might help. Below is a sample presentation you can modify to fit your needs.

Sample Layoff Statement at a Company Meeting

"Six months ago, Acme Lumber was doing well and we had lined up funding to expand. Then the economic roof fell in. Sales are down over 30% compared to last year, meaning that we are losing money. And last week, because a new housing subdivision was cancelled, we lost a $200,000 contract. That made our bank warn us that our $500,000 line of credit would be pulled if we don't quickly return to profitability.

"Unfortunately, to address these issues, today we were forced to lay off ten good workers. It pained us to have to say goodbye to our friends and colleagues, and we feel badly that economic necessity forced us to take this step. Even allowing for severance payments, this will save us $500,000 in the next calendar year. We are also taking other steps to get us back in the black.

"Here's our plan:

"1. My wife and I have each cut our pay by 40%.

"2. Effective today, all employees making more than $30,000 will experience a pay cut. The cut will start at 4% for the next $10,000 and scale up 1% for each $10,000 over that, meaning that the one person making over $90,000 will take a 9% cut. We estimate that these cuts will save about $100,000 in the next 12 months and allow us to keep two more employees than we could otherwise. In addition, starting next week, everyone will work a 4½ day week, which will save another 10% of our payroll costs. I'll do everything in my power to end these cuts and return your pay to its former level as soon as possible. But please understand I can't do that until Acme is solidly profitable—something that may take an extended period of time.

"3. We are cutting every possible expense and have already made cuts that will save us $100,000 over the next year. We plan to sell one of our trucks and a loader to reduce our lease costs.

"Probably the first two questions you'll want answered are have we cut enough to make Acme profitable, and will there be more job cuts?

Sample Layoff Statement at a Company Meeting, cont'd

"The answer to the first question is a qualified yes. If sales don't drop further than we anticipate, we should be able to avoid additional layoffs. But remember, times are tough, and even though we are stepping up our marketing efforts in a dozen ways, no one can know whether sales will get worse.

"Now, as to our immediate financial future. We think these cuts will give our bank confidence to stick with us and not pull our line of credit. But if not, Ann and I will invest our $250,000 in savings in Acme and mortgage our house if necessary. In short, we'll do everything in our power to keep this wonderful business going so that it will be still here when the economy eventually begins to expand, construction gets going again, and there is money to be made.

"I appreciate the hard work and loyalty of each and every one of you, and I'll email you once a week about how things are going. Are there any questions?"

Keeping the Great People You Hire

You may think that when unemployment is high and companies are laying people off right and left, motivating your continuing employees to stick with you and work as if their hair is on fire should be a breeze. But if employees who have already had to stomach pay cuts fear that your business might fail or that more layoffs are likely, they'll be quick to jump to any job that looks more secure. If your post-layoff workplace is poorly functioning, tense, and joyless, they are likely to leave even faster.

In good times or bad, your business will suffer if you don't keep the loyalty of your best employees. Just as it takes many small business owners three to five years to really hit their stride, top-notch employees, even those who can do skilled work from their first day, become more valuable every month they work for you. Long-term workers build a valuable mental database of useful information about your products or services, customers, coworkers, and suppliers. If they move on, you lose everything they know.

For example, at Nolo we hire legal editors, most of them lawyers who can explain legal rules in plain English (a rare combination), to edit and often write our new books. Even though we use a rigorous screening and testing process to hire highly skilled people who can immediately do good work, we've found that, on average, it takes about 18 months before a new editor can do the job without at least some mentoring from a more senior editor. It takes even longer for a new editor to acquire enough knowledge about a wide range of Nolo products to catch up with their more experienced peers. It follows that Nolo has a huge interest in hanging on to people who go through this extended apprenticeship.

To fully appreciate how valuable it is to keep good employees for as long as possible—especially during hard times when you have no time to train replacements—think about your own relationships with local businesses. If you've been dealing with the same competent person year after year, it's frustrating when that familiar face (or even familiar voice) is replaced by a less experienced one.

So how do you go about keeping productive employees working for you as long as possible, when your business is shrinking and you may even have imposed pay cuts? Start with a simple fact: If your employees feel fairly treated under the circumstances and believe you have set a course to outlast the economic downturn, they are far more likely to stick by you.

Treat—And Pay—People Fairly

"Fairness" is the best one-word prescription for keeping employees loyal to your business. Workers who believe your business can be trusted to treat them equitably are likely to be loyal; those who feel they are in untrustworthy hands are almost sure to move on. This goes double when times are tough, unemployment is high, and your business is obviously struggling. Loyalty often has less to do with the size of your employees' paychecks than it does with their belief that you will do everything possible to protect their job, not just toss them overboard on the first stormy day.

What is fairness in the workplace? Basically, that your business uses objective criteria—not whim or pique—to hand out rewards and punishments. Put another way, it means that your business establishes and follows a set of employment policies that are understandable, consistent, and evenhanded. For example, if you lay off a long-term, experienced employee but keep your lazy cousin, you risk convincing everyone in the company that despite your rhetoric about fairness, you can't be trusted. But if you adopt a merit-based system of promotion and stick to it, even though it means your cousin is asked to leave, you go far toward reassuring all employees that they will be treated fairly. True, your aunt may snub you at the next family gathering, but that's a small price to pay to run a business that your employees will respect and stick by.

When it comes to wages, most employees use three factors to judge whether or not they are being fairly treated.

How much similar jobs in your area pay. Especially for highly productive people who receive just a few dollars per hour over minimum wage, it's essential to pay slightly more than your competitors do. Especially when times are tough, you don't want to lose the best of those understandably penny-conscious employees because they can earn an extra 30 cents an hour down the street. Unfortunately, most small employers never grasp this lesson, paying the industry standard to the sales clerk who works twice as fast as the norm. Again, it's far better for employee retention, overall productivity, and workplace happiness to reward your most productive employees.

How much others with comparable skills are paid in your company. Your employees will have no trouble accepting substantial pay disparities as long as in their eyes they reflect real differences in skill, training, seniority, and job responsibilities. But dissatisfaction will quickly surface if employees conclude that one person or group receives substantially better pay or perks for no honest business reason—or worse, for a bad reason. This is not the place to tackle the details of complicated pay equity issues, such as differing pay rates for different departments, individual vs. across-the-board raises, and overtime for some job categories and not others. But it is important to grasp just how essential it is even for employers with just a handful of employees to create logical, understandable, and defensible pay policies and modify them only when objective new factors require it.

How much the boss's pay and perks are. Especially when you are asking your employees to work extra hard in an economically fraught environment, it's crucial that you not offend them by exempting yourself from your austerity program. (More on this in Chapter 10.) And unless you are happily married to your bookkeeper, don't think you can pay yourself lavishly or reward yourself with secret perks and keep it secret.

Don't Lose Your Sense of Purpose

Employees of successful small businesses are almost always imbued with a strong sense of purpose. It doesn't matter if you make or sell booties, bibles, or bagpipes—the key is to imbue your company with a commitment to excellence, something that is especially important to maintain when a business is struggling financially. There are several tried-and-true methods to help your employees believe in the value of their work. But no amount of cheerleading will work unless they really see that you run a high-quality operation. For example, if you claim your café serves the freshest baked goods in town, but now that sales are down you occasionally slip a few day-old muffins in with today's batch, you'll begin to alienate your own employees.

If you do run a quality operation, helping your employees create and participate in a larger vision will go far toward cementing their loyalty. No question it can be tougher to do this when you are fighting for every dollar, but it's not impossible. We're reminded of a veterinarian who not only ran the cleanest, most efficient animal care operation in town, but even when business flagged in an earlier recession, actually carved out the hours necessary to allow employees to participate in a variety of free animal rescue and support activities. As a result, the vet attracted a terrific crew of employees, people who were so pleased to be part of a committed business that many of them stuck around for years.

Communicate Early and Often

When people have been laid off (or if employees expect them to be), many of your employees will be fearful. Will they be laid off next? Will the business be sold? Declare bankruptcy? It's no secret that if allowed to fester, these kinds of worries can have a seriously negative effect on your business.

Productivity drops when people are distracted and anxious (or spend work time on online job sites), and your best employees may leave for what they perceive to be greener pastures.

To counter this, you need to honestly communicate how the business is doing, whether the news is good or bad. We hope you made a good start when you laid people off, when you explained to everyone the economic facts you faced. Now you should follow up with a weekly finance report. Don't give employees just a bunch of raw financial numbers and hope they make sense of them. Also give them the context that will let them understand exactly how your business is coping with the downturn, and tell them everything you are doing to increase sales.

EXAMPLE: You own the Continental Diner, a busy urban eatery with 20 employees. When the recession takes hold, business drops 25%, and you lay off five employees, explaining that Continental is losing money. You inform employees that you and your husband, who manages the day shift, have cut your salaries by 35% and loaned Continental $50,000 to catch up on past-due bills. You also explain that after slashing all discretionary expenses, Continental still needs to take in $20,000 per week to break even. If this can be achieved, you believe Continental can ride out the recession.

Each Monday you tell employees how much you took in the week before, explaining why you missed or exceeded the goal. You thank employees who work extra hard or come up with clever ideas to bring in more diners, making it clear that all ideas are welcome and valued. Who knows, it might be the newest busboy who comes up with the "can't resist" special that has customers lining up to get in.

Appreciate Your Employees

It's simple, really: Employees strive to do better when they know their hard work and creative contributions are noticed. This is even more important when business is grim and you are asking everyone for a little extra. In this context, those employees whose good work isn't acknowledged are likely to conclude that there is no point in busting their butts.

So whether you have five, 55, or 105 employees, develop an employee appreciation program. To make sure your program will be welcomed by your employees, it's best to create it with their input. If you don't, you risk adopting a plan that will be ignored or resented. For example, if your well-meaning plan to pay bonuses to salespeople who bring in new business is regarded as a cynical ploy to make your overworked employees put in extra hours, you're unlikely to achieve your objective.

EXAMPLE: When Jan's cardboard box company is hit hard by the financial melt-down, she decides that a great way to incentivize sales reps to bring in more business is to create a salesperson-of-the-quarter award and give the winner a trip for two to Hawaii. Consulting no one, she calls a company meeting and proudly announces the detailed rules of this new program. But Jan doesn't realize that her rules favor the three salespeople with the best territories, and in consequence angers several others who work in less productive areas and see the whole program as a backhanded way to criticize them, and maybe even to set them up to be laid off. Even worse, Jan fails to create a parallel award for the office staff and other support personnel who pro-cess the orders, ship the goods, collect the bills, and do other essential work, mak-ing them feel that their work isn't important. And finally, at a time when everyone is worried about layoffs, employees see a trip to Hawaii as an expensive and even insulting boondoggle.

Fortunately for Jan, after the meeting, a longtime employee marches into her office to forcefully explains that everyone, save the three already highly compensated sales-people, is offended by her plan. Reluctantly acknowledging her mistake, Jan cancels the program and sets up an employee committee to recommend a way to use the same amount of bonus money to provide incentives to everyone. To Jan's surprise, the committee proposes that whenever the entire business exceeded its quarterly sales goal, $1,500 be used for a dinner party at a nice restaurant to which everyone in the company is invited. Especially during the gloom of the recession, these events turn out to be so welcome that everyone, from the senior employees to the high school kid who helps with filing, begins paying close attention to weekly sales totals.

When thanking people for good work, be as inclusive as possible. Don't recognize or reward just the most visible person or even the person who has led a particular effort. Acknowledge everyone who contributed to the good work you are recognizing and honoring. For instance, in the example above, the thing that really made Jan's second reward program fun was that it included everyone, even the high school kid, who proudly brought the boyfriend she normally complained about.

Finally, during tough economic times when everyone is forced to pinch pennies, it's best to keep your appreciation efforts simple, sincere, and cheap. Many rewards programs are designed (or at least seem that way) to influence or even manipulate employees' future behavior, rather than to simply acknowledge their good work. Often a public thank you at a company meeting or via email, or a pizza celebration lunch for everyone, is more welcome than a more complicated system.

RESOURCE

More on rewarding employees for good work. *1001 Ways to Reward Employees*, by Bob Nelson (Workman), provides a comprehensive list of awards, rewards, and other techniques to let employees know that their contributions are important. Few of them will fit your business exactly, but reading this little book should jump-start your thinking.

Lead, Don't Dominate

Everyone associated with your enterprise will be happier and your business more productive if you are a frugal, hardworking leader, not a privileged dominator. American traditions are democratic and majoritarian, not autocratic and imperious. At all levels of our society, leaders who work hard and are in touch with ordinary people command loyalty and respect.

If your employees regard you as a decent human—and not just the big boss—they will be far more willing to share their thoughts about how to improve the business, something that can be crucial to your survival in a severe downturn. No doubt many of their "brilliant ideas" won't be. But after you put aside those that are self-serving, have already been tried and found wanting, or are just plain nonsensical, you are likely to find a few good ones. And it's very possible that an engaged employee who is genuinely concerned about the future of your business will come up with a true gem, something so valuable that it will make listening to dozens of mediocre ideas more than worthwhile.

Treat all ideas—even ones that are obviously nonstarters—with respect. Employees who see others' suggestions belittled or dismissed will be unlikely to make their own. You also need to develop a process to capture good ideas. (How to do this is discussed in detail in Chapter 6, which deals with innovation.)

EXAMPLE 1: Liam answers the phone and schedules service calls for Goodlight, a local electrical contractor. Because he talks to customers all day, Liam learns a lot about their needs and desires and sees that Goodlight is out of touch with some significant new developments in the market—one of the reasons business has been falling off recently. Liam considers talking to his boss, Peter, about how introducing two new services might really kick up profits. But Peter barely seems to have time to nod hello. And when Liam hears through the grapevine that Jen in customer service was laughed at when she tried to suggest changes in the phone system, Liam decides not to bother.

Six months later, when a competitor, Hi Tech Electric, opens, Liam applies for and receives a job at considerably higher pay, in part because at his interview, Mia, the owner, is impressed by his innovative ideas. Mia immediately introduces Liam's new services, which, because of their hefty profit margins, result in solid profits for Hi Tech. A few months later when hard times hit and Goodlight cuts back, Hi Tech remains profitable and gains substantial market share. Mia not only gives Liam full credit within the company, but also a meaningful raise.

EXAMPLE 2: Now let's imagine that, despite Goodlight's success, Peter's personal style remains a little more homespun. Not only is there a suggestion box in the employee lounge, but also a display recognizing the best suggestion of the previous month. The day after Liam has his big idea, he drops it in the box. The next day, he encounters Peter helping repair a door on one of the delivery trucks. Peter invites Liam for coffee and asks him to present his idea in more detail. Impressed, a few days later Peter convenes a meeting with several key employees to which Liam is invited. The result is that Goodlight introduces what turns out to be two highly profitable new services. Peter significantly raises Liam's pay and gives him a small bonus. A few months later, when the recession hits and profits in the traditional lighting business disappear, it's the new services Liam suggested that allow Goodlight to avoid major layoffs.

When implementing new ideas, be sure you include key employees in the process, instead of handing down the law like Moses. New policies and procedures carried out with the input of the people who will have to cope with them day to day are not only likely to be more successful—but they are far less prone to be sabotaged. Remember, employees who don't buy into new way of doing things can always find ways to subvert them.

No question, especially when money is tight and time short, it's easier and certainly quicker to issue an order or impose a decision than it is to listen, reason, and help build consensus. But especially when unpopular cutbacks are in the offing, it's essential to establish and respect a consensus-building management structure. Or put another way, a business that your employees view as being all about you won't be as successful as will one your employees see as also being about them.

We're not suggesting that you make your workplace a perfect democracy where all decisions are equally shared. Leaving aside the fact that it's your business and you have the biggest financial stake in its success or failure, it simply takes too long for everyone in the kitchen to discuss how much sugar to put in the brownies. Although a few cooperatively run businesses do well, we suspect their success has come despite the fact they elevated 100% democratic decision making to a first principle, not because of it. Far better to run your enterprise with a strong purposeful center at the same time you invite and respect employees' opinions and treat them with dignity.

Credit Is Cheap—Spread It Around

Hogging credit for the business's achievements is a huge and common faux pas of small business owners. Just as professors are sometimes guilty of putting only their names on research done largely by their graduate students, owners of small enterprises are far too prone to act as if they alone made the business a success. Few things are more disappointing and insulting to employees who have worked hard and creatively to help build the company.

Try to foster a culture in which leaders go out of the way to acknowledge everyone's contributions. If this means that your company meetings sometimes sound like a roll call of every employee's achievements, so much the better. People work more creatively when they know their efforts are acknowledged and appreciated—especially when, in a recession, they are asked to work harder for less pay and benefits. Here are just a few ways to foster this attitude:

- **Recognize hard and creative work throughout the company**—at company meetings, through companywide emails, and at parties. If your warehouse crew ships a big order in record time, everyone should hear about their great job.

- **Share kind words from outsiders with everyone.** If your business gets written up in the paper, or an employee does something newsworthy, email the story to everyone and tack up the clipping on a bulletin board people will see. If your customer service or sales people get compliments, forward them to everyone in the company. At Nolo, if a customer says, "Your book on immigration law saved me $10,000 and my sanity. Were it not for you, my parents never would have gotten their green cards," everyone in the company is thanked—which is as it should be.

- **When a perk pops up, let the people whose work was instrumental in making it happen reap the rewards.** For example, when the Nolo website was nominated for a prestigious Webby Award for best Law/Government site, the hard-to-get tickets to the awards ceremony were offered first to the Noloids who worked on the website day to day, not senior managers. (We won, by the way.)

- **If a customer admires your work, mention everyone who helped.** If someone worked long hours making your product—whether it's a report, a set of drawings, or a custom cabinet—look great, acknowledge that person, preferably in front of the pleased customer or client.

It's crucially important to encourage a culture of "we," not "me." If, when the limelight goes on, you can learn to step aside and nudge someone else forward, that's a good start. But to really help people feel appreciated, you'll need to go beyond fancy words and "employee of the month" type programs to show people you really do value them. In addition to paying decently, rewarding superior work, and providing good benefits (especially health care for all employees), adopting a simple stock option or other employee ownership plan can be the best way to literally put your money where your mouth is. That way your employees really do know that your business is about them, not just you.

> 💡 **TIP**
>
> **Thanks can be as important as money.** No question, paying people fairly is a key way to retain their loyalty (see Chapter 9 for ideas on keeping employees). But compensating people decently, or even giving them a welcome bonus or raise, isn't a substitute for publicly thanking them. When business hits a downturn and you must ask employees to give up perks, benefits, and even pay, thanking them early and often is even more important.

Don't Forget to Be Positive

When money is short and you are chewing the insides of your cheeks with worry, it's easy to transfer your grim mood to your employees. If you do, your employees are in turn likely to transfer it to your customers, never a wise move when you desperately need them to purchase more.

To avoid creating business-killing gloom, you must understand how actually encouraging workers to enjoy themselves can be a powerful motivator. Consider the mood at Southwest Airlines, one of the world's most profitable air carriers, to that at United, a company that staggers from bankruptcy to bankruptcy. In addition to charging low prices and providing reliable, if somewhat Spartan services, Southwest is surely the world's largest corporation that actually encourages its employees to enjoy themselves. Flight attendants joke around, ticket agents dress up in holiday costumes, and even pilots have been known to tell one-liners. How effective is this unique company culture? Almost alone among all the world's major airlines, which are constantly beset by strike threats from angry unions, Southwest enjoys relatively harmonious relations with its employees and consistently operates in the black.

Because workplace environments vary so much, the best advice is probably just to find simple ways to let employees enjoy themselves, and then get out of the way and let it happen. Start by loosening up a bit yourself. For example, if on St. Patrick's Day, you promote a green food potluck brunch and come dressed as a leprechaun, people will likely get the idea.

Here are a few ways to establish an upbeat workplace tone.

Food. Sharing food is probably the most basic way to build community. If you occasionally bring in some treats (homemade is best), others will, too. Be sure that when this happens everyone in your business has a few minutes to enjoy the gift. If this means that it's your turn to spell the person who answers the phone, do it with a smile.

Birthdays. Families celebrate one another's important milestones. Businesses smart enough to treat the people who work for them as part of a workplace family do, too. Keep a calendar of employee anniversaries and remember to do a few little things (balloons and a cake may be corny, but they always work) to honor major milestones.

Hats, shirts, and other tchotchkes. At Nolo we have a long tradition of occasionally giving employees Nolo T-shirts, baseball caps, coffee mugs, and other little gifts. You can always tell that the general mood is good when you see people wearing them around the building.

Wall decorations. Taking the trouble to put framed prints or other tasteful decorations on the walls is a great way to tell both employees and customers that you take pride in your workplace. This costs a few dollars, but is well worth it in many ways. For example, if an impressed visitor tells your employee, "Wow, it's really nice here, you're lucky to work in such a cool place," obviously you have received a huge dividend on your investment.

Parties and picnics. Now and then it's a great morale-builder to invite everyone to an off-site social event. There are many ways to do this, from the ubiquitous summer picnic and winter holiday party to all sorts of less common events. For example, at Nolo we usually hold an annual Play Day. We close the entire business on a weekday and go to a local park to hang out with each other (no spouses or kids) and play wacky games.

Other events. Nolo once had a Pet Parade in the parking lot as part of a lunchtime potluck. Everyone was invited to show off their pets, which included dogs to doves to cats to iguanas. Of course, there were goofy prizes for stupid pet tricks, pets that looked most like their owners, and so on.

A three-legged tortoise won a prize for jumping over a three-foot barrier. (Well, okay, we waited for ten joke-filled minutes before going along with her owner's claim that she only performed at midnight.) And we've held "no-talent" shows and encouraged every ham in the company to participate. A big favorite was a chorus line of body-part wigglers—employees who could twitch ears and noses and turn double joints inside out. We're sure you get the idea, so we'll spare you the details of our Halloween party, holiday gift exchange, and other events, some of the best of which are spontaneous.

Drive a Modest Car

In the United States, the embedded class and caste structures common in many other nations are largely absent, and even the rich often claim to be part of the middle class. Still, many affluent people buy Armani suits and Gucci bags and other expensive things they don't need, in part to signal that they are somehow above the herd. This desire to one-up the Joneses is so much a part of our national psyche that advertisers repeatedly depict the smug suburban homeowner who buys a new car and then sits back to watch the neighbors seethe with envy. Exaggerated? Certainly, but nevertheless we all notice the kind of cars our friends (and especially our foes) drive, how fancy their houses are, and whether they adorn themselves with expensive clothing and jewelry.

It isn't just social acquaintances who notice how you spend money. Your employees and those who do business with you also pay attention, especially when a business experiencing recession-driven cutbacks foots the bill. If you wear designer clothes, drive the biggest Beemer, and have your business pay your country club dues, you'll not only find yourself short of loyal employees, but also risk offending your banker, key suppliers, and customers, who sooner or later are likely to figure out that they are paying for all those perks.

The more ostentatious you are, the more harshly you are likely to be judged. Should you doubt this, ask yourself which of the two business owners briefly profiled below is more likely to be popular with coworkers:

- **Fred.** Flies first class, drives a big Mercedes paid for by his business, wears a $3,000 watch, and owns lots of flashy electronic toys and top-of-the-line sports equipment that he constantly flaunts. He also uses his business credit card to eat at pricey restaurants and makes no secret of how much he spends on exotic vacations.

- **Fredericka.** Flies coach, drives a Honda Accord that she pays for herself, wears a sensible watch and wedding band, and golfs at the local public links. She eats wherever the food tastes good—charging it to the business only when strictly appropriate—and keeps how much she spends on her holidays to herself.

If your answer is Fred, go buy that 12-cylinder Jaguar you have been lusting for. Even in today's dire times, if you work very hard, treat your employees well, and have a bit of luck, you may overcome the resentment your showy behavior is sure to engender. If your answer is Fredericka, you're already on the right track toward understanding why it makes sense in the recessionary workplace, to quickly dial back any ostentatious habits.

Now let's add a few facts. Assume that Fredericka takes home a larger paycheck than Fred does, and that she quietly spends some of her money on luxuries—a second home in the mountains, foreign travel, and a rare book collection. Who wins the popularity contest now? Again, it's Fredericka, something that won't change as long as Fred drives that big company-owned Benz and brags about flying to Bermuda for a golf weekend. Conspicuous consumption—not financial success—is what rankles.

But who, you ask, would flaunt wealth while their company was struggling even to survive? Well, you might remember that the first time the heads of the Detroit automakers went to Washington DC to beg for bailout money, they traveled by private jet. Newspaper stories detailed how GM's Rick Wagoner and Ford's Alan Mulally treated themselves to a long list of luxuries even while lobbying Congress for taxpayer money—and usually went on to note that up to a million people could lose their jobs if all three American car companies failed. If Wagoner and Mulally had flown coach, we suspect Congress would have been more sympathetic to their argument. (When they went back a second time, they drove.)

The same thing happens at small companies. Just walk around any business park or commercial neighborhood until you find a perfectly detailed, new luxury car in a reserved parking spot next to the front door. (Given the large percentage of self-important business owners, this shouldn't take long.) Hang around for a few minutes until an office or service worker enters or leaves the building, and say something like, "Cool car, huh?" Chances are good the person will make a sour comment about the boss. And why not? Especially when times are hard, and layoffs are routine, it's no fun to work for someone whose car cost three times your yearly pay.

Years ago when Jerry Brown was governor of California, he insisted on driving an old Plymouth and living in a budget apartment instead of the governor's mansion. This is overkill. Like the citizens of California, many of whom eventually concluded that the *Doonesbury* comic strip had a point when it called Brown "Governor Moonbeam," your employees want and expect you to act like the boss, not an entry-level employee. There is no need to buy your clothes at Goodwill, work in a broom closet, and drive a used Kia to work to send a message that you know times are tough. Here are a few tips:

- Choose an appropriate office and furnish it in a businesslike way. Save the oriental carpet, fancy furniture and TV-stereo combo for your living room. If you already have these perks, raise a few needed dollars by selling them.

- Share administrative help with others as needed. If you have a largely unneeded administrative assistant whose main job is to pick up your dry cleaning and make you feel important, put him to work at a real job or lay him off.

- Park in the lot or garage with everyone else, not in a "CEO" slot next to the front door. If parking is tight and others have reserved spaces, you obviously should, too, but if you are often out of the office, consider sharing with another employee.

- Roll up your sleeves and participate in periodic workplace cleanup efforts.

- Get your own coffee and snacks. If you insist, people will probably fetch and carry for you, but every one of them will think less of you for making them do it.

- Use equipment such as computers and phones that are appropriate for the work you really do. Get rid of TVs, game consoles, and other toys.

- Always address and refer to employees by their names. Never use disrespectful terms like "sport," "stud," "honey," or "babe."

Suppose now you've looked over this list and are chagrined to say that your behavior has been needlessly ostentatious and possibly even insulting. No worries—as long as you change it quickly, firmly, and sincerely, you'll regain your employees' respect. Especially if your business is facing financial difficulty and you are asking others to make sacrifices, lose your fancy ride (yes, even if you paid for it), your club memberships, your upscale lunches, and whatever else sets you apart from the people you are trying to motivate to work harder. ●

Don't Work Too Much

"Success has made failures of many men."
COLUMNIST CINDY ADAMS

When your business is struggling, nothing could be more obvious than the fact that you need to put in more time to straighten things out, right?

Wrong. It's at least as likely that people who regularly work overly long days will be less successful than those canny enough to keep their work and personal time in better balance. In a world full of cheap labor but short on intellectual capital, it rarely pays to try to substitute hours for smarts.

It's hard, though, to get past this enduring American folk myth that successful businesspeople spend every minute working. Virtually every article or book profiling a successful entrepreneur prominently mentions how hard the person works—routinely, 60 or 70 hours a week. Especially when times are tough, such super hardworking owners are frequently pictured as sacrificing heroes. But in good times and bad, loads of prosperous entrepreneurs work far less. The American media has committed itself to the notion that going without weekends is a key to attaining riches—and people who don't conform to this stereotype simply don't get profiled. Recognizing that, we suspect many savvy businesspeople exaggerate how hard they work. If so, they are part of a long tradition. Ben Franklin admitted in his autobiography that he regularly left a candle lit in his Philadelphia print shop so passersby would think he was toiling into the wee hours instead of, in fact, being snuggled cozily in bed.

Although there can be all sorts of reasons why a particular business owner chooses to work too much, in a recession surely the biggest reason is that owners assume that there is a direct relationship between the number of hours worked and money earned. It's not true. Profits flow from businesses that cost-effectively meet their customers' needs—not because a desperate entrepreneur works until midnight seven days a week. No question, when a business is caught in an economic downturn, and especially when key people have been laid off, there are times when you need to work extra hours. But the long-term solution to the problem is to work smarter, not to burn yourself out with 15-hour days.

EXAMPLE: Cecily's interior design business suffers as the hard economic times worsen. Trying to outwork the problem, Cecily begins submitting bids on more and more jobs, even highly unlikely ones, in a desperate effort to keep her office open and her staff paid. Only when her husband and children go into total revolt about never seeing her does she finally admit she is working more and more for less and less. Laying off her staff and closing her office, Cecily decides to work from home, bidding on only the most likely jobs.

She also partners with a local furniture shop to provide free, in-store 45-minute consultations, two mornings each week. After of each consultation, Cecily gives each person a brochure listing reasonable prices for a menu of additional design services. Many self-helpers who see just how talented Cecily is during the free consultation hire her for additional help. Although her new business isn't as profitable as the old one was in boom times, it puts groceries on the table and lets Cecily spend time with her family.

The Importance of a Sane Schedule

It should go almost without saying that working too many hours for too long is bad for your health and the well-being of your family—two things you absolutely need to nurture to have a chance to thrive when the economy finally recovers. Many overworking, and as a result, overstressed, business owners say they would love to work less, but argue that they can't because they absolutely know that without their 60-hour weeks they would quickly go broke. Even in a tough economy they are almost always wrong.

It's our experience that owner overwork is actually a big reason why a potentially successful business closes. If you can scrape by only because you lay off key employees and work 60 to 70 hours per week yourself, you need to face the fact that your business is not financially viable. You are not really in business at all. Instead, you have hired yourself, at a rotten wage, to do a task no one values enough to allow you to generate a decent profit.

Fortunately, even when the economy is tanking, in most instances overwork isn't necessary. Businesses that really meet customers' needs offer many opportunities for an owner to be more productive in less time. By learning to concentrate on the activities that count most, most entrepreneurs can achieve the same results in up to one-third fewer hours.

The Danger of Burnout

Most well-run small businesses become more profitable—often far more profitable—as they age. True, an economic downturn can temporarily interrupt this steady growth trend, but it's nevertheless important to realize that if you make good decisions, an economic downturn of a year or two won't derail long-term success. In fact, because an extended recession will flush out weak competitors, once it ends your business is likely to quickly grow larger and more profitable.

In short, growing a successful business is like running a marathon, not a hundred-yard dash or even a mile. To go the distance, you must adopt a work schedule that lets you pace yourself. Many new small business owners, especially those who face a profit-killing recession, fail to understand this and as a result burn themselves out and quit, in some instances just when their businesses are poised to make good money.

EXAMPLE: Sal and Patricia, each a 30-something mother of young children, open Z-Pot, a business that imports and wholesales large glazed pottery planters from Southeast Asia, and immediately begin making a solid profit wholesaling their unique wares to about 25 nurseries and half a dozen indoor garden shops. In addition, they open their own retail outlet to profitably dispose of overstock and slightly damaged goods.

But two years later, the economy turns down, and Sal and Patricia have to lay off a couple of employees and begin working much longer hours themselves. On top of their family responsibilities, this leaves both women feeling exhausted and even depressed much of the time. Patricia's husband, whose own career teaching at a university is going well, begins to strongly suggest that their family life would improve if Patricia sold her share of the business and stayed home with the kids for a few years.

Not wanting to give up Z-Pot, but recognizing their problem, Sal and Patricia decide to close their retail operation, negotiate their way out of the store lease, and concentrate all their energy on the core wholesale operation. Although they miss the additional income, they both appreciate the extra time.

And then an exciting thing happens. Because Sal, who no longer has to worry about the retail shop, has time to do more marketing, and because a competitor goes out of business, Z-Pot is able to land several large new nursery wholesale accounts. In addition, to get rid of dinged-up inventory, Sal and Patricia hold their first annual three-day blowout sale. To create a come-and-get-it sale frenzy, they mark some pots down to their cost, but they also mix in plenty of pots at a decent markup. The sale brings in enough cash to catch up their accounts payable and put some money in the bank besides.

Now working reasonable hours, Sal and Patricia are content to keep overhead low in their smaller operation so they stay in the black. They both know that when the recession ends and sales jump back to historical levels, Z-Pot will be positioned to achieve significant profits.

Working a reasonable schedule, with the occasional week or two off, lets you stay focused and interested in your work and attack your responsibilities with drive and enthusiasm. Of course, occasionally you'll need to work extra hours. But if you do it for an extended period, your sense of personal well-being begins to erode, your families' happiness declines, and your quality begins to drop off.

Maybe you are now thinking something like this, "I'd love to work a 40-, or even a 50-hour week, but if I do my business will surely go under." Perhaps, but when we look around at friends whose small businesses have done extremely well over a number of years, we see no one who consistently works more than a 50-hour week, and many who average fewer than 40. The few who regularly put in ten-hour days compensate by working fewer days per week or taking at least a month's annual vacation. In other words, virtually every successful small business owner we know has adopted a work schedule that provides them time to have a life. And it doesn't seem like a particularly lazy or pampered group—these people seem to reflect an important entrepreneurial truth: In fat or lean economic times, the ability to create a business that effectively and profitably meets the needs of its customers, not the determination to work long hours, is the key to success.

Interestingly, many successful people say that although they do not put in six 13-hour days every week, that doesn't mean business isn't on their minds. Several report coming up with their best, most creative business ideas when they're swimming laps, tossing a Frisbee to the dog, or just taking a walk—away from the emails, phone calls, meetings, and other distractions that crowd days at the office, store, or factory. One friend puts it like this, "Busy work—doing any one of thousands of little tasks at the office—doesn't improve anything important about how my business operates, certainly not its profitability. Just the opposite. To have time to focus on important initiatives—most importantly, how to better meet the needs of my customers—I must take the time to think, something I simply can't do well when I'm tired."

Don't Get Lazy

Although working too hard is the more common situation, the flip side—working too little—can also lead to problems. If during earlier times you got used to being comfortably solvent, you might have transformed from hard-working ant to showboating butterfly almost without realizing it. Now that your business has hit a rough patch, what do you do?

It is easy to understand why you wanted to take a little time to flit among the flowers, golf balls, sailboats, or motorcycles. But understandable or not, going walkabout for any extended period is always a mistake. Few, if any, of your employees who have worked so hard to help your business succeed will have a similar opportunity, and many will almost surely resent you. And especially during hard times, you're courting disaster if you withhold your attention at the same time key employees become disaffected.

If you no longer want to stay involved in the day-to-day management of your successful business, you may be able to reduce your managerial role by delegating, while concentrating on another important part of your business, such as new product development. But if there really is no part of your business that truly interests and engages you, your best bet is to sell it. That way, you allow the business to move under committed new leadership that's prepared to act quickly in tough times, while you have the freedom to do other things. Later, if you want to recommit to being a business owner, you'll have the financial wherewithal to start fresh.

Keeping Your Priorities Straight

Ask retired businesspeople you admire to tell you what they learned about keeping work, family, and personal time in perspective, and one thing you probably will not hear is, "If I had to do it all over again, I would have worked lots more hours." It's far more likely that they'll advise you to spend more of your life's energy developing personal interests, protecting your health, and spending time with family and friends. Of course, when a business is hit by a large negative event, be it a hurricane, fire, or recession, it's often necessary to work longer hours, sometimes much longer hours, to surmount the crisis. Fine, as long as you are working extra hours as part of a sensible, goal-driven plan to get the business back on its feet.

Another way to think about how to fit your work into the type of life you would like to lead is to make a list of the things you really care about. For many people, it would look something like this:

- stay close to our families
- have time to share family responsibilities and spend happy time with our spouses
- spend time on personal interests (and develop new ones)
- stay physically active and otherwise protect our health
- spend time with friends, and
- do work we enjoy and that pays well enough to adequately help support our families.

Assuming your list is even a little like this, it's crucial to notice that work is only one item. And once you do, it should be easy to see why working so many hours that you leave inadequate time for other priorities is a poor way to lead your life over the long term. Of course, if work, work, and even more work were the only way to ward off starvation or keep a roof over your head, it might be your only choice. But in 21st-century America—even in periods of sharp recession—there are a huge number of entrepreneurial opportunities. Don't become so obsessed trying to save a loss-making enterprise that you fail to see that other opportunities abound.

How to Work Less and Make More

If you already work too many hours and don't have enough black ink on your balance sheet to justify it, how can you cut back without risking financial disaster? Reading this in the middle an economic meltdown, you can be forgiven if you are thinking that it would be easier to find a unicorn in the back yard. Not so. If, unlike most small business owners, you take the time to truly understand the power of delegation, you can simultaneously cut your hours, improve your productivity, and possibly even increase profits.

The Power of Delegation

At the Acme Sandblasting Co., the New York City company Ralph's grandfather Frank "Stuke" Toors owned and ran during most of the first half of the last century, Stuke personally knew how to do almost every job in the business. He could make cost estimates for jobs, close a deal, machine a spare part, splice a rope, write payroll checks, and even collect overdue bills. A few days before he finally retired at 75, Stuke shed his three-piece suit, donned a respirator and some work clothes, and climbed a scaffold to prove he could still blast grime off a big expanse of granite.

Stuke was typical of the jack-of-all-trades American businessman whose heyday lasted from the end of the Civil War through World War II. In a far less bureaucratic, rule-bound, and technologically sophisticated world, these people really could cost-efficiently do a great many tasks themselves. Although it should be obvious in our hyperspecialized world this is no longer true, huge numbers of entrepreneurs work horrendous hours, still trying to run and control every aspect of their business. By doing so, they risk both exhausting themselves and ruining their business.

Since at least 1776, when Adam Smith famously noted in *The Wealth of Nations* that a group of people each specializing in one aspect of pin production could make far more pins in a day than could the same number of people each making whole pins, the principle of the division of labor has been well established as a huge engine of increased productivity. Even when times are tough and money is scarce, there is almost always a specialist who can accomplish all but your most core entrepreneurial tasks better, and ultimately cheaper, than you can. One good example involves preparing the payroll, something that for a modest fee you probably can farm out to a highly automated specialist, largely freeing you from the time-consuming task Ralph's grandfather performed every other Friday afternoon.

Delegation by Trading

Sometimes, you can delegate without spending money—instead, you can trade your surplus services or goods for those you need. For example, Margaret might help Jeremy with marketing in exchange for getting to share his office and equipment. One-to-one barter arrangements can be complicated to establish and sustain, but they come into vogue when cash is tight. If you engage in a barter with someone, be sure both you and the other party benefit from the deal enough that you'll both hang in over time, and write your agreement down in the form of a simple contract.

Online bartering exchanges let you barter your goods or services for "trade credits," which you can then use to buy other goods or services. Bartering has become a way to cover necessary expenses without using cash. For example, a refrigeration specialist who is having trouble moving inventory sells a display case to a florist for $3,000. The florist, who doesn't have the cash to replace her faulty old display case, pays with trade credits she earned from her bartering exchange. The refrigeration specialist gains $3,000 worth of trade credits that he can then use to pay for services from other companies, such as tax preparation or website design.

Many barter exchanges have spring up over the last few years. Three of the better known ones are bizx.com (BizXchange), bbu.com (Better Barter Unlimited), and greenapplebarter.com (Green Apple Barter).

Of course, it costs money to hire others to do routine tasks. But sensible delegation frees up your time so you can concentrate on the high-value aspects of your business including, especially, new product development and marketing, which will produce much higher profits in the long run. If, for even a moment, you doubt the wisdom of working with others, consider that without the phone company, your Internet service provider, and package delivery services, you would probably need to spend every waking hour just trying to deliver essential messages. Fortunately, because these companies are at our beck and call for a very reasonable cost, you can efficiently delegate your communications tasks for a fraction of what it would cost to personally deliver your messages.

Unfortunately, when it comes to many other business tasks—from bookkeeping to equipment maintenance and repair to graphic design to human resources management—the wisdom of delegation is less well understood. That's a big reason why so many Americans persist in wrongly believing long hours and high profits go together. People who work overlong hours often do so because they fail to grasp the crucial difference between routine work and high-value work. But what if you have so little income you can't possibly afford to delegate even the most time-consuming tasks to others? If you need to handle every routine task yourself, what you have is a bad job, not a good business.

EXAMPLE: Jeff is an architect whose firm, J&D Associates, designs big buildings such as schools and hospitals. Although he is a gifted draftsman, Jeff's real skill is selling potential customers the idea that they are in great hands with J&D. But when the recession hits and two of J&D's big projects are put on hold, Jeff begins spending his weekends and evenings in front of his computer anxiously helping do the design work for several new bids.

Fortunately, his partner Dale, a more introverted type who enjoys running the office side of the business, is smart enough to say "Get the hell out of the office. Even if we have to mortgage my house to hire another draftsperson, one thing is sure—if you don't focus all your energy on sales, we have no chance to survive."

What Do You Do Best?

Before you can delegate well, you need to understand the things you do that contribute the most black ink to your bottom line. Only then can you aggressively look for ways to get someone else to do the other bits. So your first step is to identify the tasks you must really do yourself, as opposed to those you handle either because no one else is available, you believe you can't afford to hire help, or for some other less-than-convincing reason. For example, if you are a website designer, and customers are attracted to your small design company because of your imaginative graphics skills, it makes sense for you to concentrate on the creative process. Even if money is tight, pay someone else to renegotiate the lease or collect past due debts—things that are important, but not critical to your long-term success.

How to Delegate

Many small business owners readily agree they need to learn to delegate tasks that someone else could do better. Nevertheless, they put it off. For example, one man who puts in 12-hour days at his Internet-based sports memorabilia business, whose wife had recently threatened him with divorce, came up to Ralph after he made a luncheon presentation and said, "I know I need to cut back, but I just can't spare a dime to hire help right now. How do I start?" Here's what Ralph told him.

There are two keys to making a delegation plan work. First, you need to find people who can do the necessary tasks better than you can. As long as you understand the basic point that productivity increases and costs drop when work is divided into a series of specialized tasks and assigned to people with access to state-of-the-art technology, you'll see that this shouldn't be difficult. No question, if you are a perfectionist who has trouble letting go of even the simplest tasks, learning to delegate can be a big hurdle. But perhaps it will help get you started if you are able to concede that there really are people in the world at least as competent and careful as you are. And this is just as true if you are delegating routine office tasks or work that is crucial to your business's success, such as making important sales calls.

The second key to profiting from delegation is to put at least some of the time you save into more profitable activities. For example, if finding new clients for your financial planning service is the activity that will most positively affect your bottom line and you have excellent rainmaking skills, you'll want to delegate as many routine tasks, such as bookkeeping, as possible, and use the time you save to find customers. That way you win three times: revenue goes up, the jobs you delegate get done better, and your total work hours might even go down.

EXAMPLE: Tina runs East Mountain, a rural yoga center that offers classes and retreats. Like many small business owners, Tina is stretched too thin, trying to deal with the workaday details of running the business and at the same time spend enough time with guests and teaching classes. But she's always thought she couldn't afford to hire help. Finally, realizing that something has to give, Tina makes two lists: one of the time-consuming tasks that wear her out without making much difference to East Mountain's success, and another of the tasks that attract clients. The routine jobs include meal preparation, bookkeeping, and designing promotional materials. The ones most important to customer satisfaction are teaching excellent, innovative yoga classes and spreading the word about East Mountain's unique programs.

Tina's next step is to find good people to do the non-core tasks at a reasonable price. Because she is in a rural area with endemic unemployment, it proves relatively cheap to find experienced independent contractors to take over the bookkeeping and brochure design. But hiring someone for all the meal preparation turns out to be prohibitively expensive. Instead, Tina decides to hire a cook to coordinate dinners only, relying on workshop participants willing to trade work for a tuition reduction to prepare East Mountain's simple breakfast and lunch. To cover the additional cost, Tina decides to devote one-third of the hours she saves to teaching two more classes per week and the other two-thirds to marketing.

Tina's new marketing efforts include writing a blog and articles for interested media, preparing press packages highlighting East Mountain's new and noteworthy offerings, and using email, regular mail, and the occasional phone call to stay in touch with former students, yoga teachers, and others in the yoga network. As a result, business increases by 40%. This lets Tina raise her rates by 25%, and East Mountain is more than able to cover its additional labor costs. Best of all, Tina can now afford to hire a part-time, yoga-loving publicist to help with the routine aspects of her marketing program, freeing Tina to take the occasional nap.

Work With Your Best Competitors

"The trouble with the rat race is that even if you win, you're still a rat."
LILY TOMLIN

Your spouse, best friend, and nosiest brother-in-law—combined—probably don't know your business as well as your closest competitors do. Whether you import spices, silkscreen T-shirts, set tile, run a gymnastics school, or paint nails, the entrepreneurs who vie with you for business will closely track your successes and failures. Given that you often compete with them for customers, deal with the same suppliers, and promote your businesses in similar ways, you couldn't ignore them if you tried.

Competitors will also play a significant role in defining your business reputation. If you set a high standard (the kids in your gymnastics classes love what they do and frequently win regional competitions), you will inevitably earn the respect of others in your field. They may even have to change the way they operate to better compete with your successful example. On the other hand, if you run a slipshod business, your competitors will almost surely enjoy mocking your efforts.

To fully grasp how important earning the respect of your competitors can be, talk to any established local businessperson in a competitive field, such as a doctor, house painter, or copy shop owner. Ask the person to accurately rank the business's closest competitors by competence, integrity, cost, timeliness, and other significant factors. Almost any businessperson will have no trouble doing it blindfolded. In fact, peer-based evaluation systems tend to be so accurate they are often used as a rating methodology by academics, consumer groups, and others. For example, the editors of the book *America's Top Doctors*, by Castle Connolly Medical Ltd., start their rating process by asking tens of thousands of American doctors a very simple question, "To which doctors would you send a member of your family?" Nominees are then separated by specialty and again rated, this time by teams of doctors in each major geographical area.

Even if you agree that your competitors are likely to know a lot about your business, you might still not see why you should embrace them, especially when times are tough. Traditional small business wisdom, after all, teaches that you should be wary of your rivals; you may even be coached to do everything in your power to drive them out of business. Much of the rest of this chapter explains not only why this scorched-earth approach is wrong, but also why, when most businesses are struggling, a kinder, gentler approach is far more likely to benefit your business and make your personal life more pleasant. It could even save your business.

Treat Competitors With Respect

In large business, it's at least theoretically possible for one corporation to play hardball so successfully that it largely destroys its competitors. From the Standard Oil Trust of the early 20th century, through mid-20th century category-killers such as IBM, Sears, and General Motors, to 21st-century Microsoft and Google, there are many examples of monopoly-building corporate strategies that have produced huge profits, at least until government antitrust regulators or rapidly changing technologies produced new competitors.

The rules are different in the small business world. With lots of providers in most fields, it's rarely possible for one company to dominate. Leaving aside the fact that to do so would mean that a small business would have to grow large (something that most small entrepreneurs don't want anyway), there are a variety of reasons why a local plumber, Chinese restaurant, T-shirt printer, or tax preparer can't monopolize its market. One big reason is location. Customers often choose these businesses precisely because they are nearby. That makes it hard for a big centralized operator with one or two megastores to completely take over as long as the small operators find ways to stay close to their customers and provide specialized service—for example, a hardware store that opens two hours earlier than a big competitor or a grocery store that stocks local foods.

Price competition is another big barrier, especially among service businesses, which all have similar labor costs. For example, if ClipMe, a local haircutting salon, suddenly slashes prices in half, chances are that every other budget hair stylist in town will quickly realize that survival depends on matching or beating ClipMe's prices. The likely result will be that ClipMe's initial increase in volume will dry up, and its owner, learning that in most instances no one wins a small service business price war, will put prices back to their former levels. Similarly, if Ready T-Shirt announces that it plans to move from a storefront to a large warehouse, install high-speed silk-screening equipment, and embark on an expensive advertising blitz, its local competitors, Graphic Attack, T-Shirt Express, and T-Top are almost sure to spot the danger early and move to counter it. They may lower prices even before Ready T-Shirt makes its move, forcing Ready to similarly drop its prices—and lose the profit margins necessary to justify an expansion loan.

Your Competitors, Your Friends

With some exceptions, most small business owners who succeed do so in sig-nificant part because they like what they do. The truly fortunate among them create a vocation as well as a business. Examples come to mind easily: Ann, who gives Ralph's softball-mad granddaughter pitching lessons; Antonio, who owns and runs an excellent Italian deli; and Laurie, who owns a popular yoga studio. Without exception, these men and women not only operate profitable businesses, they enjoy and care about what they do. How can you tell? Everything they do—including getting to know their customers—makes it easy to see how deeply each is committed to his or her business and the people it serves.

So here's a key question you might never have answered: Assuming there are good people like these in your chosen field, who better to be on good terms with, especially in tough times when there may not be enough business to support all local providers? After all, in our big, fast, anonymous world, you are almost sure to have much in common with people who have somehow been drawn to do the same work as you do, in the same place, and at the same time. Except for the fact you see yourself scrapping with these people for your daily bread, at least some might well turn out to be your friends, if not soul mates.

So being seen by your small business competitors as running an efficient, ambitious, and even highly competitive small business is positive, but being regarded as an unfair competitor or business predator is almost sure to be counterproductive. It's important to realize that in this context it's often what you say as much as what you do that influences how others regard you. For instance, the president of one of Nolo's competitors once bragged to a prominent journalist, "Nolo is history." The marketing director of another competitor loudly proclaimed at an industry trade show, "We'll bury Nolo." Although in both instances these executives may have been as guilty of hyperbole as they were of a real plan to flatten Nolo, we have ever since been extremely wary of both outfits.

Getting Business From Competitors

By their very size, small businesses are significantly limited in the amount of work they can handle during any given period. A busy dentist, who on average treats 80 people per week, has a very restricted ability to increase these numbers. If too many patients call in too short a time, some will have to be put off until later or, especially in the case of new patients, referred to another dentist.

Of course, it's not only a work overload that leads one small business owner to refer customers to a competitor. In an age of increased specialization, the exact specifications of the task often play a huge role in a businessperson's decision to accept work or refer it to someone else. For example, Bill's Pruning may prefer to handle high-volume jobs on hedges and small trees up to 30 feet, while sending more complicated and potentially dangerous tall tree jobs to Way-Up Tree Care, which as its name implies, specializes in caring for sky-huggers. True, the two companies compete to trim medium-sized trees and, in periods where business is in short supply, may further invade each other's vertical space. But most often they find mutual advantage in referring customers back and forth to fit each other's preferred customer profile.

Every busy small business at least occasionally refers customers to its competitors, if for no other reason than to be able to meet the needs of its established customers. True, referring an existing or potential customer to a high-quality competitor means you run the risk that the person might never come back. But making a good referral is less problematic than simply turning the customer away. And it's certainly better than recommending a marginal business—that is likely to leave the customer disappointed both by the service received and the bad steer you provided.

EXAMPLE: Millie, a regular customer of the Pour Vous' catering company, recommends the company to Jeannie, who is helping plan her daughter's wedding. When Jeannie calls Pour Vous, it's already fully booked for the date of the wedding, so Jeannie asks Tad, Pour Vous' owner, to recommend another caterer. A savvy businessperson, Tad knows that Pour Vous has a lot riding on the success of his recommendation. If Jeannie is satisfied by the caterer he suggests, Millie and probably others Jeannie talks to will hear about it. But if the second caterer turns out to be a bust, Jeannie will let Millie know, and at least some of the discredit is sure to rub off on Pour Vous. So Tad recommends Good Hands, a business he considers thoroughly reliable.

A few days later he calls Deb, Good Hands' owner, to be sure she realizes where the referral came from. Fortunately, Good Hands lives up to its name, and a pleased Jeannie tells Pour Vous' longtime customer Millie how well the referral worked out. As a result, Millie emails Tad her thanks and asks him to begin planning to cater the big Christmas party.

A year later, when a recession hits and both businesses and individuals cut way back on parties, many local caterers, including Pour Vous and Good Hands, feel the economic pain. But based on mutual respect and the success of a number of back-and-forth referrals like the one to Jeannie, Good Hands and Pour Vous decide to combine some of their operations, including an office, trucks, and catering staff. For now at least, the businesses will remain independently owned and operated, but sharing costly overhead will allow each to survive until business picks up.

Working for Your Competitors

In many fields, it's common for independent businesspeople to work at least part time for one another. This is especially likely when a business is in the start-up phase. A freshly minted CPA who opens her own tax preparation service and has a short roster of clients might contact several established accounting firms to see whether part-time work is available during the tax season rush. Or a carpet installer might work two days a week for a floor covering megastore, while devoting the other three to establishing an independent carpet-laying service.

To make these sorts of relationships work typically takes patience, discretion, and good judgment by everyone involved, but particularly on the part of the new entrepreneur who, after all, is in the weaker bargaining position. Until proven otherwise, the established businessperson is likely to worry that the upstart might try to steal customers or clients. This explains why the independent businessperson is often asked to handle only the bits and pieces of jobs that require little or no customer contact.

But if, over time, the newbie is smart enough to demonstrate that he or she is not a client poacher, the established business's defensive attitude will typically relax. The established business may even begin sending the new business some of the very same accounts it was initially protective of. Although this behavior—first paranoid, then generous—might strike you as bizarre, in fact it makes sense. That's because by the time the referral actually takes place, the established business owner has had ample time to judge the upstart's work and character. Assuming both prove solid—and given the new entrepreneur's clear determination to establish her own business—the established business owner may sensibly conclude that over the long term it will be more beneficial to maintain cordial and cooperative relations than to compete tooth and claw.

Working With Your Competitors

When a recession hits and business declines, many small businesses fail because overhead costs gobble up such a high percentage of their income that no profit is possible. For example, assume Jen's financial planning business loses one-third of its clients as recession-shocked customers pull out of the stock market. The result is that when Jen subtracts her rent, salary for her part-time receptionist, utilities, office cleaning expenses, and so on, she is making less than $15 per hour. Then when two wealthy clients move all their money to Treasuries and fire Jen, she is suddenly working for nothing at all.

Jen and other service providers, from caterers and barbers to car mechanics and tax preparers, who face a similar business meltdown must either quickly reduce overhead so as to be able to ride out the recession with reduced income—or close down.

One of the best ways to lower overhead expenses is to combine operations with another high-quality business. For instance, if Jen started to share her office and receptionist with another similar business, she would immediately be back in the black, something that could give her enough time to increase marketing efforts designed to reconnect with former clients and find new ones.

The keys to making an arrangement like this work are trust and respect. For example, two small metal bending shops whose owners have known and liked each other for years might be able to operate out of the same facility. People who regard each other as unfair competitors never will.

EXAMPLE: When the economic downturn hits, there are five nail salons in a city neighborhood. Salon #1 is bigger, better financed, and more successful than the others. Salon #5 is a recent start-up that hasn't yet developed a loyal clientele. The other three are more or less indistinguishable storefronts whose owners work hard for a modest profit. After three months of declining business, Min, the owner of salon #2, decides that if her business is to survive, she needs to do something fairly radical.

So she visits her distant cousin Lai, who owns salon #4, with a proposal. Since Lai's lease is up, why not combine operations in Min's salon? The businesses would operate independently, with signage, invoices, and licenses making this clear. But by operating out of one facility with shared rent and receptionist, and lending technicians back and forth, each business could make a small profit. It works. And that small profit even grows somewhat when salons #3 and #5 close due to slow business and high overhead.

RESOURCE

More on combining resources. *The Sharing Solution*, by Janelle Orsi and Emily Doskow (Nolo), offers some great ideas for businesses interested in sharing space and equipment with other businesses.

Of course it's also possible to formally merge two or more businesses into one legal entity. But unless one business can afford to buy the other, this strategy is almost always problematic. That's because in addition to establishing a limited liability company or small corporation, assets must be valued, and owners who are used to running their own show must agree on how to jointly run the merged business. In our experience, this is difficult in normal economic times—and almost impossible when businesses are under economic pressure and their owners are stressed and short of funds. ●

How to Close Down Your Business

"When the horse dies, get off."

KINKY FRIEDMAN

Especially if you can't make required tax payments or are slipping behind on your house or car payments, chances are you are past the point where trimming expenses or adopting a clever marketing campaign will salvage your business. If you conclude that there's little or no chance of getting back in the black anytime soon, it may be time to cease operations, pay off as many debts as possible, and close down in an orderly fashion, before your creditors force you to do it.

It can take months to wind up a business properly. You need to come up with a plan that will offer the most protection possible to your personal assets, your credit, and your reputation in the community—and to those of your spouse, cosigners, and lenders. If you simply close down and let the pieces fall where they may, you could end up haunted by unnecessary headaches, lawsuits, and debts.

A proper shut-down process will give your creditors and customers clear notice of your business's closure, an important step toward limiting the amount of time you may be subjected to lawsuits. Take your time even announcing your decision to close. The order in which you notify people of your intention to quit business can greatly affect your ability to make the most of your last weeks or months. The sequence of the closing steps in this chapter is not fixed, and many of them will overlap—arrange the steps in a way that makes sense for your business. For instance, if your restaurant needs goods from your main supplier until the end, wait until the last week to let it know of your closure.

This chapter gives an overview of the closing-down process. But every business is different. It's almost always a good idea to get individualized advice from a lawyer, accountant, or tax expert along the way.

CROSS-REFERENCE

Should you file for bankruptcy? The majority of small business owners can wind up their business affairs without filing for bankruptcy. But if you have many creditors and a heavy debt load, bankruptcy may be your best, or only, option.

Chapter 13 discusses bankruptcy and other ways to deal with significant debt. If you do file for bankruptcy, it will be your first step in the closing process; the rest of the steps discussed below will follow, shaped by the bankruptcy process.

Closing a Business: What You'll Need to Do

- Create a closing team.
- Look at your contractual obligations.
- Deal with your landlord.
- Collect bills and sell off inventory.
- Notify and pay your employees.
- Liquidate all business assets in an orderly fashion.
- Notify customers and creditors.
- Prioritize your debts and pay them to the extent possible.
- Pay your taxes and file final tax returns.
- If your business is an LLC, corporation, or partnership, dissolve your legal entity.
- Cancel permits, licenses, and fictitious business names.
- After debts are paid, distribute any assets remaining to yourself and other owners.

Create a Closing Team

It will make the closing process smoother if you can get advice from people who've been through this before, especially if yours is a complicated situation with a long list of creditors. It's possible that your existing advisory board will have the requisite experience, but if not, try to add someone who does.

You'll probably also need to hire some experts. A business attorney who's been through business closings can be a huge help in dealing with recalcitrant landlords and other creditors. In addition, consulting an attorney can alert you to any potential liabilities you haven't considered or any steps you might omit. Even more important may be seeking the advice of an accountant or tax expert, who can advise you on the tax consequences of selling assets, the various tax forms you'll need to file, and ways to take advantage of your business losses for tax purposes.

Look at Your Contractual Obligations

An important part of ending any business consists of examining all of your contractual commitments, with the goal of either fulfilling them or negotiating a termination. That way your business ends cleanly, with no danger of being sued for unfulfilled contracts.

If you can complete your contractual commitments, do it—it's the best way to avoid future hassles. For example, a furniture reupholsterer might sensibly plan to complete all the jobs in his shop, while not taking any new ones.

If you have signed a long-term contract for ongoing performance of work or delivery of goods that you simply can't complete, check first to see whether the contract has a cancellation provision. If it's reasonable (for instance, you have to pay an early termination fee, or "liquidated damages," of $300 to cancel a $15,000 contract), exercise it. If not, call the other party, explain that you are going out of business, and ask whether they would like to end the contract. This will often be possible, especially if you can suggest another quality provider willing to complete the work for the same price. If the other party asks for a payment in exchange for a written termination agreement, don't pay much. Instead, consider having a lawyer call the other party to negotiate. When you do arrive at an agreement to end the contract, get it in writing.

EXAMPLE: Talia and Aaron run Blue Egg Web Design, which designs and builds websites for local small businesses. In January, Blue Egg signs a contract to build a small e-commerce website for a local sporting goods store. The contract states that Blue Egg will deliver a completed website by August for $15,000. In February, the economy takes a turn for the worse, and Blue Egg's main client goes out of business, meaning that Blue Egg loses a maintenance contract that paid $3,000 per month. Without that business, Blue Egg will have trouble paying the rent.

Aaron and Talia, now expecting a baby, decide that Aaron has to get a stable, well-paying job while Talia is off work. They decide to close down Blue Egg and tell the sporting goods store they won't be able to complete the contract. Their contract calls for a refund of any payments made to Blue Egg for work not performed but doesn't say anything about what happens if Blue Egg doesn't complete the contract. Fortunately, Aaron and Talia know the principals of an excellent Web design firm, Fluid Web, and recommend them to the sporting goods store. Fluid Web signs a contract with the sporting goods store, which then releases Blue Egg from the contract after Blue Egg returns the sporting good store's first payment.

Deal With Your Landlord

If you've been renting space, that's probably a big expense for your business —one you want to take care of. Your options depend on whether you're a month-to-month tenant or have a lease for a certain period of time.

If you have been renting month to month, give your landlord written notice to that you're terminating your agreement. You'll probably have to give 30 days' notice, but some commercial leases require 60 to 90 days. Check your agreement.

If you have a long-term lease, you will be liable for any rent payments for the remainder of the lease. Depending on your state's law, however, your landlord may have a legal duty to reduce (mitigate) his losses by looking for a new tenant. That's something you might be able to help with, to lessen the chance that you'll be liable for paying those remaining months. If the landlord can rerent the place for the same amount (or more) than you pay, you are off the hook for the rent (but the landlord can charge you for the time the space was vacant, plus costs of rerenting the place). If the landlord is not able to rerent the place with reasonable effort, however, you will be on the hook for the rent for the remainder of the lease.

You might be able to negotiate a lease termination in exchange for paying several months' rent up-front. Your landlord will probably be happy to arrive at a negotiated solution rather than having to chase you down for the money or risk that you'll file for bankruptcy.

If you paid a security deposit, ask your landlord to inspect the premises with you well before you vacate, so that you can deal with all issues and possible misunderstandings that could keep you from getting your whole deposit back promptly. Especially if you have rented premises for some time, you shouldn't be charged for normal wear and tear—for example, if, after several years, the walls need repainting or the carpet should be replaced.

TIP

Prepare an inspection checklist. It can be a good idea to prepare a one-page list of the premises' main features—walls, floors, windows, and so on. As part of your walk-through with the landlord, ask the landlord to check off all features that are in good shape before signing the form. Nolo offers a downloadable form, the Landlord-Tenant Checklist, available on nolo.com.

RESOURCE

More information on commercial leases. See *Negotiate the Best Lease for Your Business*, by Janet Portman and Fred Steingold (Nolo).

Collect Bills and Sell Off Inventory

Now is the time to try to collect money owed to you and to get rid of all remaining inventory. Here are some tactics.

Collect Accounts Receivable

Before you send out a general notification that you're going out of business, do your best to collect money that's owed to you. Don't wait—it's much harder, and sometimes impossible, to collect accounts receivable after you've ceased operations. Companies and customers—who may themselves be strapped for cash—who owe you money will have far less incentive to pay once they find out you're no longer going to be providing them with goods and services. (For tips on how to collect receivables, including offering discounts for prompt payments, see Chapter 3.)

Sell as Much Inventory as Possible

If your business has excess inventory, it's time for a big sale. If you aren't yet ready to tell employees and suppliers about your plan to close, you may want to start with a "Blow-Out Sale" and announce you are going out of business only during your last week or two, further discounting prices then.

Especially if you are a retailer with deep roots in your community, a going-out-of-business sale may be a big event, a chance to recoup some of the money you've lost in recent months. To do this, in the early days of the sale, consider restocking just the popular items that you know you can sell at modest but still profitable markups.

If, after you've publicly announced your closing and had your going-out-of-business sale, you still have more inventory than you can possibly sell, consider using websites like eBay and craigslist to sell the excess. A last resort is to sell surplus inventory by the pallet or truckload at a site such as liquidation.com, or to consider contacting a liquidator or discount outlet, which will often buy surplus inventory in bulk for pennies on the dollar.

Notify and Pay Your Employees

If your business had employees, you've probably had to lay off some of them already. If not, now's the time to lay off all but the people you'll need for the next few weeks or months to help wind down the business. In particular, it is helpful if you can keep employees who have worked in the finance or bookkeeping area to help wind up the business—especially if they may know more about the business's finances and accounting procedures than you do.

You could—and some employers do—simply wait until the last day of operations to notify the employees of the business's closing, to avoid a premature exodus. (Obviously, this isn't an option if you're a retail business and have been having a going-out-of-business sale.) But it's usually unwise, especially when it will take months to close down your business and you'll need to take a number of steps that will surely alert employees. Especially if you plan to make some layoffs before others, it's usually best to 'fess up to what's going on sooner, when you need to make the first layoffs. Then consider incentivizing the essential people to stay, by committing to pay them a small bonus for hanging in there until the last day.

For more about laying off employees—including legal rules about advance notice, final paychecks, and some thoughts about severance pay—see Chapter 9.

Liquidate the Business's Assets

Your next step is to turn your remaining business assets, such as office equipment, tools, and furniture, into cash to pay your creditors—or in a best-case scenario, to put in your pocket.

Identify the Assets

Make a list of the physical property your business owns, as well as any money owed to the business in the form of rent, security deposits, and unpaid bills you expect to collect. Your list should include:

- business equipment, such as computers, phones, cash registers, and credit card machines
- office furniture, art, and supplies
- vehicles
- real estate
- security deposits with landlords, utilities, or taxing agencies, and
- prepaid insurance premiums you can get refunded to you.

For your records, write down a description of each item or category of property, the condition of the property, and who owns it—that is, what money was used to purchase the property—personal or business funds. In addition, you'll want to list how you tried to sell it (save copies of ads or Web listings) and the amount you received. This list not only will help you conduct your liquidation process, but also, keeping good records of your property and what happens to it will protect you in case a creditor later questions your liquidation of assets or in case you have to file for bankruptcy. You will also need this information for your tax returns.

In addition to tangible property, you may be able to sell intangible property that your business owns, such as:

- a commercial lease at below-market rent or at a super location (but you'll probably need the permission of your landlord)
- contracts with suppliers at below-market rates
- contracts with customers at profitable rates (you may need your customers' permission)
- works in progress that could have some value
- your customer list and your company name (essentially, the goodwill your company has built up)
- intellectual property such as copyrights, patents, and trademarks, and
- remaining accounts receivable.

Deal Separately With Secured and Leased Assets

Set aside assets that you have pledged as collateral for a debt or loan. You cannot sell them without the permission of the creditor; selling loan collateral is fraudulent and may be punishable as a crime. You'll need to speak to the creditor about how to handle the collateral—whether you will give it back as is or sell it with the creditor's permission, giving the proceeds to the creditor.

Likewise, leased property belongs to the lessor, not to you. Your main options are to return the property or assign the lease contract to someone else (the lessor will usually have the right to refuse an assignment, however). For more information on settling the amount you owe on secured or leased assets, see "Pay Your Debts," below.

Find Buyers for Assets You Own

Next you'll want to find buyers for property that is fully paid for and that you have not pledged as collateral for another loan. Use your industry contacts, including appropriate suppliers and competitors. Competitors may also be interested in buying your intellectual property (trademarks, copyrights, and patents) and any works in progress, as well as your customer lists and company name or product names.

You might find buyers for fixtures, furniture, and equipment by listing them on websites like eBay, craigslist, or bid4assets.com. Also search for websites that specialize in auctions for your industry; there are sites that specialize in restaurant equipment, industrial machinery, high-tech equipment, construction equipment, and so on. Contacting a business broker or professional liquidator can be a good idea if you have numerous assets with significant value.

Again, don't forget that while accounts receivable are valuable now, they will be much less valuable after you close. So make a high-energy effort to collect them. Or, as discussed in Chapter 3, transfer high-quality accounts receivable to a factor, or debt buyer, who, for a fee, will pay you a certain percentage of the debt up front and the rest when they collect it.

> **TIP**
>
> **Don't cheat your creditors.** Do what you can to get a good price for your business assets—not just for yourself, but because you have a legal responsibility to your creditors to try to get fair market value for your assets. In particular, the directors and officers of an insolvent corporation or LLC (one whose assets are worth less than its liabilities) have a statutory duty to minimize losses to the company's creditors. But no matter how your business is organized, you commit fraud if you give away or sell business assets at below market rates or put your interests ahead of those of creditors. In other words, forget about selling assets cheaply and pocketing the cash or giving assets to friends or family.

Get Prepaid Insurance Premiums Refunded

Request refunds on your workers' compensation premiums and liability insurance premiums, if your policies' terms allow it. Because businesses pay workers' comp premiums in advance based on payroll estimates, workers' comp carriers are accustomed to adjusting accounts each year to return overpaid money, and you should get a refund without a problem. With liability insurance, whether you'll get a refund depends on the terms of your policy.

Notify Creditors and Customers

You need to notify the people and businesses you've relied on—banks, insurers, big customers, and so on—that you're closing. In some instances this is a legal requirement; in others, you are required to by contract, and in all, it's of matter of good business practice.

Secured Creditors

If you owe a debt that's secured by collateral, such as a vehicle or equipment, let the creditor know you'll no longer be needing the item. If you used the loan to buy the collateral, find out how you can return it. For example, if you were still making payments on a loan for your company car, you could voluntarily surrender the vehicle to the lender or you could sell the vehicle and give the lender the proceeds. If you are going to try to sell a vehicle, check with the lender to find out its procedures to get the lien released on your vehicle—most lenders won't release the vehicle without money in hand, so this may require both you and the buyer going to the lender to pay off the loan.

Even after you turn over a secured asset or the proceeds from selling it, there may be a deficiency, meaning that you owe the difference between what the property was sold for and what you owed on it. Before you turn over the property or sales proceeds, try to negotiate with the creditor to give you a signed release that you will no longer owe money or the debt. Selling the property rather than voluntarily surrendering it may decrease your chance of owing a deficiency on the loan.

Lenders

If you have a bank loan or line of credit, your bank may call the entire loan in immediately, or will at least want to know how you plan on paying it off. Your loan agreement may give your bank the right to deduct from your business bank account any amount you owe at any time—this is called a right to setoff. So if your business account is at the same bank (which most loan agreements require), don't be surprised to find money taken out of it soon after your bank learns your business will be closing. If there are debts you'd rather pay before paying off your loan, such as payroll taxes or other personally guaranteed debts, be sure to do it before notifying the bank of your impending closure.

If the bank has a security interest in some of your business assets or in your accounts receivable, it may grab this collateral. If not, it might at least want to examine it (and your financial statements) to be sure it's both physically secure and of sufficient value to cover your debt, should you not be able to repay it.

Service Providers

Service providers, such as utilities and payroll preparers, will want to know the final day you'll require services and how to collect their final bill. Provide this information at least a few days before you cease operations so as not to be charged for extra days. But if you signed any long-term contracts with service providers, such as credit card processors and payroll providers, try to give as much notice of the cancellation as possible to try to avoid any early termination fees. Also, if you have made any deposits with utility companies, find out how to get them back.

Insurance Carriers

Before you tell your liability insurance carrier to cancel your policy because you are going out of business, read through the terms of your policy to determine whether it covers past acts or whether you'll need to keep it in force for a year or two in case you are sued. If there is a pending legal threat or even a whisper that you might be sued, speak to the insurance company about it—hiding issues when winding up coverage can cause your coverage to fail if you are subsequently sued.

If you find you don't need to keep your liability policy active, the best way to cancel it is to send a written request, by certified mail, return receipt requested. If you think you're entitled to a refund on your premium, ask that it be sent to you and give an address where you can be reached after your business closes.

Cancel other types of policies such as car insurance and workers' compensation if you haven't already.

Suppliers and Other Unsecured Creditors

Suppliers who provide you with inventory or materials will want to know when the last delivery should be made, whether you're returning any goods, and when and how they'll get paid for goods they've supplied. If you want to continue to receive supplies until you close your doors, wait until the last week to let suppliers know of your impending closure. Obviously, don't be ordering anything unless you know you can pay for it!

When you decide it's time to let your suppliers and unsecured creditors know of your closure, send them a certified letter saying that you will be closing your business and are requesting claims for payment—in other words, final bills.

Special State Rules

If your business is in retail, wholesale, or manufacturing, in California, Virginia, Georgia, Maryland, Wisconsin, or DC, you need to also comply with your state's bulk sales law. (This law applies to corporations, LLCs, partnerships, and sole proprietors alike.) This law requires you to notify your creditors a specific number of days before you close your business, and in some states, to publish a notice of your impending closure in a local newspaper. (In California, this law also applies to restaurants.) Your local newspaper or recorder's office should be able to help you with the bulk sales notice. In most of these states, sending a certified letter to all known creditors and publishing the notice in a newspaper in order to notify unknown creditors, as discussed above, will take care of the bulk sales requirement as well.

Corporations and LLCs

Your letter should include the deadline for submitting claims, a statement that claims will be barred if not received by the deadline, a list of the information that the creditor should send to file a claim, and the mailing address to which the creditor must send the claim. You must allow 90 to 180 days (120 days in the vast majority of states) for creditors to submit claims, depending on your state's corporate or LLC statute. To find out the rule in your state, go to www.nolo.com/legal-research and choose your state. Then search for "known claims corporation" or "known claim limited liability company." If a creditor does not respond within the time period, your corporation or LLC can generally disregard that creditor's claim.

Sample Letter to Creditor

Dear Mr. Lee:

We are saddened to inform you that Torchlight Productions, LLC, will be closing its doors on September 20. We are in the process of liquidating our assets and will be paying off our debts to the fullest extent possible. Unfortunately, our insolvency will prevent us from paying our debts in full. Please send any claim for payment, including details on goods or services rendered and address for payment, to the above address within 120 days. Claims received after this date may be barred by law.

We have been proud to provide quality services over the years and regret that economic realities force us to close. Thank you for your attention to this difficult matter.

Very truly yours,

Emme Lorenz

CEO, Torchlight Productions, LLC

If a particular creditor does not receive notice that your LLC or corporation is closing down, that creditor's claim may survive the closing. Because you may not be aware of all potential creditors, to limit the time period in which a creditor can file claims, you should publish a notice in your local newspaper (and on your website if you have one), that your business is closing down. The notice should state that a claim will be barred unless a proceeding to enforce the claim is started within a certain time period and include a list of the information that the creditor should send to file a claim and the mailing address to which these unknown creditors may send claims. In most states, the time period for unknown creditors to make a claim is two years, but in some states it is five. To find out the rule in your state, go to www.nolo.com/legal-research and choose your state. Then search for "unknown claims corporation" or "unknown claim limited liability company." If you are concerned about cutting off significant claims that might be out there, run your letter and notice past a local business lawyer before sending it, to make sure you fulfill all of your state's requirements.

Sole Proprietorships and Partnerships

Lawsuits by creditors against sole proprietorships or partnerships must be filed within the time set out by your state's statute of limitations (usually three to ten years) or be barred. To find out the statute of limitations in your state, visit www.nolo.com and search for "statute of limitations," which will pull up a state-by-state table.

Even though sole proprietors and partners can't limit the time period in which claims must be made, you may want to send a short letter to known creditors, as well as publish a simple notice for unknown creditors, stating that your business is closing. This should help flush out creditors, which is something you might want to do before your partners disappear. If you'd rather not remind customers to send a bill or make a claim, as is true for many sole proprietors, don't (but see "Special State Rules," above, if you live in California, Virginia, Georgia, Maryland, Wisconsin, or DC).

Customers

Give your customers notice that you are going out of business and as mentioned above, fill any last orders, complete any final projects, and fulfill any contractual obligations. If you can't fulfill an obligation, let the customer know and return any deposits or payments for goods not delivered or services not rendered.

If your business is big enough, you can send out a press release to newspapers to notify your customers that your business is closing. You can cite economic downturn, rising costs, or competitive realities as the explanation for closing, or just that you are moving on to new ventures. If your business is on the small end, when you publish your statement in a local newspaper that you are closing your business (see above), also consider thanking your customers for their support.

Pay Your Debts

You probably have a good-sized pile of debts—to landlords, suppliers, utilities, service providers, and possibly a bank or private lender. After you notify these creditors of your upcoming closure, you'll want to make plans to either pay these bills in full, settle them for less than full payment, or consider filing for bankruptcy. The fourth possible approach—ignoring your debts and hoping your creditors will ignore you—might be tempting, but don't go that route. It will almost surely result in your spending the next couple of years hounded by collection agencies, repo people, lawyers, and lawsuits.

TIP

If you can't pay all of your debts, consider bankruptcy. Bankruptcy lets you wipe out debts you have no hope of paying—and if your business owes a pile of debts it can't pay, it could offer the fresh start you need. To decide whether bankruptcy or a bankruptcy-like alternative such as an assignment for the benefit of creditors is your best course of action, see Chapter 13.

Negotiating a Deal

If you can't pay all your creditors in full, the question becomes: How little will they settle for? As you might guess, it depends on the type of creditor, the legal details of the debt, and the attitude of the creditor. For example, if your business is an LLC or corporation without any personally guaranteed debts, a creditor will know that it doesn't have the option of collecting from you personally, so it may be more willing to accept a small portion of what your business owes as complete payment. But if you owe a debt personally, or worse, a friend or relative cosigned for it, the creditor has much more leverage.

But no matter what the legal status of your debts, in our experience, if you can pay 30% to 70% cash on the barrelhead, it's worth trying to settle them. Many creditors, knowing that they will have a hard time collecting the debt once you are out of business, may agree to settle your debt for 50, 60, or 70 cents on the dollar—or even less if you hire a lawyer to negotiate for you.

Keep in mind that it won't help you much to settle one or two small debts for a reasonable amount while not being able to settle larger ones. So it might make sense to tell your creditors that your offers are contingent upon all of your creditors agreeing to settle their debts.

> ## CAUTION
>
> **Debt forgiveness can be taxed as income.** If creditors agree to settle your debts for less than the amount you owe, the IRS and state tax agencies may view this debt forgiveness as taxable income. (In other words, you don't have to pay the money, so it's like getting the same amount as income.) This could result in your actually having positive taxable income, rather than an operating loss, in the year you close. Owners of corporations and LLCs won't be personally liable to pay these taxes, but sole proprietors and partners should talk to a tax adviser to see whether this income can be applied to previous years' net operating losses or otherwise wiped out.

Prioritizing Your Debts

First, if you've pledged an asset that you own personally as collateral, if you want to keep it, you'll want to pay that debt first. You will then want to pay:

- any wages and benefits owed to employees, and
- loans for which you are personally liable (in particular, court judgments).

If there is money left over, then you can pay suppliers, credit card companies, lease deficiencies, and bills for garden-variety business expenses—advertising, travel and entertainment charges, dues and subscriptions, and repairs and maintenance. Let's look at how you might handle each type of creditor.

Equipment Lessors

Make arrangements to return leased equipment such as copiers, machinery, and vehicles. If you return equipment before your lease term is up, you will no doubt be liable for either the remainder of the payments in the lease term or for an early return penalty. Try to negotiate a better deal while you've still got the equipment. For example, you might offer to return two forklifts and a pallet jack to the leasing company along with two months' additional payments, in exchange for a complete release of further obligations.

Again, if lots of money is at stake and the lessor is not willing to cooperate, having a lawyer call, possibly with the suggestion that you may file for bankruptcy, can be a huge help. No lessor wants to cope with bankruptcy court and the fact that their property may deteriorate in the meantime.

Secured Creditors

If you weren't able to negotiate with a secured creditor to release you from owing a deficiency after you turned over the secured asset or the proceeds from selling it (see "Notify Creditors and Customers," above), the deficiency is now like any other unsecured debt (see "Unsecured Creditors," just below).

Unsecured Creditors

After you notify your unsecured creditors that you are going out of business (see "Notify Creditors and Customers," above), they will start calling you, demanding to be paid. Often it's best simply to explain that you are preparing as fair a settlement offer as you can and will be in touch. Even if it takes a few weeks to be sure how much you owe and how much cash you have to divide among creditors, it's worth the time to get it right.

When you are ready to discuss settlements, if you have just a few creditors, you can explain your terms personally or by phone. Explain that your business doesn't have the money to pay the creditor in full but that you can offer a partial payment to settle the debt. If the creditors accept, great. Get each creditor to sign a release for the entire amount in exchange for your partial payment, and you're done. The release is critical—without it, you have no proof that the debt has been satisfied. Creditors could sue you or the business, which would be expensive and time-consuming to defend, even if you end up not being liable for the debt.

If you have more than a few creditors, offering a settlement in writing is often your best course of action. In your letters, spell out what you can pay as settlement of the debt in full, that you're offering each creditor the same percentage, and that you'll need all creditors to agree to sign a settlement releasing the debt before you can make the payments.

Sample Settlement Offer to Creditor

Dear Mr. Lee:

As you know, Torchlight Productions, LLC, is insolvent and closing its doors. We regret that we are not able to pay your bill in full, but in an attempt to be fair we are offering to pay all of our creditors 60% of their submitted claims. This means we can pay you $9,000 of the $15,000 we owe you.

If you are willing to accept this amount as payment in full, please sign the included release. This offer is contingent on all creditors accepting a settlement of 60% of the amount owed. Thank you for your attention to this difficult matter.

Very truly yours,

Emme Lorenz

CEO, Torchlight Productions, LLC

If some creditors want to negotiate for substantially more, and others are threateningly uncooperative, it's time to involve a lawyer. This will immediately raise the seriousness of the negotiations, because the lawyer will be able to convincingly let the creditors know that you may file for bankruptcy if settlements aren't reached. Creditors know that the costs and delays inherent in bankruptcy would mean they will almost surely receive less than you are offering and they wouldn't get the money for many months, so most will accept your settlement.

A lawyer can also advise you on whether or not it makes sense to fully pay a creditor who refuses to accept less. Likewise, if a creditor makes a request for payment that you dispute, a business attorney can tell you what your next steps should be.

If, after making settlements with your creditors, you have any cash or assets left, you should set aside some money for potential future claims. Invariably, after you close up shop, a creditor will come out of the woodwork. Do your best to estimate any unpaid bills that might later surface or any potential lawsuits that could be brought against your business. Some experts recommend you set aside 1% of your annual revenue to provide for surprise creditors, but a reasonable amount depends on the hazards of your particular business. You can keep the money in your regular business bank account, a savings account, or, if the amount is significant, an escrow account. Some states actually require you to deposit the money into a trust account with the state controller or commissioner of revenue.

If your business is an LLC or corporation, keep the money set aside for two to five years, depending on your state's statute. (See "Notify Creditors and Customers," above.) This is important because, if a corporation or LLC distributes its assets to its owners after it dissolves and then a creditor appears within the two- to five-year period, the creditor can sue the business owners personally, to the extent of the assets distributed. If your business is a sole proprietorship or partnership, you may want to keep a contingency fund for three to ten years, depending on your state's statutes of limitation.

EXAMPLE: QuickClean Cleaners, Inc., closes its door after months of competing with three different dry cleaners within a three-block radius in downtown Stamford, Connecticut. After laying off employees, paying suppliers and creditors, and dissolving their corporation, the owners want to tie up loose ends. They know that customers take a while to make claims for lost or damaged apparel and that Quick-Clean usually has to pay out about $6,000 per year in claims not covered by insurance. Wanting closure but not wanting to risk later personal lawsuits, QuickClean sets aside $6,000 in a savings account, distributes the remaining assets to its three shareholders, and dissolves the corporation. If there is money left over in the account in two to five years, they can split the money among themselves.

SEE AN EXPERT

Get help if you expect big creditors' claims. If you think significant claims could surface after you close your business, see a lawyer. Your state may impose specific requirements that you'll need to know about. Nolo's website features a free lawyer directory with comprehensive profiles of business attorneys in your area; to find one, go to http://lawyers.nolo.com.

Pay Your Business Taxes

Your tax obligations are your most important debts because governments are given extraordinary legal powers to collect them. (See Chapter 4.) In addition, you are personally liable for some tax debts, even if your business is a corporation or LLC. So before you pay off even one trade creditor, make sure you've met of all your tax obligations, as discussed below.

Payroll Taxes and Sales Tax

First and most important, if you have employees, make your final payroll tax deposits and file all of your final employment tax paperwork on time. First priority should go to federal taxes withheld from employees' paychecks— income tax withholding and Social Security and Medicare taxes. Next in line are state income withholding taxes and sales taxes that you have collected. (When you file the final sales tax forms, be sure to write FINAL across the top of the return.) With these serious tax obligations behind you, it's time to take care of the employer's share of the Social Security and Medicare taxes.

TIP

Negotiate with the IRS. If you owe the IRS more than you can pay, you might be able to pay less than you owe through an offer in compromise or installment payments. To start the offer in compromise process, fill out IRS Form 656, *Offer in Compromise*. To obtain an installment payment plan with the IRS, use Form 433A, *Collection Information Statement*. For more information on the advantages and disadvantages of each, as well as how to calculate the amount you should offer to pay, see *Stand Up to the IRS*, by Frederick W. Daily (Nolo).

Final Income Tax Returns

There are a number of IRS requirements you need to take care of when ceasing business operations; similar state requirements apply as well. Because tax requirements can get complicated in a hurry, consider enlisting the help of a tax professional, especially if your business makes over $50,000 per year or has several owners.

Sole proprietors. As usual, report your income and expenses, including information on gains or losses, on Schedule C of your Form 1040. File your return by April 15 the year after you close your business. There is no "final return" box to check on Schedule C.

Partnerships and LLCs. File Form 1065, *U.S. Partnership Return of Income,* and check the box that says this is your final return. Also report any profits or losses allocated to each partner for the year by filing Form 1065 (Schedule K-1), *Partner's Share of Income, Credits, Deductions, etc.* File both forms by April 15 the year after your partnership closes.

Corporations. File Form 1120, *U.S. Corporation Income Tax Return,* and check the box that this is your final return. Also report any income allocated to each shareholder by filing Form 1120S (Schedule K-1), *Shareholder's Share of Income, Credits, Deductions, etc.* Shareholders will also need to report a personal capital gain or loss when they return their shares to the corporation. Finally, corporations also need to file IRS Form 966, *Corporate Dissolution or Liquidation,* to report their dissolution. You need to file these forms two months and 15 days after your tax year ends—that is, two months and 15 days after you close your business.

Reporting asset sales. You will experience a taxable gain or loss when you liquidate your business's assets. You'll need to file Form 4797, *Sales of Business Property,* to calculate your gain or loss. After calculating the gain or loss on this form, you record the total from this form on your personal or corporate income tax return, depending on your form of business. (For more information, see IRS Publication 544, *Sales and Other Dispositions of Assets.*)

For Employers

If you had employees or independent contractors working for you, you'll also need to take the following steps—even if you were the sole employee of your corporation.

Employer returns. File your final employer's federal tax return, IRS Form 941 or 944, and your final federal unemployment tax return, IRS Form 940 or 940EZ, by their regular due dates. Mark the returns as final and include the proper amount of taxes. You must attach to both of these forms a statement showing the name of the person who will be storing the payroll records for the business and the address where the records will be kept. Also, don't forget to file your state's version of the wage and withholding report.

Withholding statements. Issue final wage and withholding information to your employees on Form W-2, *Wage and Tax Statement,* by January 31 of the year after your business closes. Report the information from the W-2s to the IRS using Form W-3, *Transmittal of Income and Tax Statements.* (If you were in the restaurant business, you must also file information on tip income with Form 8027, *Employer's Annual Information Return of Tip Income and Allocated Tips.)*

Contractor statements. Issue payment information to freelancers and contractors using Form 1099-MISC, *Miscellaneous Income.* Report the information from the 1099s to the IRS using Form 1096, *Annual Summary and Transmittal of U.S. Information Returns,* (unless you file the 1099-MISC forms electronically).

Pension plans. If you provided your employees with a pension plan, you'll need to close it down. If the plan was a simplified employee pension (SEP) plan, simply notify the financial institution running the plan that you won't be making any more contributions. If you had a savings incentive match plan (SIMPLE), you need to wait until the end of the year to shut it down. Legally, you are required to continue to fund the plan until the end of the year.

Taxpayer IDs

You won't need your business ID numbers anymore, so take steps to cancel them.

Federal employer identification number. The IRS will not cancel your EIN, but if you no longer need the number for your business, the IRS will deactivate your business account (and reactivate it if you ever go back into business). To deactivate your account, write to the IRS at: Internal Revenue Service, Cincinnati, OH 45999 and say that you're going out of business and want to close your account. If you have the EIN Assignment Notice that was issued when your EIN was assigned, include a copy of it when you send your letter. Otherwise, be sure to include the complete legal name of your company, your name, the EIN, and the business address. You must file all tax returns due before the IRS will close your account.

State employer tax ID number and business tax account. To close your state tax account, contact your state tax agency. Some state agencies have a notice of discontinuance form that you must file; in other states you have to write a letter to the tax agency. Most state tax agencies have clear instructions for what you need to do on their website. You must file all tax returns due before a state tax agency will close your account.

> **SEE AN EXPERT**
>
> **Get tax help.** You would be well advised to hire a tax preparer or accountant to file your final tax forms for you. It saves you the headache of preparing them yourself, ensures their accuracy, and will no doubt gain you some deductions for business losses that you can take against other income you or your spouse bring home.

> **TIP**
>
> **Put away the shredder.** After you've wrapped up all of your tax paperwork, the IRS recommends that you keep tax records for seven years after closing your business.

Dissolve Your Corporation or LLC

Several months after you send notice to your creditors, and after you've settled debts with all known creditors, it's time to officially end your corporation or limited liability company (LLC). You need to dissolve your entity with the secretary of state or the corporations division in your state by filing a form or two. By dissolving your entity, you ensure that you are no longer liable for paying annual fees, filing annual reports, and paying business taxes. If you don't dissolve your corporation or LLC, you could be looking at thousands of dollars in accumulated fees and penalties.

Officially dissolving your business also puts creditors on notice that your business can no longer incur business debts. In fact, in some states, if you don't notify them by officially dissolving your business, creditors and customers could sue you for a longer period of time.

Vote to Dissolve

The first step to dissolving your company is for your shareholders or members to officially agree to dissolve the business. The vote to dissolve the entity should be recorded in a resolution in the minutes of a meeting or with a written consent form and put it in your records book.

File the Proper Forms

Next, visit your state's secretary of state or corporations division website to find the dissolution form. It will be called a certificate of dissolution, certificate of cancellation, articles of dissolution, or something similar. Typically, the form merely asks for identifying information, but some states also ask whether all debts and liabilities have been paid (or assumed by another company or provided for in a bank or escrow account) and whether the remaining assets, if any, were distributed. Most states charge a small fee for filing the form—check the form instructions for the amount.

When you send in your dissolution form to the state, include a cover letter with your business name and corporation or LLC number as well as your name, return address, and telephone number. If there is a fee, be sure to include it. To be safe, send the form by certified mail, with return receipt requested. The state should send you back a certificate of dissolution or similar document, which you should file with the rest of your corporate or LLC records. If you have questions on the paperwork, most states provide very clear rules for dissolution on their websites.

RESOURCE

Online state offices. To find a link to your secretary of state or corporations division website, go to www.statelocalgov.net.

If your corporation or LLC has qualified (registered) to do business in other states, you'll also need to file a form to withdraw your right to transact business in that state. This form may be called an application of withdrawal, certificate of termination of existence, termination of registration, or certificate of surrender of right to transact business. If you neglect to file the appropriate form, you will continue to be liable for paying annual report fees as well as minimum taxes to those states, even if you cease all operations.

Corporations, don't forget to also file IRS Form 966, *Corporate Dissolution or Liquidation.* LLCs, because they don't have stock to liquidate, don't need to notify the IRS of their dissolution, except through checking the final return box on Form 1065 (for LLCs with multiple members).

Get a Tax Clearance If Necessary

In some states, before you may formally dissolve your corporation or LLC, you are required to obtain something called a tax clearance, consent to dissolution, or verification of good standing from your state tax agency. The secretary of state or corporations division will not allow your corporation or LLC to dissolve if you have not filed your last tax return (checking the "Final tax return" box and writing FINAL at the top) and paid all taxes owed. To get the clearance or consent of the tax agency, you submit a request by phone or fax. If you are current on filing tax returns and paying state taxes, you will receive a letter or certificate declaring that you have no tax liability.

> **TIP**
> **Hang on to the evidence.** Keep all dissolution and winding-up paperwork for at least six or seven years.

Dissolve Your Partnership

If you have been doing business as a partnership, you and your business partners need to vote to dissolve the partnership and record the decision in writing. Also record in writing the responsibilities of each partner regarding the debts and any future liabilities of the partnership. For instance, if Partner #1 pays off half of the partnership's debt but Partner #2 fails to pay off his half (or files for bankruptcy), creditors can still come after Partner #1 for the rest of the partnership's debts. Without a written agreement that Partner #2 was to pay a certain debt, Partner #1 is out of luck. (Even with an agreement, Partner #1 might not be able to collect if Partner #2 has no assets or files for bankruptcy.)

> **SEE AN EXPERT**
> **If your partnership is insolvent, consult a lawyer.** If there aren't enough business funds to pay partnership debts, each partner would be wise to seek the advice of a lawyer to protect their interests. To find a business attorney, go to http://lawyers.nolo.com.

It's a good idea to file the state's dissolution of partnership form (available from your state's secretary of state or corporations division website) as additional proof that the partnership has been terminated. Typically, filing a partnership dissolution form with the state isn't legally required unless you filed paperwork with the state when you formed your partnership. (For instance, in California, a partnership needs to file a certificate of dissolution form only if it filed a statement of authority with the secretary of state when the partners formed the partnership.)

It also makes sense to publish a notice in the local newspaper that the partnership is no longer in business. This puts creditors on notice that the partnership, as well as any of the partners, can no longer incur debts. This is especially important for partnerships, because any partner can bind the partnership to a deal without letting the other partners know. You could be on the hook for debts you don't know about.

Cancel Permits, Licenses, and Fictitious Business Names

No matter what kind of business you have, you probably applied for and received a business license or tax registration, seller's permit, and perhaps a fictitious business name or dba ("doing business as") statement from the state or local government. You should cancel any kind of permit or license you hold with the state, city, or county so that no one else can use it. You could be responsible for any taxes and penalties incurred after you no longer operate the business if, for instance, someone else were to get hold of your seller's permit number and use it to buy goods at wholesale.

Fictitious name. If you filed a fictitious business name or dba statement, file an abandonment form of the name with the same agency. Most agencies require you to also publish the abandonment in a local newspaper for several weeks.

Seller's permit or resale license. A seller's permit goes by many different names in different states, including a resale certificate, reseller license, wholesale license, or sales tax ID number. If you hold one, contact the agency that issued it and ask for the form to cancel it. (Don't be tempted to continue to use your seller's permit or resale certificate for your personal use—in most states this is a crime.) If you made a security deposit when you obtained your seller's permit or resale certificate, to get it back you'll have to turn in your permit and certificate and provide documentation that you have made your full sales tax remittance.

Business license. To cancel your local business license—called a tax registration in some areas—contract your city or county for the appropriate form.

Distribute Any Remaining Assets to Owners

After you have paid creditors' claims, you can pay off any loans to existing owners and sign the appropriate paperwork to document it. If there is still money left over, the remaining cash and assets can usually be distributed to the owners based on their pro rata share of ownership. But as discussed above, if there is a possibility that a creditor may bring a claim after the company is dissolved, you and the other owners should set aside a contingency fund to pay any liabilities (or taxes) that surface after the dissolution, rather than distributing the assets to yourselves.

When all is said and done, be sure to close out your business bank account and cancel your business credit cards. However, you may want to wait a few weeks or months to close your checking account—no matter how organized you are, a bill or debt or two are certain to arise after you close.

CAUTION

Don't distribute assets to owners if debts aren't paid. State law prohibits a corporation, LLC, or partnership from distributing its assets to the owners if the company cannot pay all of its debts. Not only are there penalties for doing so, but unpaid creditors can sue for the return of the assets from the owners. And the directors, officers, members, or partners of the company who approved the illegal distributions of assets can be held personally liable for the amount of the distributions.

If there are any assets left to be distributed, how the remaining cash and assets are distributed to the owners depends on the structure of the company.

Corporations. In a corporation, the remaining cash and assets are totaled and then divided by the number of shares owned by shareholders. The corporation pays the shareholders the amount of cash or assets that's proportionate to the number of shares each shareholder owns, and in exchange the shareholders return their outstanding shares.

Partnerships and LLCs. In a partnership or LLC, distributions are made to members and partners according to the balance in each member or partner's capital account. (All partners or members have capital accounts that start off with their initial investments in the business and are increased when profits are allocated to them and decreased when profits are distributed to them.) If there isn't sufficient cash to pay each owner the amount in the capital account, as is likely, whatever cash or assets that remain are split among the owners based on the relative size of each one's capital account.

> **TIP**
>
> **Stay available.** Even though your business is ending on a not-so-successful note, make sure that people who might need to get in touch with you have your contact information. For instance, a former customer may need a referral, or a former employee may need a reference. Leave contact information with your business contacts, colleagues, employees, and customers. You never know when a contact can help you out in the future, so it pays to keep your network alive.

Dealing With Debt:
Bankruptcy and Its Alternatives

"Capitalism without bankruptcy is like Christianity without hell."
FRANK BORMAN

If you've run up big debts (business or personal) and are worried about never being able to repay them, it may be time to sell business assets, pay off your debts as best you can, and move on. This chapter discusses the three main ways to proceed:

- Negotiate with your creditors and agree on a settlement that releases you from further liability.
- Hire a company or lawyer that specializes in this process to do it for you.
- File for bankruptcy and let the court sell your assets and wipe out remaining debt.

Which liquidation option works best for you depends on the size of your business, the amount of your debts, and your personal inclination.

Bankruptcy is a powerful tool. You can use it to wipe out most unsecured debts—for example, credit card bills, lawsuit judgments, and debts to suppliers (unless they were secured by inventory). It can give you a fresh start, and maybe even the opportunity to start a profitable new business. After all, bankruptcy laws exist at least in part to encourage entrepreneurship and give business owners the chance to start over. But if one of the alternative solutions fits your situation, it will probably be less expensive, less time-consuming, and less gut-wrenching than a bankruptcy filing.

SEE AN EXPERT

Consult a lawyer. Especially if a lot of money is at stake, check any conclusions you reach after reading this chapter with a bankruptcy attorney. Look for someone who will quote you a reasonable fee to review your business and personal affairs and advise you on how to proceed in your particular situation. A knowledgeable business associate may be able to direct you to an excellent attorney, or you can check Nolo's lawyer directory (www.nolo.com), which contains detailed profiles of hundreds of bankruptcy lawyers.

Negotiating With Your Creditors

Many sole proprietors, as well as owners of small insolvent corporations, LLCs, and partnerships, liquidate their own assets and negotiate their own settlements.

The Process

The idea is simple: You or your lawyer calls each of your creditors and asks them to release you from the debt, in exchange for some fraction of the full amount you owe. Why should creditors do this? Because it's often a better choice than suing you and trying to chase down your remaining assets while hoping you don't file for bankruptcy, which creditors know will leave little or nothing for them after costs and fees are paid. Obviously, you need to have enough business cash and assets that you can make at least partial payments on your debts. If you are flat broke, your creditors will have no incentive to negotiate with you.

EXAMPLE: Darla runs the BookNook LLC, which sells new books upstairs and used books downstairs. It has a diehard following, but when the economic downturn hits the book industry especially hard, Darla can't keep her income above expenses. When she decides to close the business, she owes three publishers a total of $80,000, $4,000 to her landlord on the month-to-month lease that she personally guaranteed, and $1,000 to utility companies. She gives her landlord the required 30 days' notice. She returns as much book inventory as possible to the publishers, lowering the amount she owes them to $40,000, and notifies them in writing that she's going out of business. Of course they call her immediately to press for payment on their invoices, but Darla tells them she'll get back to them.

She then sells off her used book inventory as well as her bookshelves, cash registers, and computers (mostly to a competitor, the rest on craigslist), leaving her with $25,000 in cash. She pays her landlord the $4,000 past due—this is a high priority because she personally guaranteed the lease—and writes checks to the utilities. Darla then writes to each of the publishers offering a final payment of 50 cents on the dollar ($20,000 to satisfy her debts of $40,000). She makes the offer contingent upon the publishers' signing a written release that releases BookNook, Darla, and her spouse from any liability for the debts. The publishers, knowing that BookNook is an LLC and that Darla can either walk away from the business or file a Chapter 7 business bankruptcy, much prefer getting half their money immediately, so they take the deal.

Liquidating your own business and settling its debts outside of bankruptcy will take work on your part, and unless you have only a few debts and thoroughly understand the legal effect of each, is best done with the help of a lawyer who specializes in debt issues. Having a lawyer negotiate for you is often a big advantage if, as is likely, some of your creditors can no longer stand the sound of your voice. In addition, the lawyer will know how and when to mention the bankruptcy alternative in an effort to convince all of your creditors to accept your settlement as a better choice. If your creditors agree to settle, your lawyer can also help you prepare the necessary releases to be sure that, in exchange for your partial payment, you, your spouse, and any cosigners will be fully absolved from future liability.

If your business is a corporation or LLC and you haven't signed any personal guarantees or become personally liable for any debts (such as unpaid payroll taxes), you don't actually have to wait around for creditors to sign releases. You can simply close the business, sell its assets, and pay your creditors on a pro rata basis until the business's cash is exhausted. The downside of this approach is that by not getting signed releases, you open yourself up to being hounded for years by collection agencies and possibly even being sued. If you are sued, you'll at least have to file a response in court pointing out that you aren't personally liable for the debt, and you may have to hire a lawyer or appear in court. Worse, a creditor might even argue that your corporation or LLC was just a sham to help you defraud creditors and that it was really just you running the business (this is called trying to "pierce the veil" of the corporation or LLC). If the creditor were to succeed, you would be personally liable for paying the business's debts. Getting releases on all of your debts can avoid this, as can going through Chapter 7 individual bankruptcy.

On the other hand, if you are personally liable for some business debts because you're a sole proprietor or a partner, or because you signed some personal guarantees, you'll absolutely need to get all of your creditors to settle with you and release your from the debts. If even one creditor refuses to release you from a debt you're personally liable for, all of your other settlements may be for naught, if the creditor sues you and takes your property or you end up having to file for bankruptcy anyway. Again, a business lawyer can help you keep this from happening.

Advantages of Doing It Yourself

Selling business assets yourself, rather than turning them over to a bankruptcy court for liquidation, will likely bring in more money for your creditors. And you won't have to pay the costs of bankruptcy (court and lawyers' fees). So if you feel an ethical duty to creditors and want to see that they receive as much money as possible, this may be the way to go. Keep in mind, though, that if you hire a lawyer to liquidate your company for you, these savings could disappear.

Managing the liquidation outside of bankruptcy also gives you far more control over which debts are paid. For instance, if you don't file for personal bankruptcy, you can choose to first pay the debts for which you are personally liable, such as:

- trust fund taxes
- a line of credit that you personally guaranteed, or
- contracts or leases with your personal signature.

You might even be able to buy the business's assets back yourself—something you might want to do if you are planning to start up a new business after the liquidation. For example, you might want to buy back a patent, copyright, or specialized technology to use in a new business. By contrast, in a Chapter 7 business bankruptcy, the bankruptcy trustee (the person in charge of gathering and selling the assets) may not let the owners of a corporation or LLC purchase the company's assets (though this is standard procedure for sole proprietors in individual Chapter 7 bankruptcies). Keep in mind that, especially if yours is a business that required little capital to start up, such as a service business, you can easily and legally start up a similar business after a Chapter 7 bankruptcy.

Finally, if before the liquidation you paid some creditors (perhaps family and friends) at the expense of others, these preference payments won't be taken away when you wind down your business yourself, as they would in bankruptcy. (For instance, if you made payments on a loan to a relative or close business associate in the year before filing, or transferred property for little or no payment in the two years before filing, a bankruptcy court could take back these payments or property to divide them equally among all creditors.)

For a discussion of how to liquidate your business and negotiate settlements with your creditors, see "Pay Your Debts" in Chapter 12.

CAUTION
Once you start negotiating, bankruptcy may not be an option. You often can't go back and file bankruptcy once you start liquidating assets and negotiating settlements yourself. That's because if you have made any preference payments or invalid transfers, these things will come back to bite you if you file for bankruptcy. For more information, see "If You Might File for Bankruptcy," below.

Hiring Help: Assignment for Benefit of Creditors

An alternative to liquidating your own business or filing for bankruptcy is to follow a procedure called an "assignment for the benefit of creditors," or ABC. Here you work with one of the many ABC companies or law firms that specialize in liquidating insolvent businesses. Basically, the company will liquidate your assets and pay off your creditors (for a percentage of what it is able to sell your assets for), while you and your co-owners move forward with your lives.

This option generally works well if your business is a corporation or LLC with a lot of debts and assets. A large liquidation can take months or years to wind up—something you probably can't afford to spend your time doing.

Here's how it generally works. Your business assigns (transfers) all of its assets and debts to the ABC company or law firm, meaning that liability for the business's debts moves to the ABC company or firm. You might still be liable for debts with personal guarantees (or all debts if you are a sole proprietor or partner), however, so you want to discuss with the ABC company paying these debts first.

An ABC company will almost always get more for your assets than a bankruptcy trustee will, and it may be able to sell any intellectual property you own to help pay debts, something a bankruptcy trustee usually will not do. Going the ABC route is also usually faster and more private (and less embarrassing) than a bankruptcy. To learn more about ABCs, speak to a local business lawyer or search online.

EXAMPLE: Angelo's Meatpacking, Inc., has been suffering from poor sales for the past year, and now Angelo's accounts payable list is growing, creditors are demanding payment, and the company will be out of cash within a few months. Angelo consults with two ABC companies and finds that one company has experience with liquidating meatpacking companies, meaning that this company is more likely to get top dollar selling Angelo's business equipment. Angelo signs a contract with the ABC company (now called the assignee) and provides a list of the company's creditors as well as all of the business assets to be assigned.

First, the ABC company investigates whether Angelo's company can be sold as a going concern. If not, it will send a letter to all creditors notifying them of the fact that the assignment has been made and providing a claim form for each creditor to submit a claim to the ABC company. At the same time, the company advertises the assets for sale in industry publications and, using its contacts, searches for another company to take over Angelo's lease, for a fee. It also publishes a press release simply stating that it has acquired the assets of Angelo's Meatpacking, Inc. After all of the assets have been liquidated, the ABC company takes a percentage of the proceeds as its fee and distributes the rest based on the creditors' claims. In six months, it's all done.

Filing for Bankruptcy

Most people who talk of bankruptcy are referring to Chapter 7 bankruptcy, also called "straight" or "liquidation" bankruptcy, which is by far the most common type. However, there are several others. Let's take a look at each and how it might help you when you're swamped by debt.

CROSS-REFERENCE

Understanding the legal status of your debts. Before you can decide whether bankruptcy is right for you, it's essential that you know whether you are personally liable to repay your debts. Review Chapter 4 if you are unsure.

Chapter 7 Personal Bankruptcy

In a Chapter 7 personal bankruptcy, you ask the bankruptcy court to wipe out (discharge) your debts. In return, you might have to let the bankruptcy court sell some of your personal or business property and use the proceeds to pay down your debt. An individual Chapter 7 bankruptcy typically takes three to six months to move through federal bankruptcy court and generally costs less than other types of bankruptcy.

Chapter 7 bankruptcy can efficiently wipe out most unsecured debts—for example, credit card bills, lawsuit judgments, and debts to suppliers (unless they were secured by inventory). Secured debts are different. If you pledged property—such as your home or car—as collateral for a loan, the creditor is entitled to take the property if you don't make the payments, even if you file for bankruptcy. If you owe more on a secured debt (say a truck loan) than the collateral (the truck), is worth, the difference ("deficiency") is discharged in bankruptcy. However, the lender can still take the collateral if you don't make the payments.

Whether bankruptcy will solve your pressing debt problems depends on a combination of factors, including the legal types of debt you have, how your business is legally organized, and the nature and amount of the personal assets you hope to protect.

Chapter 7 Business Bankruptcy

If your business is not a sole proprietorship, you can file a business Chapter 7 bankruptcy. This lets you turn over your business to the bankruptcy trustee for an orderly liquidation. The business stops operating, and the court liquidates all its assets to pay business creditors. The court doesn't touch your personal assets if your business is a corporation or LLC.

The court takes the proceeds from the sale of the business assets and pays what it can to creditors. When that's done, you won't owe any remaining debts—including leases, contracts, credit cards, loans, and overdue accounts —unless you personally guaranteed them.

The process is very similar to that of a personal Chapter 7 bankruptcy. The court fees are the same, but the bankruptcy trustee is likely to get a bigger fee. And you'll almost certainly need to hire a lawyer.

Can You File for Bankruptcy but Keep Running Your Business?

If you're hoping that bankruptcy is a magic solution that will both wipe out your debts and let you continue your business debt-free almost as if nothing happened, you may be disappointed.

Especially if you have a business that sells or manufactures products or owns significant assets, Chapter 7 bankruptcy is unlikely to allow you to continue in the same business. That's because the bankruptcy court will sell the business assets. If you have enough money, though, you could buy back some of the assets and start a new business—this happens all the time.

If your business is so deep in debt that you're considering bankruptcy, your best and most realistic alternative is to close it down and rid yourself of as many debts as possible. Then you can start a new, debt-free business.

Chapter 13 Bankruptcy

Businesses can't file for Chapter 13 bankruptcy, but business owners can. You can use it to repay and discharge business-related debts for which you're personally liable. To be eligible, your unsecured debts can't exceed $336,900 and secured debts can't exceed $1,010,650.

In a Chapter 13 bankruptcy, you don't lose any property. Instead, you pay off part of your debts under a repayment plan (approved by the bankruptcy court) over three to five years. Depending on your income and expenses, you may actually have to pay only pennies on the dollar. (Some debts, however, must be paid in full, including most tax debts, some employee pay, and back alimony and child support.) If you complete the plan, you'll be debt-free.

Chapter 13 bankruptcy requires continuing your business under the scrutiny of a bankruptcy trustee (if you decide to continue it) and repaying a portion of the business's debts—a difficult task for a struggling enterprise. Only about 35% of Chapter 13 filers complete their repayment plans. It's usually cheaper and easier to liquidate your failing company and then start a new, debt-free company.

It's hard for a business owner to keep up with payments—imagine never being late on a monthly payment when your income is seasonal, or fluctuates with the economy and what your competition is doing. If you're a sole proprietor, all of your personal and business property would be under the bankruptcy court's control. You would need court permission to borrow money or to buy or sell business assets (other than in the normal course of business). You couldn't use credit cards, and you would have to submit monthly reports to the bankruptcy trustee. If business picked up or you took a side job, the extra money would have to go toward your debts.

If you missed a payment, the bankruptcy judge would probably convert your case to a Chapter 7 bankruptcy or dismiss it, and order your business to be liquidated. If that happened, you would owe your creditors the balance of your debts—that is, what you owed at the start of your bankruptcy case, plus the interest that stopped accruing while you were in bankruptcy, less whatever you paid through your repayment plan.

One advantage of a Chapter 13 over a Chapter 7 bankruptcy is that it lets you reduce even secured debts. You can reduce a secured debt down to the value of the collateral, rather than the amount you owe, which might be much higher. Called "cramming down" your debt, this can let you hold on to the collateral.

For example, if you owe $15,000 on a car loan and the car is worth only $9,000, you can propose a plan that pays the creditor $9,000. Once you pay the $9,000, the rest of the loan is discharged. You can't cram down the mortgage on your primary residence or debts for cars or other property you bought shortly before filing.

Although Chapter 13 bankruptcy is unlikely to help most small business owners, there can be exceptions. A sole proprietor who doesn't want to lose assets that wouldn't be exempt in a Chapter 7 bankruptcy, for example, might want to consider Chapter 13. On the other end of the scale, it might work for a business owner who has few assets, because in that case the owner wouldn't be required to pay off many unsecured debts, if any. (That's because the amount you have to repay toward your unsecured debts is equal to the amount of your nonexempt assets.) So if you have the patience and perseverance to repay at least some of your debt, don't rule Chapter 13 out.

RESOURCE

More on Chapter 13 bankruptcy. See *Chapter 13 Bankruptcy: Keep Your Property & Repay Debts Over Time*, by Stephen Elias and Robin Leonard (Nolo).

Other Bankruptcy for Business: Chapters 11 and 12

Most small businesses use Chapter 7 bankruptcy, if they use bankruptcy at all. But there are a couple of other kinds of bankruptcy you might have heard of and be curious about.

Chapter 11. This type of reorganization bankruptcy is appropriate only for large businesses and for individuals with very large debts: over $336,900 in unsecured debts or $1,010,650 in secured debts. Because Chapter 11 is very expensive—think $50,000 in attorney's fees—and extraordinarily complex, businesses with fewer than 100 employees really don't use it.

Chapter 12. This type of reorganization bankruptcy is for people whose debts come mainly from the operation of a family farm.

SEE AN EXPERT

Time for an expert. If you think either of these kinds of bankruptcy might help you, see a lawyer who's got experience with their special issues.

What's Your Best Strategy?

Is a business or personal bankruptcy better, or should you try to settle your debts with creditors and stay out of bankruptcy court altogether? It depends on your situation. Generally, most small business owners file an individual Chapter 7 bankruptcy to get rid of large personally guaranteed business debts, rather than a business bankruptcy.

Ways to Sell Business Assets and Settle Debts			
Settle with creditors yourself or hire lawyer to do it	Turn liquidation over to "ABC" company or law firm	File for business Chapter 7 bankruptcy	File for personal Chapter 7 bankruptcy
Private process	Private process	Available only to LLC, corporation, or partnership	Lets you wipe out personal obligations, including those for business debts
Assets likely to bring more than if sold by bankruptcy court	Assets likely to bring more than if sold by bankruptcy court	Doesn't affect personal obligations for business debts	Public process
You choose which debts get paid first, and how much each creditor gets	Lets you turn negotiations over to professional and move on with your life	Public process	Assets sold in bankruptcy always fetch a low price; you may lose personal assets
If you've made payments to family or friends, those payments won't be taken back as they would in bankruptcy	If you've made payments to family or friends, those payments won't be taken back as they would in bankruptcy	Assets sold in bankruptcy always fetch a low price	Bankruptcy trustee controls how much each creditor gets
		Bankruptcy trustee controls how much each creditor gets	If you've made payments to family or friends, the bankruptcy trustee will demand that the money be returned and given to other creditors
		If you've made payments to family or friends, the bankruptcy trustee will demand that the money be returned and given to other creditors	Bankruptcy goes on your credit record for ten years
		Won't affect your personal credit record	

Sole Proprietors

All business debts are personal when your business is organized as a sole proprietorship. That means your bankruptcy choices are to file for individual Chapter 7 bankruptcy, which will wipe out most of your debts, or for Chapter 13 bankruptcy, which will let you repay some or all of your debts over time. Sole proprietors generally don't make assignments for the benefit of creditors because an assignment doesn't offer a discharge of debts like Chapter 7 bankruptcy does.

However, if the value of your business assets is almost enough to pay your debts, you might just be able to sell your assets and settle your debts yourself, without bankruptcy—a process that's cheaper and less public than bankruptcy. See "Negotiating With Your Creditors," above.

Corporations and LLCs

If your business is a corporation or LLC, your decision will depend primarily on whether or not you are personally liable for any of the business debts.

Generally, you don't need to file for personal bankruptcy to escape most business debts, because you are not personally liable for them. The corporation or LLC, as a separate legal entity, is liable. But if your business can't pay all of its debts, you'll want to negotiate a settlement with your creditors, assign your debts to an ABC company, or file a business Chapter 7 bankruptcy. If you go the ABC or bankruptcy route, someone else (the bankruptcy trustee) will handle the orderly liquidation of business assets and payment of debts. Whatever business debts can't be paid will be wiped out at the end of the bankruptcy case.

If, however, you personally guaranteed business debts and want to wipe out those debts, you'll need to file for personal bankruptcy. (You can file both a business bankruptcy for business debts and a personal bankruptcy for your individual debts.) For example, if you rented a space for your business and the landlord insisted that you personally guarantee the lease, then you are on the hook for back rent if there aren't enough business assets to pay it. If you file for personal Chapter 7 bankruptcy, you can get that debt discharged.

Partnerships

When you're a partner, you're personally liable for business debts—so in almost all cases, you'll need to file for Chapter 7 personal bankruptcy to wipe out those debts. Of course, you can try to negotiate a deal with your creditors on your own (see "Negotiating With Your Creditors," above) or assign your debts to an ABC company or law firm.

Partnerships rarely file for Chapter 7 business bankruptcy because it doesn't rid the partners of their personal liability for any of the business's debts. In fact, it actually makes it easier for creditors to reach the partners' personal assets, because a bankruptcy trustee in a Chapter 7 bankruptcy case can sue the partners personally to recover some cash to pay the partnership's debts.

More About Chapter 7 Personal Bankruptcy

Let's look in more detail at how filing for Chapter 7 bankruptcy can help you get rid of most of your debt and give you a fresh start.

Debts That Can Be Discharged

Not all debts are dischargeable in Chapter 7 bankruptcy, but most are. As a general rule, most unsecured credit card, medical, legal, and business debts, including debts to landlords, suppliers, independent contractors, and equipment rental companies, can be discharged, as can most court judgments and unsecured loans. In addition, some taxes can actually be discharged in bankruptcy—back taxes more than three years old and the employer's portion of various payroll taxes.

The following debts are not dischargeable in bankruptcy:

- recent back taxes; back taxes if no tax return was filed, regardless of when due; and trust fund taxes

- debts incurred to pay nondischargeable taxes (for example, if you took a loan or cash advance from your credit card to pay your trust fund taxes)

- recent debts for luxuries (for example, you buy a Mercedes three weeks before filing)

- cash advances of more than $825 within 70 days before you file
- loans owed to a pension plan (say you borrowed money from your 401(k) plan)
- student loans (unless repaying them would constitute an extreme hardship, such as a permanent disability that prevents you from ever working)
- court-imposed fines and restitution (money damages you owe)
- back child support and alimony, and
- debts owed under divorce settlement agreements.

In addition, if a creditor objects to the discharge of a debt on the basis of fraud, such as lying on a credit application or writing a bad check, or because the debt was caused by willfully and maliciously damaging another's property, the bankruptcy judge can rule the debt to be nondischargeable.

> **CAUTION**
>
> **Codebtors will still be on the hook.** A Chapter 7 personal bankruptcy discharges only your debt obligations, not those of a codebtor, such as a person who has cosigned for your loan, or a business partner who is equally liable for the debt. (For more on codebtors' obligations, see Chapter 4.)

Are You Eligible for Chapter 7 Bankruptcy?

Although individuals have to meet certain financial criteria to be eligible for Chapter 7 consumer bankruptcy, business owners whose debts are primarily due to business operations don't have to.

If, however, the majority of your debts (51% or more) are not from your business, you must meet these financial criteria. To determine whether you can file for Chapter 7, first you measure your income for the last six months against the median income for a family of your size in your state. If your income is below your state's median income, it's assumed you don't have enough income to repay your debts and you can file a Chapter 7. To give you an idea, the median annual income in the United States for a family of four ranges from about $53,000 in Mississippi and New Mexico to $99,000 in Connecticut, Maryland, and New Jersey.

If your income is more than the median, you have another hurdle to clear, called the "means test," which is designed to determine whether you have enough disposable income, after subtracting allowed expenses and required debt payments, to repay at least a portion of your unsecured debts over five years.

In our experience, very few entrepreneurs whose businesses are so troubled that they are contemplating bankruptcy fail the means test. But if for some reason you don't pass, you are limited to using Chapter 13 bankruptcy for your personal debts.

RESOURCE

Finding median income figures and the means test. To determine whether you pass the means test (and to find the monthly income in your area), use our free means test calculator at www.legalconsumer.com/bankruptcy/nolo. Enter your zip code and then scroll down and enter your family size.

What Happens to Your Property

The biggest downside to Chapter 7 is that you may have to give up some property. If, despite your business's money problems, you still have a significant amount of property you own free and clear, including investments, real estate, vehicles, or business assets, the bankruptcy trustee will take at least some of it, sell it, and distribute the proceeds to your creditors.

However, if you have few personal assets, or you owe a lot of money on them, you aren't likely to lose much. And in any case, you will get to keep the basic necessities of life, including clothing, furniture, possibly a vehicle, and some or all of your equity in your house, depending on your state's laws. Now let's look at what you're likely to lose, if anything.

Your House

If you put your house up as collateral for a business loan or line of credit, and you default on that loan—or if you stop making mortgage payments on the house—the lender can foreclose. Bankruptcy can delay the foreclosure for a while, but ultimately, if you don't make the payments, you'll lose your house.

But what about debts not tied to your house? To determine whether your house might be sold to pay debts to your landlord, suppliers, or any other business obligations, you need to understand how your state's "homestead exemption" works. Most states let you keep your principal residence if your equity in it doesn't exceed a certain limit (and, of course, you keep making mortgage payments). In other words, it can't be taken by creditors or by the bankruptcy trustee to pay your debts. In Texas, Florida, and a few other states, your residence is exempt no matter how much it's worth. In most states, only $10,000 to $50,000 of your equity is exempt from creditors. However, in a few states, such as Tennessee, Ohio, Maryland, Kentucky, and Alabama, the homestead exemption is $5,000 or less, and in New Jersey and Pennsylvania, it's zero. (Note that the homestead exemption applies only to main residences, not second houses, vacation houses, or rental property.)

If the amount of equity you have in your home is less than your state's exempt amount, there's no equity for the trustee to take. You'll be able to keep your house—assuming you keep up on your mortgage payments after the bankruptcy. But if the equity you have in your home is worth significantly more than the exempt amount, the trustee in a Chapter 7 bankruptcy will want to sell the house, give you the exempt amount (which in most states you can continue to protect by investing it another house), and use the rest of your equity to pay off your creditors.

EXAMPLE: Nathan's New York adventure travel company fails owing a $60,000 small business loan. Because the company was a sole proprietorship, Nathan is 100% personally liable for its debts, and he files for Chapter 7 personal bankruptcy. Because he has more consumer debts than personal debts (he owes $8,000 on credit cards and $245,000 on his house), Nathan is required to take the Chapter 7 means test. He passes it easily because for the last six months his income has been low and his expenses high.

Nathan's house is worth $300,000, giving him $55,000 in equity. In New York, $50,000 of home equity is exempt from being taken to pay creditors. The bankruptcy trustee could sell the house, give Nathan the $50,000 in equity that is exempt, and pay the remaining $5,000 toward Nathan's creditors. However, the trustee knows that the costs of selling the house would be more than $5,000, making it a losing proposition for the trustee, so he doesn't sell the house and Nathan gets to keep it.

TIP

Bankruptcy can buy you time. Some small business people file bankruptcy just to get some badly needed breathing room. That's because when you file for bankruptcy, the court issues an "automatic stay," an order that requires all creditors to immediately stop collection activities, including foreclosure, and prevents them from filing lawsuits or shutting off utilities. This delay might give you at least a few months to bring in the income you need to get current on your secured debts, so you can keep the collateral. After a month or two, however, secured lenders can get court permission to proceed with a foreclosure, repossession, or collection.

Your Car, SUV, or Pickup

If your car is security for your car loan, and you default on that loan, the lender can repossess your car. Bankruptcy can delay the repossession for a while—giving you an opportunity to get current—but ultimately, if you don't make the payments, you'll lose the car.

If your car isn't collateral for a debt, it still might be taken and sold by the bankruptcy trustee to pay your business debts. It depends on your state's vehicle exemption limit. Most states allow you to keep one vehicle with equity up to a certain exempt amount—usually between $1,000 and $5,000. However, some states, such as Texas, give you a lump sum exemption you can use for any type of personal property—including vehicles—up to a total of $20,000 or $30,000. (To find out your state's vehicle exemption limit, go to www.legalconsumer.com/bankruptcy/exemptions and enter your zip code.)

EXAMPLE: Jose and Jessica have two vehicles. One is a newish pickup on which they are making payments; they have no equity in it since its value went down quite a bit in the last year. The other is a ten-year-old car they own free and clear, worth $1,000.

In bankruptcy, because Jose and Jessica can't afford the payments, the pickup goes back to the lender. The amount the lender is able to sell it for doesn't cover the amount they owe on the loan plus costs, but this debt will be wiped out in bankruptcy. Because the older car is worth only $1,000, it is exempt from being taken to pay other debts, meaning Jose and Jessica can keep it.

If you bought your vehicle in the last year or two and don't have much equity in it, chances are you will be allowed to keep it after bankruptcy—if you can make the payments. On the other hand, if you have equity in your car that's worth more than your state's exemption amount (say you finished paying for your car and it's worth $12,000), you will probably have to give it up to the bankruptcy trustee. However, the trustee is likely to give you an opportunity to buy back the car at a greatly reduced price. If you decline, the trustee will sell it, give you the exempt amount, and use the rest to pay your creditors.

> **CAUTION**
>
> **Don't pay off your car before you file for bankruptcy.** Many people are under the erroneous impression that they get to keep one vehicle when they file for bankruptcy, so they do whatever they can to pay off their best car or truck before they file. As you can see from the discussion above, because exemption laws protect only a limited dollar amount in most states, it's better to owe money on your car when you go into bankruptcy.

Leased Vehicles or Equipment

If you want to keep paying for a leased car or other equipment, you can usually hold on to the leased property even after filing for Chapter 7 bankruptcy, by contacting the lease company and arranging to continue making the payments.

Business Assets

The bankruptcy trustee has the power to take valuable business equipment and supplies and sell them for cash, to at least partially repay your creditors. However, most states let you keep a couple of thousand dollars worth of tools or equipment—called the "tools of the trade" exemption—if you will continue to use them to make a living. And again, some states give you a lump sum exemption to use for any type of property, including business property, up to a total of $20,000 or $30,000.

Having your business set up as a corporation or LLC won't protect your business assets if you file personal bankruptcy—if you are the sole owner of your corporation or LLC. The bankruptcy trustee can simply take over your shares or membership interest and vote to sell or liquidate the business and distribute the proceeds to the business's creditors. In deciding whether to dissolve the corporation or LLC, the trustee will take a cost/benefit approach: The trustee will look at the cost of dissolving and liquidating the business, how much the assets can be sold for, and whether you can claim any exemptions in the assets. In many cases, the business's debts are equal to or close to the value of the business's assets, so the trustee decides liquidating the business wouldn't be worth it. But if the business has little debt and some valuable nonexempt assets, it's likely that the trustee will dissolve the corporation or LLC and sell the assets.

Other Valuable Assets

Every state allows you to keep a certain amount of essential personal property, such as clothing, appliances, and furniture. Even if your property is worth somewhat more than the exempt amount of personal property, the bankruptcy trustee is not likely to take it to sell, because the considerable costs of a legal sale would typically eat up the overage. However, expensive art, collectibles, boats, antiques, stocks, bonds, and highly valuable jewelry are likely to be taken and sold by the bankruptcy trustee. Fortunately, federal law exempts virtually all pensions and retirement plans from being taken in bankruptcy.

EXAMPLE: Arcelia, with her husband Alejandro's help, starts a high-end chocolat-erie called Viva Chocolat! in Austin, Texas. Unfortunately, Arcelia's timing is bad, and a month after she spends $50,000 on rent, remodeling, permits, and equipment, the economy goes south. After bringing in only $1,000 her first three months, Arcelia buys her way out of her lease and closes down.

As a sole proprietor, she is personally liable for all of the business's debts. Unable to pay them, she files for Chapter 7 bankruptcy to protect their house and Alejandro's income (Texas is a community property state, so Alejandro and Arcelia are jointly liable for Arcelia's business debts). Because their debts are primarily business—$50,000 in business debts and $30,000 in personal unsecured debts—they don't need to pass the means test.

In bankruptcy, their house is entirely exempt from being taken to pay their debts, even though they have $350,000 equity in it, because the Texas homestead exemption is unlimited. They are also able to keep up to $60,000 in personal possessions—both of their vehicles, in which they have a total of $30,000 equity, and all of their furniture, art, jewelry, and family heirlooms (Texas law exempts all of these). Arcelia does have to sell the business equipment she bought to pay her business debts—they don't fall under the tools of the trade exemption since she won't continue to use them to make a living. Fortunately, federal law protects the money in Alejandro's 401(k) plan.

Other Consequences of a Chapter 7 Bankruptcy

Obviously, there's a lot to think about before you decide whether filing Chapter 7 bankruptcy is in your best interest. In addition to the possibility of losing property, here are a couple of other consequences that may be important to you.

Payments you made to family or friends may be reversed. The bankruptcy trustee will look at all payments and asset transfers you made during the year or two before the bankruptcy filing to make sure that you didn't make "preference" payments to certain creditors. If you made payments on a loan to relatives or close business associates in the year before filing, or transferred property to them for little or no payment in the two years before filing, a bankruptcy court can reverse the payment or transfer. The trustee can and will "recapture" (take back) payments you made to family or friends to divide them equally between all creditors. If the money you paid to family or friends has been spent, the trustee can sue the recipient of the payment to get it back. To make things worse, if the bankruptcy judge decides you made the payment or transfer for fraudulent purposes, your bankruptcy case could be dismissed.

Your credit rating will be damaged. A Chapter 7 bankruptcy will go on your credit report and stay there for ten years. In theory, this information may hurt your chance of getting a subsequent mortgage, car loan, other credit, or possibly even a job. But in practice, if you are far over your head in debt, it's a good thing that you won't be able to immediately run up more debt (after all, you can file Chapter 7 bankruptcy only every eight years). It's also true that, if you take sensible steps to rebuild your credit and can show you have a job, many lenders will extend at least some new credit within a year or two. Keep in mind, though, that none of us yet knows what upcoming credit markets will look like.

RESOURCE

In-depth information on filing Chapter 7. See *How to File for Chapter 7 Bankruptcy*, by Stephen Elias, Albin Renauer, and Robin Leonard (Nolo).

CAUTION

You may need to get out of a partnership or LLC before filing for bankruptcy. If you are a partner in a partnership or a member of a multi-member LLC, you may have signed a buy-sell agreement that requires you to terminate your ownership interest before filing for bankruptcy. If you don't, you open yourself up to a lawsuit from your co-owners. A small business attorney can help you assess your obligations and options here.

More About Chapter 7 Bankruptcy for Business

Corporations, LLCs, and partnerships can use Chapter 7 business bankruptcy (though it's rarely used for partnerships, and for good reason, as discussed above). But if you file for personal bankruptcy to get rid of your personal liability for your business debts—or you aren't personally liable for any business debts—there may be little reason to file a business bankruptcy. However, there are a few practical reasons business might want to file.

A Chapter 7 business bankruptcy is similar to a Chapter 7 personal bankruptcy. The bankruptcy trustee sells the business's assets and pays off the creditors, priority debts (back taxes, wages, and benefits) first. No business property is exempt, so the trustee can take anything the business owns—the entire company is liquidated. In theory, after the creditors are paid, the business owners (shareholders, members, or partners) receive anything left over. In fact, when a business files for bankruptcy, its liabilities usually exceed its assets, and there is nothing left for the owners.

When a corporation or LLC files for bankruptcy, that's the end of its debts (unless the owners personally guaranteed some of them). If creditors aren't fully paid, too bad—the owners of the business are off the hook.

The bankruptcy trustee is paid from the business's assets, so in actuality your creditors, not you, pay the bankruptcy costs. What about your credit rating? A corporation or LLC bankruptcy shouldn't affect your personal credit if you're not personally liable for any of the business's debts.

If You Might File for Bankruptcy

If you decide that personal or business bankruptcy is probably the best strategy for you, you'll need to plan ahead to steer clear of some common missteps. Fortunately, even if you end up solving your debt problems without bankruptcy, these tips make good sense anyway.

Don't Make Preference Payments to Creditors

If a friend, relative, or business associate has lent you money, you may be tempted to try to repay some or all of it before filing bankruptcy. Bad idea. When you file for bankruptcy, the bankruptcy trustee will scrutinize all payments you make during the year before the filing, to make sure that some creditors weren't given an unfair advantage (called "preference payments"). As mentioned above, the trustee will want to "recapture" (take back) any preference payments you made to creditors within the 90 days before you file—or within one year if those payments were made to a relative or close business associate (an "insider")—and will divide them equally among all creditors. If your relatives or associates can't come up with the money that you paid them, the bankruptcy trustee can sue them to recover it.

You are legally allowed to pay one unsecured creditor ahead of the others if the creditor is not a close relative or associate—for example, you can choose to pay the business line of credit that you signed a personal guarantee on before you pay your suppliers. The bankruptcy trustee will, however, look back 90 days at payments you made to your regular creditors. The trustee can make a company that was paid "disgorge" (return) payments of over $5,475 and spread the money among all of your creditors. (But if fewer than 51% of your debts are from your business operations, the trustee can force a company to disgorge only payments of more than $600 from a regular creditor.)

Don't Borrow From Friends or Family Unless They Can Afford to Lose It

If you borrow money from family and friends to repay your business debts but then end up filing for bankruptcy, none of the money you borrowed can be paid back, even if your business property is sold and the proceeds distributed to your creditors. That's because the bankruptcy court is likely to classify a loan from a relative or close associate as a gift, not a loan.

Don't Pay Yourself a Bonus or Back Pay

The bankruptcy system treats you like an insider creditor. So if you pay yourself a bonus, repay a loan you made to the business, or otherwise take money out of the company during the 12 months prior to filing for bankruptcy, it will be considered a recoverable preference payment. It might even be considered bankruptcy fraud, which can result in jail time or at least in the dismissal of your bankruptcy case.

EXAMPLE: Julieta runs an insurance brokerage with five employees. When her sales slump for three months in a row, Julieta realizes she has to cut her biggest expense: payroll. First she lets her employees know that she cut her own salary from $8,000 per month to $4,000, and then she cuts everyone else's salary by 10%. Two months later, business hasn't picked up, and she finds herself with even lower sales and $120,000 in personally guaranteed debt. With her creditors threatening lawsuits, she decides to file for Chapter 7 personal bankruptcy.

In the last month of business, she is able to collect an $8,000 commission payment from a client insurance company. Reasoning that she gave up $8,000 in salary over two months, she repays herself the $8,000 before filing for bankruptcy. After she files, the court requires her to pay back the $8,000 to the bankruptcy trustee. Fortunately, the bankruptcy judge does not find that her intent was fraudulent, so her bankruptcy case is not dismissed.

Don't Go on a Shopping Spree

Some people, realizing that bankruptcy is inevitable, grab whatever cash they can and buy a car, luxury items, or go on a trip before they file. Another bad idea. If you buy luxury goods or services within three months of filing, you are considered to have had the intent to defraud the bankruptcy court, and the resulting debts won't be discharged in bankruptcy.

Even if you make big purchases, such as a vacation time-share, country club dues, or even a pricey new wardrobe, *more* than three months before filing, the creditor can still claim that your intent was fraudulent and you never meant to pay the money back—but in this case, the creditor has to prove that your intent was fraudulent. If the creditor is successful, these debts won't be discharged in bankruptcy.

Don't Take Equipment or Supplies From Your LLC or Corporation

If you are headed into bankruptcy, taking goods from your LLC or corporation, like laptops, forklifts, vehicles, inventory, or supplies, is considered stealing from your creditors and bankruptcy fraud, which can result in the dismissal of your bankruptcy case or even criminal charges.

Avoid Taking Cash Advances on a Credit Card

If you take a large cash advance on a credit card before filing for bankruptcy, the credit card company can assert that you were trying to defraud it and that you had no intent of paying the money back. In consequence, the bankruptcy trustee can treat the cash advance as a nondischargeable debt, or even throw your case out of court entirely because of it. Any cash advance over $825 taken within 70 days of filing for bankruptcy is usually nondischargeable. Lesser amounts should be dischargeable unless the creditor argues successfully that you had no intent to pay the money back.

Don't Pay Off Your Car Loan

As mentioned, many people erroneously believe that they get to keep one car when they file for bankruptcy (regardless of the amount of equity) and do whatever they can to pay off their car loan before they file. In truth, as mentioned above, under the exemption laws of most states, you get to keep only a limited amount of equity in a vehicle, typically $1,000 to $5,000. If you have more equity in your car, the bankruptcy trustee will grab it to pay down your debts. So find out your state's equity limit for vehicles and stay within it.

Don't Panic About Utilities or Your Lease

If you declare bankruptcy, the utility companies can't use this as an excuse for immediately shutting off services (although they can require you to post a reasonable deposit to keep on the lights, phone service, and heat). As long as you pay future bills on time, you should be fine. Similarly, as long as you keep paying your rent, your landlord can't evict you. Don't be spooked by the clause, common in commercial leases, that says that you're automatically in default (in violation of your lease) if you file for bankruptcy. These clauses are generally not enforceable (except against sublessees and assignees).

Consider Returning Some Leased Property

If you're leasing equipment and are going out of business, return the equipment to the leasing company before you file for bankruptcy. No doubt the company will bill you for the amount owed under the remainder of the lease, but this debt will be discharged in bankruptcy. On the other hand, if you will try to soldier on with your business postbankruptcy and want to keep leased property, you'll need to keep making payments on time. Your obligation won't be discharged by your bankruptcy, because the debt is secured by the equipment.

Don't Pay All of Your Unsecured Debt

If you are certain that you'll file for bankruptcy and there are certain unsecured debts you plan to wipe out, such as credit card bills and medical bills, it often makes sense to stop paying anything toward them. They will be fully discharged in bankruptcy, so you don't really gain anything by paying them down now. Better to put the money toward secured loans, such as your mortgage or car loan, and debts you're personally liable for, such as payroll taxes or bankruptcy fees. Just be really sure the unsecured debt you stop paying on is dischargeable in bankruptcy before you stop making payments.

Consider Selling Some Nonexempt Property

If you own valuable property that you are likely to lose in a Chapter 7 bankruptcy, such as a boat, vehicle, or business equipment, you might be able to sell it before you file and use the proceeds to pay personally guaranteed loans and bankruptcy fees. However, you shouldn't use the proceeds to increase your exempt property—for example, paying the proceeds toward your mortgage when your home equity will be protected by your state's homestead exemption. If you do, and the court determines that you intended to defraud your unsecured creditors, your case could be dismissed and charges filed against you.

Don't Let Your Insurance Coverage Lapse

If you need to keep your liability insurance in force to cover unknown liabilities, file for bankruptcy just after you renew your policy. That's because when you file, you'll want to have insurance in place that extends at least 12 months into the future. Otherwise you may have a tough time finding an insurance carrier willing to renew your business coverage or issue a new policy. As long as you continue to pay on time for existing coverage, the insurance can't be canceled because of your bankruptcy, and you'll enjoy some peace of mind. ●

How to Prepare a Profit and Loss Forecast and Cash Flow Analysis

To determine with a reasonable degree of accuracy whether your business can return to profitability, you need to master two essential spreadsheet tools: a profit and loss forecast and a cash flow analysis. If you haven't prepared these yet, it's high time you learned. (Good news: It's not hard.)

Why do you need both of these tools? Basically, because they tell you different things. The P&L forecast is a very useful long-term management tool, which you can use to predict your business's viability six months or a year into the future. But it doesn't give you a picture of how and when money comes in and out of your business. A P&L could show that you were making a profit while your bank account was below empty. So it's also essential that you accurately track cash using a cash flow analysis.

RESOURCE

More on making a plan. If you want more detailed step-by-step help, complete with far more detailed explanations and examples, check out *How to Write a Business Plan*, by Mike McKeever (Nolo).

Profit and Loss Forecast

A profit and loss, or P&L, forecast is a projection of how much money you will bring in by selling products or services and how much profit you will make from these sales. In good times, you use it to ensure that there will be enough money coming in to exceed the costs of providing the goods and services so you can make a solid profit. In tough times, your P&L can play an essential role in showing you what kind of a plan you need to return to breakeven, so that you'll be able to survive until better times come.

If you use accounting software, such as Intuit's *QuickBooks*, Sage's *Peachtree Accounting*, or *Accounting Express* by Microsoft, it will generate a P&L forecast for you once you enter monthly sales and expense estimates. You can also create your own forecast, using a basic spreadsheet. Just look at the sample P&L below and you'll see how to set it up.

Step 1. Estimate Future Revenue

Start by estimating how much you'll take in each month during the next six to 12 months. No question, this will be a guesstimate, but if you extrapolate from current sales levels and allow for significant seasonal fluctuations and other known variables, you shouldn't be too far off.

EXAMPLE: Emme owns and operates a consignment shop that sells gently used clothes for women and children. She buys her inventory from moms who bring in their own and their children's clothing to sell. Emme is careful to buy mostly well-known brands (and when possible, high-end ones) that she can sell for a premium.

Before the economy took a dive, Emme was selling $15,000 of clothing per month. But sales have been down almost 30% lately. For her profit and loss forecast, she estimates that she'll bring in an average of $10,000 per month in sales over the next year—more at back-to-school time and the holidays, less during the slow summer months.

Step 2. Estimate Your Variable Costs

Now estimate the monthly cost to you of the goods or services you'll sell as part of achieving your sales estimate. These are your variable costs. They're called variable, or sometimes incremental, because they go up or down depending on the volume of products or services you produce or sell. (And in retail, they're called "cost of goods.") For example, if you're a mail-order business, then the more you sell, the more you'll pay for shipping costs.

Other variable costs include inventory, supplies, materials, packaging, and sometimes labor used in providing your product or service. In the case of services, count labor costs as variable costs only if they will go up or down depending on how many sales you make. For instance, if you have to hire independent contractors or temps to cover busy periods, those labor costs are variable. But if you employ a manager, bookkeeper, or marketing employee, you'll have to pay their salaries no matter how much sales go up or down, meaning their wages should be listed under fixed costs (overhead) in Step 5, below.

Your Gross Profit Margin

It's also useful to know your gross profit margin. Gross profit margin measures the difference between the costs of producing a product or providing a service and what you're selling it for. In short, it lets you know how profitable your products and services are.

To get your profit margin, divide your estimated average monthly gross profit by your estimated monthly sales.

EXAMPLE: Emme divides her monthly gross profit of $5,500 by her $10,000 of sales, to get a profit margin of 55%. Now she knows she will get to keep, on average, about 55 cents of every sales dollar she takes in (before paying for overhead).

Profit margins can be used in many different ways. Some businesses regularly calculate their profit margin to monitor the profitability of their products or services. A decrease in profit margin over time usually means that variable costs have gone up—costs for raw materials, manufacturing, or labor—which should nudge the company to either look for new suppliers or raise prices. Other businesses use their anticipated profit margin to help them price products or services (and increase profitability). For example, a business that requires a profit margin of 60% and produces a product that costs $20 to make would set the retail price at around $50 ($20 ÷ (100% − 60%)). (However, some experts disagree with this use of profit margin, recommending instead that businesses start with the price they think customers will pay and then making sure the costs are low enough to make a profit.) Another way to use profit margins is to screen new products and services to sell. For instance, a retail gift shop might decide to add only new products that can be bought and sold at a price that yields a profit margin of 50%.

What's a good profit margin? The answer varies across industries. For example, most airlines have low profit margins, around 5%; the software industry has traditionally had high profit margins, around 80%–90%; wholesalers' profit margins are somewhere in the middle, between 15% and 35%. But without looking at the costs of a company's overhead, such as marketing and administration, profit margins don't give the whole picture of a company's profitability.

EXAMPLE: Emme used to spend more than $6,500 per month to buy used clothing to resell. But because sales have been down so much, she will need less inventory and estimates that she will probably spend only about $4,500 per month.

Step 3. Estimate Your Gross Profit

Now simply subtract your average monthly variable costs from your estimated average monthly sales revenue to get your estimated monthly gross profit. This number will let you calculate how much of each dollar of sales you get to keep. From that amount, however, you'll have to pay for overhead costs; anything left over is your net profit.

EXAMPLE: Subtracting her inventory costs of $4,500 per month from her sales esti-mate of $10,000 per month, Emme estimates her average monthly gross profit will be $5,500. (This is before subtracting her overhead, which is discussed below.)

Step 4. Calculate Your Net Profit

Your net profit is the most important number you need to determine. This lets you see whether you'll have any money left after paying your overhead costs or, failing that, whether you can at least break even. To arrive at your net profit, make a list of your monthly fixed costs, which are items such as:

- rent
- employees' wages (including payroll taxes, benefits, and workers' comp costs)
- your wages, if you plan to pay yourself a regular wage regardless of how profitable the business is (but if, as is typical, you'll just take what's left over after costs are paid, don't include your salary as a fixed cost)
- utilities
- telephone
- insurance
- office equipment

- advertising, and

- accounting, bookkeeping, or tax preparation fees.

Divide any annual expenses, such as insurance premiums, by 12 to get a monthly amount.

To arrive at your monthly net profit (or loss), subtract your average estimated monthly fixed costs from your monthly gross profit.

EXAMPLE: Over the past year, Emme has been able to pay herself $60,000 from the business, but she knows that with sales dropping this won't be possible in the coming year. She guesses she'll need to cut her take-home wages to $30,000—and if she can't bring home at least that amount, she won't keep the shop open.

Emme adds up her fixed costs, including these and a few others:

- $1,000 for rent

- $100 for utilities

- $4,000 for wages (this includes $12,000 per year for a part-time assistant as well as employment taxes and costs), and

- $100 for insurance (her annual premium is $1,200), and so on.

The total of her fixed costs comes to $5,500 per month. When she puts one month's numbers together in a spreadsheet, here is what it looks like.

January		
Sales Revenue		10,000
Cost of Goods		4,500
Gross Profit		5,500
Fixed Costs		
Rent	1,000	
Wages	4,000	
Utilities	100	
Telephone	30	
Insurance	100	
Advertising	40	
Accounting	130	
Miscellaneous	100	
Total Fixed Costs		5,500
Net Profit (Loss)		0

When you are satisfied with your cost estimates for an average month, fill in estimates for six or 12 months. Then, for each month, subtract your total fixed expenses from your gross profit to get the net profit.

EXAMPLE: Emme fills in an entire year of sales estimates, with the usual dip in sales she experiences in summer and then upswings in September when the kids go back to school and in December, traditionally her best month. Then, using her estimate of $4,500 in monthly variable costs and her estimate of $5,500 in monthly fixed costs, she comes up with a net profit for each month. Emme notices that in the summer she'll lose a little over $1,000 per month for a few months in a row, but will make it back up by December.

Emme's Profit and Loss Forecast					
	January	February	March	April	May
Sales Revenue	10,000	10,000	10,000	10,000	10,000
Variable costs	4,500	4,500	4,500	4,500	4,500
Gross Profit	5,500	5,500	5,500	5,500	5,500
Fixed Costs					
Rent	1,000	1,000	1,000	1,000	1,000
Wages	4,000	4,000	4,000	4,000	4,000
Utilities	100	100	100	100	100
Phone	30	30	30	30	30
Insurance	100	100	100	100	100
Advertising	40	40	40	40	40
Accounting	130	130	130	130	130
Miscellaneous	100	100	100	100	100
Total Fixed Costs	**5,500**	**5,500**	**5,500**	**5,500**	**5,500**
Net Profit (Loss)	0	0	0	0	0

June	July	August	September	October	November	December
8,000	8,000	7,000	12,000	10,000	10,000	15,000
4,500	4,500	4,500	4,500	4,500	4,500	4,500
4,400	4,400	3,850	6,600	5,500	5,500	8,250
1,000	1,000	1,000	1,000	1,000	1,000	1,000
4,000	4,000	4,000	4,000	4,000	4,000	4,000
100	100	100	100	100	100	100
30	30	30	30	30	30	30
100	100	100	100	100	100	100
40	40	40	40	40	40	40
130	130	130	130	130	130	130
100	100	100	100	100	100	100
5,500	**5,500**	**5,500**	**5,500**	**5,500**	**5,500**	**5,500**
−1,100	−1,100	−1,650	1,100	0	0	2,750

Cash Flow Analysis

To prepare a cash flow analysis, you'll use many of the same figures you came up with for your profit and loss forecast. The main difference is that you'll include all cash inflows and outflows, not just sales revenue and business expenses. For example, you'll include loans, loan payments, transfers of personal money into and out of the business, taxes, and other money that isn't earned or spent as part of your core business operation.

Also, in your cash flow analysis, you'll record costs in the month that you expect to incur them, rather than spreading annual amounts equally over 12 months. This is important because it's easy to show a monthly profit on a spreadsheet but go belly up from lack of cash if you can't pay your bills on time. For example, if you have a $4,000 workers' comp premium and a $3,000 liability insurance premium due each July 1, you'll need to find a way to come up with real dollars then, not later. Plus, if you make sales to some customers on credit (for example, a painter who invoices customers after the job is done rather requiring full payment up front), your cash flow analysis should account for the fact that you won't get paid right away, as well as the fact that you might not collect some of the credit sales at all.

Here are the steps you need to follow to create a cash flow analysis like the sample below. Do one month at a time.

Step 1. Enter Your Beginning Balance

For the first month, start your projection with the actual amount of cash your business will have in your bank account.

Step 2. Estimate Cash Coming In

Fill in all amounts you expect to take in during the month. Include sales revenue that will actually be in hand, collections of previous sales made on credit, transfers of personal money into the business, and any loans coming into the business—basically, every dollar that will flow into your business checking account.

Step 3. Estimate Cash Going Out

Enter all your projected payments for the month. Include your variable costs (cost of goods), your fixed costs such as rent, tax payments, and any loan payments. Add them to get your monthly total.

Step 4. Subtract Outlays From Income

Finally, subtract your total monthly cash-outs from your total monthly income; the result will be your cash left at the end of the month. That figure is also your beginning cash balance at the start of the next month. Copy this amount to the top of the next month's column and go through the whole process over again.

EXAMPLE: On January 2 (as a New Year's resolution), Emme starts work on a cash flow projection for the next 12 months. She starts by putting the $5,000 she has in her business bank account in the "Cash at Start of Month" column for January. In her "Cash Coming In" section, she includes her cash sales (which are about 75% of her sales) and her credit sales (about 25% of her sales) on separate lines. She adds in all of the cash sales, but only 80% of her credit sales, because some percentage of her credit customers always take longer than 30 days to pay. In the "Cash Going Out" section, Emme includes her variable and fixed costs, putting the annual insurance premium she's about to pay in the January column rather than spreading it over 12 months.

Emme's Cash Flow Analysis					
	January	February	March	April	May
Cash at Start of Month	5,000	3,340	3,080	2,220	1,960
Cash Coming In					
Sales Paid (75%)	7,500	7,500	7,500	7,500	7,500
Collections of Credit Sales	2,000	2,000	2,000	2,000	2,000
Loans & transfers	0	0	0	0	0
Total Cash In	9,500	9,500	9,500	9,500	9,500
Cash Going Out					
Inventory	4,500	4,500	4,500	4,500	4,500
Rent	1,000	1,000	1,000	1,000	1,000
Wages	4,000	4,000	4,000	4,000	4,000
Utilities	100	100	100	100	100
Phone	30	30	30	30	30
Insurance	1,200	0	0	0	0
Ads	200	0	0	0	0
Accounting	130	130	130	130	130
Miscellaneous	0	0	600	0	0
Loan payments	0	0	0	0	0
Taxes					
Total Cash Out	**11,160**	**9,760**	**10,360**	**9,760**	**9,760**
Cash at End of Month	3,340	3,080	2,220	1,960	1,700

June	July	August	September	October	November	December
1,700	−740	−2,900	−6,410	−4,770	−5,030	−5,290
6,000	6,000	5,250	9,000	7,500	7,500	11,250
1,600	1,600	1,400	2,400	2,000	2,000	3,000
0	0	0	0	0	0	0
7,600	7,600	6,650	11,400	9,500	9,500	14,250
4,500	4,500	4,500	4,500	4,500	4,500	4,500
1,000	1,000	1,000	1,000	1,000	1,000	1,000
4,000	4,000	4,000	4,000	4,000	4,000	4,000
100	100	100	100	100	100	100
30	30	30	30	30	30	30
0	0	0	0	0	0	0
280	0	0	0	0	0	0
130	130	130	130	130	130	130
0	0	400	0	0	0	200
0	0	0	0	0	0	0
10,040	9,760	10,160	9,760	9,760	9,760	9,960
−740	−2,900	−6,410	−4,770	−5,030	−5,290	−1,000

It's easy to see why a cash flow analysis can give you a more realistic picture of whether your business will have the money to pay its expenses—in other words, sufficient cash flow to stay afloat—than a P&L forecast. This is especially true for companies that make sales on credit, because typically some credit sales are not paid within the expected 30 days (and others not at all). A P&L forecast does not account for late or missing payments, and this is why it's so important to do a cash flow analysis as well.

EXAMPLE: After filling in her cash flow projection, Emme realizes that her account will go significantly negative in the slow summer months. She may not even be back in the black in December, her biggest sales month, because she has estimated that about $500 per month in payments on credit sales will be late. (Though if she eventually gets caught up collecting her accounts receivable, she will be profitable for the year.) But given that some customers will always pay late, she knows that if she can't reduce her costs in some way, she will need some cash to tide herself over in some months, especially during the summer. Because she has already cut her own pay in half and trimmed other expenses to the bone, she'll have to bring in money from extra sales, provide extra services, or get a loan from family, friends, or a bank line of credit.

Despite what your P&L forecast says about your company being profitable or breaking even over the next six to 12 months, if your cash flow is projected to go negative, it means you're not going to be able to pay your bills when they become due, and you'll have to bring in more income or borrow some cash to cover the shortfalls.

EXAMPLE: Going back to her spreadsheet, Emme sees that a loan of $8,000 would cover the shortfall, even accounting for making a small loan payment. After December sales are in, she'd still have a balance of $5,000. But she also sees that even if she gets a loan, it would let her business survive only about 12 to 18 months of lower sales before again going cash-negative the next summer. In short, she needs to make sure that she can boost her sales back to her previous levels within the next 12 to 18 months, or she risks going in the red again before paying back the loan.

Emme's Cash Flow Analysis With $8,000 Loan					
	January	February	March	April	May
Cash at Start of Month	5,000	11,180	10,760	9,740	9,320
Cash Coming In					
Sales Paid (75%)	7,500	7,500	7,500	7,500	7,500
Collections of Credit Sales	2,000	2,000	2,000	2,000	2,000
Loans & Transfers	8,000	0	0	0	0
Total Cash In	**17,500**	**9,500**	**9,500**	**9,500**	**9,500**
Cash Going Out					
Inventory	4,500	4,500	4,500	4,500	4,500
Rent	1,000	1,000	1,000	1,000	1,000
Wages	4,000	4,000	4,000	4,000	4,000
Utilities	100	100	100	100	100
Phone	30	30	30	30	30
Insurance	1,200	0	0	0	0
Advertising	200	0	0	0	0
Accounting	130	130	130	130	130
Miscellaneous	0	0	600	0	0
Loan payments	160	160	160	160	160
Taxes					
Total Cash Out	**11,320**	**9,920**	**10,520**	**9,920**	**9,920**
Cash at End of Month	11,180	10,760	9,740	9,320	8,900

June	July	August	September	October	November	December
8,900	6,300	3,980	310	1,790	1,370	950
6,000	6,000	5,250	9,000	7,500	7,500	11,250
1,600	1,600	1,400	2,400	2,000	2,000	3,000
0	0	0	0	0	0	0
7,600	**7,600**	**6,650**	**11,400**	**9,500**	**9,500**	**14,250**
4,500	4,500	4,500	4,500	4,500	4,500	4,500
1,000	1,000	1,000	1,000	1,000	1,000	1,000
4,000	4,000	4,000	4,000	4,000	4,000	4,000
100	100	100	100	100	100	100
30	30	30	30	30	30	30
0	0	0	0	0	0	0
280	0	0	0	0	0	0
130	130	130	130	130	130	130
0	0	400	0	0	0	200
160	160	160	160	160	160	160
10,200	**9,920**	**10,320**	**9,920**	**9,920**	**9,920**	**10,120**
6,300	3,980	310	1,790	1,370	950	5,080

Emme sets about thinking how to come up with the extra $8,000. Her first thought is having a one-time sale. But even at her usual 55% profit margin, she would need to sell an extra $14,500 in clothes to generate that much gross profit. Discounting prices for a big sale would lower her profit margin, meaning she'd have to sell more. (If she sold her inventory at a 20% discount, her profit margin would be less than 45%, and she'd need to bring in more than $18,000 in additional sales.)

Realizing that she doesn't have a realistic chance of selling that much inventory, she goes looking for a loan. When family, friends, and the bank turn her down, her last resort is to take $8,000 from her home equity line of credit to tide her over. In the meantime, she gets to work on a clever marketing plan to boost sales until better times are here.

Index

R

Reaffirming a debt, 75

Recapture, 276, 278

Recession rate/discount, 54, 105, 113, 156

Reciprocal discounting program, 156

Recourse factoring, 64

Refinancing, 82

Release of debt, 241–242, 259

Rent, 87–88, 93, 281

Repossessions, 80–81, 92, 273

Resale certificate/license cancellation, 251

Resource combining, 48, 220

Restaurants
bulk sales laws and, 99, 236
changing business direction, 32–33
importance of cleanliness in, 164–165
marketing and innovation, 21, 123–124, 147
special considerations for, 20–22

Retailers
adding a service component, 116
asking for customer support, 162, 173
bulk sales laws and, 99, 236
calculating gross profit margin, 286
discounting, 57
embracing long-term trends, 125–127
hibernation, 10
identifying your customers, 147, 148, 149
innovation and marketing, 128, 131, 156, 157
marketing vs. advertising, 159–161
negotiating with creditors, 258–259
profit and loss forecast example, 285, 287–291
renegotiating your lease, 48–49
selling your business, 10
special considerations for, 12–16
understanding profitability, 113–116
working reasonable hours, 204–205

Retirement plans, 86, 246, 275

Right to setoff, 234

S

Sales, 156, 172–173, 230

Sales taxes, 88, 244

Sales tax ID number cancellation, 251

Saving your business
changing business direction, 11, 30–33
choosing hibernation, 8–9
choosing to sell, 7–8, 33
construction businesses, 19–20
creating an advisory board, 4–6
franchises, 23–24
importance of acting fast, 26–27
objectivity in, 4–5, 9–10
overview on choice of, 9–12
restaurants, 20–22
retailers, 12–16
service businesses, 16–19

NOLO *Keep Up to Date*

1   Go to **Nolo.com/newsletter** to sign up for free newsletters and discounts on Nolo products.

- **Nolo Briefs.** Our monthly email newsletter with great deals and free information.

- **Nolo's Special Offer.** A monthly newsletter with the biggest Nolo discounts around.

- **BizBriefs.** Tips and discounts on Nolo products for business owners and managers.

- **Landlord's Quarterly.** Deals and free tips just for landlords and property managers, too.

2   And don't forget to check **Nolo.com/updates** to find free legal updates to this book.

Let Us Hear From You

3   Comments on this book? We want to hear 'em. Email us at feedback@nolo.com.

SAVE1

NOLO Catalog

BUSINESS

	PRICE	CODE
Business Buyout Agreements (Book w/CD-ROM)	$49.99	BSAG
The California Nonprofit Corporation Kit (Binder w/CD-ROM)	$69.99	CNP
California Workers' Comp	$34.99	WORK
The Complete Guide to Buying a Business (Book w/CD-ROM)	$24.99	BUYBU
The Complete Guide to Selling a Business (Book w/CD-ROM)	$34.99	SELBU
Consultant & Independent Contractor Agreements (Book w/CD-ROM)	$34.99	CICA
The Corporate Records Handbook (Book w/CD-ROM)	$69.99	CORMI
Create Your Own Employee Handbook (Book w/CD-ROM)	$49.99	EMHA
Dealing With Problem Employees	$44.99	PROBM
Deduct It! Lower Your Small Business Taxes	$34.99	DEDU
The eBay Business Start-Up Kit (Book w/CD-ROM)	$24.99	EBIZ
Effective Fundraising for Nonprofits	$24.99	EFFN
The Employer's Legal Handbook	$49.99	EMPL
The Essential Guide to Family & Medical Leave (Book w/CD-ROM)	$49.99	FMLA
The Essential Guide to Federal Employment Laws	$44.99	FEMP
The Essential Guide to Workplace Investigations (Book w/CD-ROM)	$39.99	NVST
Every Nonprofit's Guide to Publishing	$29.99	EPNO
Form a Partnership (Book w/CD-ROM)	$39.99	PART
Hiring Your First Employee: A Step-by-Step Guide	$24.99	HEMP
Form Your Own Limited Liability Company (Book w/CD-ROM)	$44.99	LIAB
Home Business Tax Deductions: Keep What You Earn	$34.99	DEHB
How to Form a Nonprofit Corporation (Book w/CD-ROM)—National Edition	$49.99	NNP
How to Form a Nonprofit Corporation in California (Book w/CD-ROM)	$49.99	NON
How to Form Your Own California Corporation (Binder w/CD-ROM)	$59.99	CACI
How to Form Your Own California Corporation (Book w/CD-ROM)	$39.99	CCOR
How to Run a Thriving Business: Strategies for Success & Satisfaction	$19.99	THRV
How to Write a Business Plan (Book w/CD-ROM)	$34.99	SBS
Incorporate Your Business (Book w/CD-ROM)—National Edition	$49.99	NIBS
Investors in Your Backyard (Book w/CD-ROM)	$24.99	FINBUS
The Job Description Handbook (Book w/CD-ROM)	$29.99	JOB
Legal Guide for Starting & Running a Small Business	$34.99	RUNS
Legal Forms for Starting & Running a Small Business (Book w/CD-ROM)	$29.99	RUNSF
LLC or Corporation?	$24.99	CHENT
The Manager's Legal Handbook	$39.99	ELBA
Marketing Without Advertising	$20.00	MWAD
Music Law: How to Run Your Band's Business (Book w/CD-ROM)	$39.99	ML
Negotiate the Best Lease for Your Business	$24.99	LESP

Nolo's Crash Course in Small Business Basics (Audiobook on 5 CDs) .... $34.99   ABBIZ
Nolo's Quick LLC .... $29.99   LLCQ
Nonprofit Meetings, Minutes & Records (Book w/CD-ROM) .... $39.99   NORM
The Performance Appraisal Handbook (Book w/CD-ROM) .... $29.99   PERF
The Progressive Discipline Handbook (Book w/CD-ROM) .... $34.99   SDHB
Retire—And Start Your Own Business (Book w/CD-ROM) .... $34.99   BOSS
Small Business in Paradise: Working for Yourself in a Place You Love .... $19.99   SPAR
The Small Business Start-Up Kit (Book w/CD-ROM)—National Edition .... $29.99   SMBU
The Small Business Start-Up Kit for California (Book w/CD-ROM) .... $29.99   OPEN
Smart Policies for Workplace Technologies: Email, Blogs,
    Cell Phones & More (Book w/CD-ROM) .... $29.99   TECH
Starting & Building a Nonprofit: A Practical Guide (Book w/CD-ROM) .... $29.99   SNON
Starting & Running a Successful Newsletter or Magazine .... $29.99   MAG
Tax Deductions for Professionals .... $34.99   DEPO
Tax Savvy for Small Business .... $36.99   SAVVY
The Work From Home Handbook .... $19.99   USHOM
Wow! I'm in Business .... $21.99   WHOO
Working for Yourself: Law & Taxes for Independent Contractors,
    Freelancers & Consultants .... $39.99   WAGE
Working With Independent Contractors (Book w/CD-ROM) .... $34.99   HICI
Your Limited Liability Company (Book w/CD-ROM) .... $49.99   LOP
Your Rights in the Workplace .... $29.99   YRW

CONSUMER

How to Win Your Personal Injury Claim .... $34.99   PICL
Nolo's Encyclopedia of Everyday Law .... $29.99   EVL
Nolo's Guide to California Law .... $34.99   CLAW
Your Little Legal Companion (Hardcover) .... $9.95   ANNIS

ESTATE PLANNING & PROBATE

8 Ways to Avoid Probate .... $21.99   PRAV
The Busy Family's Guide to Estate Planning (Book w/CD) .... $24.99   FAM
Estate Planning Basics .... $21.99   ESPN
Estate Planning for Blended Families: Providing for Your Spouse & Children in a
    Second Marriage .... $34.99   SMAR
The Executor's Guide: Settling a Loved One's Estate or Trust .... $39.99   EXEC
Get It Together: Organize Your Records (Book w/CD-ROM) .... $21.99   GET
How to Probate an Estate in California .... $49.99   PAE
Make Your Own Living Trust (Book w/CD-ROM) .... $39.99   LITR
Nolo's Simple Will Book (Book w/CD-ROM) .... $36.99   SWIL
Plan Your Estate .... $44.99   NEST
Quick & Legal Will Book (Book w/CD-ROM) .... $21.99   QUIC
Special Needs Trusts: Protect Your Child's Financial Future (Book w/CD-ROM) .... $34.99   SPNT

FAMILY MATTERS

Always Dad: Being a Great Father During & After a Divorce	$16.99	DIFA
Building a Parenting Agreement That Works	$24.99	CUST
The Complete IEP Guide: How to Advocate for Your Special Ed Child	$34.99	IEP
Divorce & Money: How to Make the Best Financial Decisions During Divorce	$34.99	DIMO
Divorce Without Court: A Guide to Mediation & Collaborative Divorce	$34.99	DWCT
Do Your Own California Adoption (Book w/CD-ROM)	$34.99	ADOP
Every Dog's Legal Guide: A Must-Have for Your Owner	$19.99	DOG
The Guardianship Book for California	$34.99	GB
A Judge's Guide to Divorce (Book w/CD-ROM)	$24.99	JDIV
A Legal Guide for Lesbian & Gay Couples (Book w/CD-ROM)	$34.99	LG
Living Together: A Legal Guide for Unmarried Couples (Book w/CD-ROM)	$34.99	LTK
Nolo's Essential Guide to Divorce	$24.99	NODV
Nolo's IEP Guide: Learning Disabilities	$29.99	IELD
Parent Savvy	$19.99	PRNT
Prenuptial Agreements (Book w/CD-ROM)	$34.99	PNUP

GOING TO COURT

Becoming a Mediator	$29.99	BECM
Beat Your Ticket: Go to Court & Win—National Edition	$21.99	BEYT
The Criminal Law Handbook: Know Your Rights, Survive the System	$39.99	KYR
Everybody's Guide to Small Claims Court—National Edition	$29.99	NSCC
Everybody's Guide to Small Claims Court in California	$29.99	CSCC
Fight Your Ticket & Win in California	$29.99	FYT
How to Change Your Name in California (Book w/CD-ROM)	$34.99	NAME
Legal Research: How to Find & Understand the Law	$39.99	LRES
Nolo's Deposition Handbook	$34.99	DEP
Nolo's Plain-English Law Dictionary	$29.99	DICT
Represent Yourself in Court: How to Prepare & Try a Winning Case	$39.99	RYC
Win Your Lawsuit: A Judge's Guide to Representing Yourself in California Superior Court	$39.99	SLWY

HOMEOWNERS, LANDLORDS & TENANTS

Buying a Second Home (Book w/CD-ROM)	$24.99	SCND
The California Landlord's Law Book: Evictions (Book w/CD-ROM)	$44.99	LBEV
The California Landlord's Law Book: Rights & Responsibilities (Book w/CD-ROM)	$44.99	LBRT
California Tenants' Rights	$29.99	CTEN
Deeds for California Real Estate	$27.99	DEED
The Essential Guide for First-Time Homeowners	$19.99	USOWN
Every Landlord's Guide to Finding Great Tenants (Book w/CD-ROM)	$24.99	FIND
Every Landlord's Legal Guide (Book w/CD-ROM)	$44.99	ELLI
Every Landlord's Property Protection Guide (Book w/CD-ROM)	$29.99	RISK
Every Landlord's Tax Deduction Guide	$34.99	DELL
Every Tenant's Legal Guide	$34.99	EVTEN

First-Time Landlord: Your Guide to Renting Out a Single-Family Home......................... $19.99 USFTL
For Sale by Owner in California (Book w/CD-ROM).. $29.99 FSBO
How to Buy a House in California .... $34.99 BHCA
Leases & Rental Agreements (Book w/CD-ROM) .... $29.99 LEAR
Neighbor Law: Fences, Trees, Boundaries & Noise... $29.99 NEI
Nolo's Essential Guide to Buying Your First Home (Book w/CD-ROM) .... $24.99 HTBH
Renters' Rights: The Basics .... $24.99 RENT
Saving the Family Cottage: A Guide to Succession Planning for Your
    Cottage, Cabin, Camp or Vacation Home.. $29.99 COTT
Selling Your House in a Tough Market: 10 Strategies That Work................................... $24.99 DOWN

IMMIGRATION
Becoming a U.S. Citizen: A Guide to the Law, Exam & Interview .... $24.99 USCIT
Fiancé & Marriage Visas... $34.99 IMAR
How to Get a Green Card .... $29.99 GRN
Student & Tourist Visas.. $29.99 ISTU
U.S. Immigration Made Easy .... $39.99 IMEZ

MONEY MATTERS
101 Law Forms for Personal Use (Book w/CD-ROM) .... $29.99 SPOT
The Busy Family's Guide to Money .... $19.99 USMONY
Chapter 13 Bankruptcy: Keep Your Property & Repay Debts Over Time........................ $39.99 CHB
Credit Repair (Book w/CD-ROM) .... $24.99 CREP
Easy Ways to Lower Your Taxes .... $19.99 USLOT
The Foreclosure Survival Guide .... $21.99 FIFO
How to File for Chapter 7 Bankruptcy .... $29.99 HFB
The New Bankruptcy: Will It Work for You?.. $24.99 FIBA
Nolo's Guide to Social Security Disability (Book w/CD-ROM) .... $29.99 QSS
The Sharing Solution: How to Prosper by Sharing Resources, Simplifying Your Life &
    Building Community .... $24.99 SHAR
Solve Your Money Troubles: Debt, Credit & Bankruptcy .... $24.99 MT
Stand Up to the IRS... $29.99 SIRS
Stopping Identity Theft: 10 Easy Steps to Security .... $19.99 USID
Surviving an IRS Tax Audit .... $24.95 SAUD

RETIREMENT & SENIORS
Get a Life: You Don't Need a Million to Retire Well.. $24.99 LIFE
IRAs, 401(k)s & Other Retirement Plans: Taking Your Money Out............................... $34.99 RET
Long-Term Care: How to Plan & Pay for It .... $24.99 ELD
Nolo's Essential Retirement Tax Guide .... $24.99 RTAX
Retire Happy: What You Can Do Now to Guarantee a Great Retirement .... $19.99 USRICH
Social Security, Medicare & Goverment Pensions... $29.99 SOA
Work Less, Live More: The Way to Semi-Retirement .... $17.99 RECL
The Work Less, Live More Workbook (Book w/CD)... $19.99 RECW

PATENTS AND COPYRIGHTS

SOFTWARE

Call or check our website at www.nolo.com for special discounts on Software!

Order Form

Name
Address
City
State, Zip
Daytime Phone
E-mail

Item Code	Quantity	Item	Unit Price	Total Price

Method of payment

☐ Check   ☐ VISA

☐ American Express

☐ MasterCard

☐ Discover Card

Subtotal	
Add your local sales tax (California only)	
Shipping: RUSH $12, Basic $6 (See below)	
"I bought 2, ship it to me FREE!"(Ground shipping only)	
TOTAL	

Account Number
Expiration Date
Signature

Shipping and Handling

Rush Delivery—Only $12

We'll ship any order to any street address in the U.S. by UPS 2nd Day Air* for only $12!

* Order by 9:30 AM Pacific Time and get your order in 2 business days. Orders placed after 9:30 AM Pacific Time will arrive in 3 business days. P.O. boxes and S.F. Bay Area use basic shipping. Alaska and Hawaii use 2nd Day Air or Priority Mail.

Basic Shipping—$6

Use for P.O. Boxes, Northern California and Ground Service.

Allow 1-2 weeks for delivery.

U.S. addresses only.

For faster service, use your credit card and our toll-free numbers

Call our customer service group Monday thru Friday 7am to 6pm PST

 Phone
1-800-728-3555

 Fax
1-800-645-0895

Mail
Nolo
950 Parker St.
Berkeley, CA 94710

Order 24 hours a day @ www.nolo.com